Conceptualizing
Sexual Harassment
as
Discursive
Practice

Conceptualizing Sexual Harassment as Discursive Practice

Edited by
Shereen G. Bingham

PRAEGER

Westport, Connecticut
London

Library of Congress Cataloging-in-Publication Data

Conceptualizing sexual harassment as discursive practice / edited by
    Shereen G. Bingham.
        p.   cm.
    Includes bibliographical references and index.
    ISBN 0–275–94593–6 (alk. paper)
    1. Sexual harassment of women.   2. Sexual harassment.
    I. Bingham, Shereen G.
    HQ1237.C657   1994
    305.42—dc20   93–37025

British Library Cataloguing in Publication Data is available.

Library of Congress Catalog Card Number: 93–37025
ISBN: 0–275–94593–6

First published in 1994

Praeger Publishers, 88 Post Road West, Westport, CT 06881
An imprint of Greenwood Publishing Group, Inc.

Printed in the United States of America

The paper used in this book complies with the
Permanent Paper Standard issued by the National
Information Standards Organization (Z39.48–1984).

10 9 8 7 6 5 4 3 2

Copyright Acknowledgments

Contents

Acknowledgments

I would like to thank the people whose professional and personal support helped me during the process of editing this book. Julia T. Wood has been, and continues to be, an extraordinary source of encouragement and new ideas. Her suggestions and criticisms at various stages of this project were straight-forward, helpful, and wise. I am grateful to Julia and to all the contributing authors whose insights have transformed my thinking and whose cooperation and kindness brought me joy. My colleagues and friends at the University of Nebraska at Omaha provided an important sounding board and were always willing to listen. I wish especially to thank Hollis Glaser, Randy Rose, and Deborah Smith-Howell for reading and commenting on drafts of my essays. I also am indebted to Inga Ronke for invaluable secretarial assistance and Heidi Hess for proofreading and preparing the index. Finally, as in all aspects of my life, the love and support of my family sustained me throughout the project. The faith and wisdom of my mother, Vonne Irish, made the completion of this book possible.

Conceptualizing
Sexual Harassment
as
Discursive
Practice

Introduction: Framing Sexual Harassment—Defining a Discursive Focus of Study

Shereen G. Bingham

By clarifying that which we oppose, we set the groundwork for creating a vision of that for which we long.

—M. Westkott, 1983, p. 212

Over the past two decades researchers have been sketching a portrait of sexual harassment that is becoming more detailed. We have learned what behaviors seem to comprise sexual harassment, how victims typically respond, and what negative effects sexual harassment has on individuals and institutions. We have established that a number of variables influence perceptions and evaluations of sexual harassment, and that a victim's perceptions are considered by many to be more important than a harasser's intent. We also recognize gender and power as central in sexual harassment, and that harassers often, but do not necessarily, have more formal authority than their victims. Given all that we seem to know about sexual harassment, we may wonder why we have not had more success in dealing with it. Men continue to harass women sexually with alarming frequency, and the typical solutions (e.g., saying "no" or filing a complaint) have not proven very helpful.

Clearer understanding of sexual harassment, how it keeps happening, and the ways it might be stopped may require us to develop different ways of understanding the phenomenon and, with that, alternative ways of studying and responding to it. It may be prudent for those who study sexual harassment to step back at this juncture in our work so that we may assess where we have been and why we went there and so we may reflect on alternative directions we might pursue. Scholars might ask what we have learned from two decades of study, what issues we have not yet been able to address and/or understand, and what factors both in ourselves as researchers and in the phenomenon we study are impeding our understandings.

Conceptual frameworks are important to researchers because they predispose us to grasp and study a phenomenon in particular ways and shape our interpretation of findings. They govern how researchers deal with fundamental issues such as what questions are important, what categories of analysis are appropriate and acceptable, what count as data, and what the goals of analysis can be (Fisher, 1978; Foss & Foss, 1989). Conceptual frameworks also have valuative implications; they serve the interests and concerns of some groups while marginalizing and sometimes even disparaging other groups' values and assumptions (Foss & Foss, 1989; Kersten, 1986; Spitzack & Carter, 1989). According to Astrid Kersten (1986), we have ample evidence from a variety of disciplines that "scientific activities are far from being a neutral, objective, and value-free enterprise" (p. 138). Thus, our conceptual frameworks for studying sexual harassment are likely to generate particular ways of understanding and studying the phenomenon which, in turn, serve and legitimate the concerns and interests of some groups more than others.

Because research frameworks have both conceptual and valuative implications (Kersten, 1986), the study of sexual harassment may be enhanced by exploring a plurality of perspectives. A pluralistic orientation views all scientific knowledge as partial because knowledge is bound by theory, culture, and particular moments in history (Nielsen, 1990). Although pluralistic thinking implies that all versions of reality have validity, the need to choose between many perspectives need not pose a dilemma for pluralists (Nielsen, 1990). Puzzling over conflicts and contradictions between opposing perspectives can actually stimulate theory development, expose one's taken-for-granted assumptions, and result in enlarged and enriched vision and understanding (McNamee, 1989; Nielsen, 1990; Poole & Van de Van, 1989; Putnam, 1983a; Spender, 1985).

The pluralistic ideal of exploring contradictions between opposing perspectives, however, depends on a context of equality (Ehrenreich, 1990; Nielsen, 1990).[1] When inequalities exist between scientific or social groups, the dominant version of reality may be presumed to be everyone's reality, the dominant group's standards for judgment may be assumed to be neutral and objective rather than partial, and consensus among dominant group members often passes as universal consensus. According to some legal critics and theorists (e.g., Ehrenreich, 1990; Fechner, 1990; Pollock, 1990), this is precisely what has happened in many court trials on sexual harassment; the perspective of dominant groups (e.g., males, whites, businesses) has tended to prevail, and the full benefits of exploring diverse viewpoints have been unrealized.

Researchers have not routinely analyzed which conceptual frameworks have dominated or compared different frameworks that are used to study sexual harassment.[2] However, given the potential power of these frameworks to influence what and how we study and whose interests we serve, scrutiny seems both warranted and wise. My task in this introduction, then, is to examine a conceptual framework that appears predominantly in sexual harassment research, identify the sorts of conceptualizations of sexual harassment that arise within this framework, and consider whose interests these may be serving. I will then compare these conceptions of sexual harassment with those that are encouraged by a discursive approach explored in this volume. Since a discursive approach to studying sexual harassment is relatively new to the literature,[3] juxtaposing these different frameworks should broaden our thinking about sexual harassment and help us grapple with the conceptual and valuative implications of our work.

PREVALENT CONCEPTIONS OF SEXUAL HARASSMENT

The literature on sexual harassment is expansive and interdisciplinary, including contributions from fields such as business, communication, education, labor and human resources, psychology, social work, sociology, and women's studies. Although a variety of conceptual frameworks are reflected in this diverse literature, one broad framework, functionalism, is apparent in much of the literature across many fields. After briefly reviewing the feminist roots of sexual harassment theorizing and research, I will turn to the functionalist framework and the kinds of conceptions of sexual harassment that arise within it.

Feminist Framework

The first studies of sexual harassment were conducted and published by feminist activists and scholars working collaboratively in the 1970s (Evans, 1978; McCaghy, 1985). Feminists named and conceptualized sexual harassment as an expression of power and a form of sex discrimination (MacKinnon, 1979) rooted in male dominance and privilege in the capitalist workplace, perpetuated through sex-role socialization and the sexual objectification of women (McCaghy, 1985), and obscured by patriarchal myths (Evans, 1978). As Julia Wood suggests in chapter 1 of this book, early conceptions of sexual harassment were in the best interest of women who previously had no fitting language available to describe their experiences. The import of early research on sexual harassment, then, was that it validated women's reality and demonstrated that sexual harassment is not an isolated or individual problem (McCaghy, 1985). Feminist and pro-feminist conceptualizations of sexual harassment continue to evolve, with increasing attention to diversity among women in terms of race, ethnicity, class, and sexual orientation (e.g., Brodkey & Fine, 1991; Ehrenreich, 1990; Kramarae, 1992; LaFontaine & Tredeau, 1986).[4] Because the activism and scholarship of feminists brought sexual harassment into both the public consciousness and the legal system, implicitly or otherwise most subsequent research has reflected feminist insights, albeit it has frequently not partaken of feminist modes of inquiry.

Functionalist Framework

Researchers who were not necessarily feminists began to conduct studies on sexual harassment with greater and greater frequency during the 1980s. These authors often cited feminist and legal definitions of sexual harassment, but tended to define themselves implicitly or explicitly as "social scientists" (e.g., Maypole, 1986) or "academics" (e.g., Wilson & Kraus, 1983). Although most of the initial studies were entirely exploratory and pragmatic, a broad conceptual framework for studying sexual harassment—functionalism—gradually took shape.

Functionalism, as described by Linda Putnam (1983b), is "a generic or generalized paradigm based upon positivist orientations to research" (p. 34). Functionalist researchers tend to view social reality and social structures as existing "independent from the processes that create and transform them" (p. 36). Thus, social phenomena are treated as "entities" that are concrete and materialistic. Moreover, as functionalist researchers ignore the processes by which structures are created, social processes become "reified" and individual actions are recast into "fixed properties" such as "levels, departments, and boundaries" (p. 35). Functionalist researchers also view causality as linear and unilateral; they are particularly interested in identifying "cause-effect relationships" and predicting "patterns of behavior across situations" (p. 41). Finally, a functionalist view of human communication locates the meaning of verbal and nonverbal messages in the messages themselves, or in the "perceptual filters" of the receiver (p. 39).

Most research that fits the functionalist framework seems to emanate from a general, three-part conceptualization of sexual harassment. The three elements of this conceptualization correspond closely with the focus of the behavioral, legal, and power-oriented definitions of sexual harassment offered in the literature (e.g., see the reviews by McKinney & Maroules, 1991; Paludi & Barickman, 1991). Specifically, I understand a functionalist conceptualization of sexual harassment as consisting of behavioral, psychological, and structural elements, envisioning (1) verbal and nonverbal behaviors or interactions that have negative effects on victims and that (2) are coercive, discriminatory, or perceived as inappropriate and hostile, and that (3) are inspired or enabled by organizational and social structures and processes.

All three elements of this functionalist conceptualization are often reflected within a single author's work. However, researchers sometimes emphasize one element more than the others. Since the particular element that is accentuated tends to vary with the focus of research, I will discuss and illustrate each one separately. Each element seems to highlight certain aspects of sexual harassment and encourages particular ways of understanding the phenomenon. Once

I have reviewed the primary conceptualizations of sexual harassment that arise within functionalism, I will consider whose interests these conceptions may be serving. Because I have embraced functionalist conceptualizations of sexual harassment in my own research (e.g., Bingham & Burleson, 1989; Bingham & Scherer, 1993), I have both personal and scholarly investment in contemplating them.

First, functionalist conceptualizations that emphasize the *behavioral* element of sexual harassment tend to portray the phenomenon as something harassers *do*. Sexual harassment is viewed as consisting of a behavior, a type of behavior, a behavioral episode, or a series of episodes, all situated between antecedents and consequences which may or may not be specified. The behavioral emphasis can be seen most clearly in the genre of descriptive surveys that emerged in the 1980s. These studies were designed primarily to identify the extent, nature, and effects of sexual harassment in organizational and university settings (e.g., Allen & Okawa, 1987; Baldridge & McLean, 1980; Crull, 1980; Grieco, 1987; Maihoff & Forrest, 1983; Maypole, 1986; Mazer & Percival, 1989; Rosco, Goodwin, Repp, & Rose, 1987). Researchers developed survey instruments which divided sexual harassment into units, and they explored these units separately and in relation to each other. They asked who was being harassed by whom, what the harassers were doing, how often they were doing it, where the harassment was happening, how victims were responding, and with what effects. Thus, the behavioral emphasis transforms sexual harassment into a linear, chain-like process involving a series of causes and effects. This compartmentalized portrayal reflects a mechanistic view of human communication (Fisher, 1978), in which harassers transmit various forms of messages to victims, victims experience negative effects as a result of these messages, and then victims send responses back to the harassers and/or to various third parties via a variety of communication channels.

Several researchers have developed organizing tools to facilitate more systematic research on sexual harassment from a behavioral point of view. For example, Gruber developed what he described as two mutually exclusive and exhaustive category systems for classifying different types of sexual harassment (1992) and women's responses to the problem (1989). Fitzgerald and her colleagues (1988) noted that researchers were employing incompatible definitions and research methodologies, and developed a standardized instrument for measuring the frequency of different forms of sexual harassment. Finally, Terpstra and Baker (1986) proposed a four-part research framework that identified a network of potentially related variables including "causal factors," "sexual harassment behavior," "individual responses and outcomes," and "organizational consequences." Although none of these researchers conceptualizes sexual harassment solely as a behavioral phenomenon, the research tools they have developed encourage emphasis on the behavioral element of the functionalist conceptualization.

Second, the *psychological* element of the functionalist conceptualization locates sexual harassment in the cognitive processes, or "conceptual filters" (Fisher, 1978, p. 147), of victims and other observers. These conceptions correspond with legal definitions of what is termed "hostile environment" sexual harassment, which focuses on the "unwelcomeness" of the behavior, the perceived hostility of the work environment, and the reasonableness of the victim's perceptions (Forell, 1993). Although few authors conceptualize sexual harassment as an entirely psychological phenomenon, this element is emphasized in numerous studies which investigate individual and normative perceptions and evaluations of social-sexual behaviors. Some of these studies explore the cognitive processes involved when people interpret harassing behaviors and episodes (e.g., Thomann & Wiener, 1987; Williams & Cry, 1992; York, 1989), while many more studies have examined the impact of situational, behavioral, and individual difference variables on subjects' perceptions and evaluations of real and hypothetical sexual harassment situations (e.g., Gutek, Morasch, & Cohen, 1983; Reilly, Carpenter, Dull, & Bartlett, 1982; Terpstra & Baker, 1986; Valentine-French & Radtke, 1989).

Third, conceptualizations of sexual harassment that emphasize the *structural* element focus on the reified social and organizational structures that give rise to or enable sexual harassment, such as power structures, sex roles, sex ratios, and types of jobs. The structural emphasis is reflected in theories that attempt to explain how and why sexual harassment occurs (e.g., Gutek & Morasch, 1982; Tangri, Burt, & Johnson, 1982), as well as studies and essays that explore the effects of organizational and social power structures on the nature and occurrence of sexual harassment (e.g., Fain & Anderton, 1987; Livingston, 1982; Tuana, 1985). Many of these studies conceptualize power as the relative authority or status of the harasser and the victim (e.g., Benson & Thomson, 1982; Littler-Bishop, Seidler-Feller, & Opaluch, 1982).

A functionalist framework for studying sexual harassment, then, calls attention to particular aspects of the phenomenon and has several scholarly and pragmatic advantages. The behavioral element of the conceptualization focuses especially on the enactment of sexual harassment. By identifying variables involved in sexual harassment situations and the types of behaviors performed, the researcher is able to document what is happening in sexual harassment situations, measure key variables in a variety of contexts, test for causal relationships between and among variables, and begin to predict patterns across situations. The psychological element of the functionalist conceptualization turns our attention to perceptions. It allows researchers to tap the subjective judgments and cognitive processes of different types of individuals, to gain insight into psychological reactions, and to understand what people tend to believe comprises sexual harassment. By manipulating variables in written sexual harassment scenarios, researchers are also able to assess the impact of situational variables on perceptions. Finally, the structural element of the functionalist conceptualization moves the conception more in line with early feminist theorizing (e.g., Crull, 1982). The structural element prepares researchers to recognize the influences of social conditioning, gender hierarchy, and other social and organizational power structures on the nature and occurrences of sexual harassment. The structural element exposes sexual harassment as an abuse of power and highlights the need for laws, policies, and fundamental social change.

Returning to my earlier point that social inquiry is not value-free, it is important for researchers to consider the valuative implications of their work. The conceptions of sexual harassment that arise in a functionalist framework are likely to represent and serve the interests of some groups more than others. Most sexual harassment researchers appear to view themselves as contributing to the elimination of sexual harassment, whether by clarifying the problem and its causes or offering solutions. Thus, we would expect conceptions of sexual harassment represented in this research to be especially helpful to victims of sexual harassment and society at large.

However, consistent with functionalist research on organizational communication (Putnam, 1983b), a significant part of the sexual harassment literature reflects a managerial bias. Many researchers and authors focus on and market their work for the organizational elite, such as when they highlight sexual harassment as a legal risk and a threat to productivity and profit (e.g., Machlowitz & Machlowitz, 1987; Terpstra, 1986; Wagner, 1992; Webb, 1992). Moreover, since the behavioral element of a functionalist conception of sexual harassment divides it into reified units, it is likely to make "the problem" appear orderly and manageable. A book that claims sexual harassment can be stopped in "six simple steps" (Webb, 1992, p. 37), for example, implies that the phenomenon is containable and readily resolved, a view that enhances palatability of this approach to organizations hoping to find quick fixes.

Although simplified portrayals of sexual harassment may be helpful and attractive to managers, they may not do as well at representing the interests of sexual harassment victims. Women who have been sexually harassed by men do not tend toward reductionism, and they rarely describe their experiences as a series of linearly arranged, causally related segments (e.g., "Our Stories," 1992). To the contrary, women describe nonlinear, tangled, emotionally charged experiences involving feelings of violation, vulnerability, shame, confusion, entrapment, self-doubt, resentment, and rage (Wood, 1992). Helping victims of sexual harassment may require alternative conceptualizations that defy reification and simple categorization—conceptions that are holistic, contextual, dynamic, circular, and temporal, and which expose rather than conceal the paradoxical and illogical elements and the contextual constraints in and surrounding these experiences.

The psychological element of the functionalist conceptualization may also subtly serve the interests of dominant groups. For example, a focus on normative perceptions and evaluations of sexual harassment seems particularly helpful to judges and other decision makers who are in a position to determine whether a particular charge of sexual harassment should be considered legit-

imate. A focus on normative perceptions and interpretations has a homogenizing effect, allowing majority consensus within groups and the standpoint of
only some victims to define what counts as sexual harassment. Women who
feel they have been sexually harassed but do not concur with normative perceptions may be too easily dismissed as unreasonable, irrational, or deviant
(Ehrenreich, 1990). Research that relies entirely upon psychological and behavioral conceptualizations of sexual harassment ignores the organizational
contexts, cultural practices, material conditions, and individual experiences
that shape individual identities and interpretations.

The structural element of functionalist conceptualizations also may not contribute as effectively to the elimination of sexual harassment or be as helpful
to victims as we might suppose. Because functionalists envision power structures as preexisting, static entities, dominant group members are ensured control over the solutions to sexual harassment that will be endorsed and
implemented. Further, since reified social structures and social roles appear
to be almost impossible to change through human action, the stability of these
structures can be used to justify the continuation of the status quo. Even
individuals who wish to effect structural changes at social and organizational
levels may believe their cause is unrealistic. McKinney and Maroules (1991)
contend regarding the sexual harassment literature that "[a]uthors and researchers in this area...have not yet dealt with the complexities of the concept
of power" (p. 42). What may be needed are conceptualizations of sexual harassment that envision power structures as more malleable and open to the
influences of human activity.

In summary, different conceptual frameworks lead us to understand the
essence of sexual harassment in particular ways, and serve the interests of
certain groups more than others. I have argued that a functionalist framework
portrays sexual harassment as enacted behaviors that are causally related to
antecedents and consequences, interpreted in the perceptual filters of human
beings, and occur within the context of particular social and organizational
structures. I also have suggested that functionalist conceptualizations may be
serving interests of organizations and/or certain groups of victims rather than
serving the diverse interests of all victims of sexual harassment. Thus, what
researchers know about sexual harassment through research that arises within
a functionalist framework may not be the kind of knowledge—at least not by
itself—that will alter the status quo. New ways of envisioning sexual harassment are likely to emerge from juxtaposing what is presently known with
understandings that emanate from other conceptual frameworks.

The chapters that comprise this anthology explore an alternative framework
for studying sexual harassment that we call a discursive approach. Like all
conceptual frameworks for understanding and studying sexual harassment, a
discursive approach is encumbered—both enlightened and limited—by the
perspective it embraces.

DISCURSIVE CONCEPTUALIZATION OF SEXUAL HARASSMENT

The discursive conceptions of sexual harassment explored in this collection differ in important ways from the conceptualizations that arise in a functionalist paradigm. Here I will discuss briefly three of these differences that contrast conspicuously with a functionalist approach as I have represented it. First, a discursive conceptualization recognizes a larger, more creative role of human communication. Communication is not understood merely as what occurs during the enactment of harassing behavior or in the reception/interpretation of harassing messages. A discursive framework understands communication as creating and shaping social reality rather than just being influenced by it. Second, and more specifically, a discursive approach views social structures as produced and reproduced in discursive practices. Since structures are not viewed as static and unchangeable, a discursive approach invites a more expansive critique of the status quo. Discurisve practices and everyday communication activities, particularly those of powerful group members, are seen as reproducing and sustaining oppressive social conditions which normalize sexual harassment. Third, a discursive conceptualization offers more promising avenues for bringing about changes. Discourse is recognized not only as reproducing oppressive conditions which sustain sexual harassment, but also as a means for transforming and freeing people from those conditions. In sum, a discursive approach elucidates how cultural discourses create frames—material, psychological, and social—within which sexual harassment and responses to it transpire. It illuminates how sexual harassment is enacted, interpreted, and especially how it is normalized and challenged through discursive practices.

The chapters in this collection explore the nature and parameters of sexual harassment as discursive activity. Since a discursive approach encourages ways of understanding and studying sexual harassment that are in tension with conceptions that arise within functionalism, this collection enables researchers to compare and contrast ideas, and should inspire new insights and result in enlarged viewpoints. Moreover, a discursive framework is itself pluralistic in its embracing of diverse perspectives. There are differences and ambiguities in both the starting premises authors embrace and the directions in which they lead us. Thus, readers have a rich array of viewpoints and readings to consider in their own thinking about sexual harassment, both as a social practice and as a topic of research.

Part I of this four-part collection, "A Discursive Approach: An Overview," contains the chapter by Julia T. Wood. In it Wood sketches some of the broad influences on the discursive tradition and suggests how their common philosophical commitments illuminate understanding of sexual harassment. She describes sexual harassment as sustained by discourses that reproduce oppressive gender ideologies both in social life and individual consciousness. She argues that social-discursive processes give rise to conditions and subject positionings that legitimate and normalize sexual harassment. At the same time, she proposes, it is through discursive activities that oppressive conditions, identities, and practices which enable sexual harassment can be critiqued and contested by activists and researchers. Perhaps no site for contesting conventional gender ideologies has been more visible than the legal system. Wood highlights the legal naming of sexual harassment and the use of the "reasonableness" standard for defining sexual harassment in the courts in order to demonstrate how divergent discourses shape institutional and personal interpretations of activities. Thus, this chapter provides a broad, theoretical foundation for conceptualizing sexual harassment as discursive practice, and it highlights major themes addressed in the rest of the collection.

Part II, "Discursive Activity Sustaining Sexual Harassment," explores further the question of how particular discursive forms create a reality in which sexual harassment is naturalized and legitimated. Working from a range of theoretical perspectives, the chapters in this section reveal how social practices, identities, and material conditions sustaining sexual harassment are constituted and reconstituted in discurisve practices and everyday communication activities. These chapters unmask the workings of dominant discourses as they inscribe oppressive ideologies into social and organizational practices and individual consciousness. A theme of silence emerges in this section, as the chapters reveal how discourses silence victims of sexual harassment by reproducing and instilling in individuals the normalcy of oppressive conditions and practices, and by reconstructing experiences that would oppose the status quo.

In chapter 2, Elizabeth Grauerholz writes from a symbolic interactionist perspective to trace intersections among gender socialization, sexuality, and dominance as they are constituted in discursive interactions. Focusing on white, middle-class women and men, she argues that cultural level power inequities give rise to gender differences in socialization experiences and communication styles, and that sexual harassment is an expectable outcome of these differences. Grauerholz suggests that institutional power is translated into the personal expression of power primarily through language and communication. She integrates research findings on gender socialization and communication differences throughout the chapter to show how these interact to make sexual harassment prevalent and to shape men's and women's perceptions of and reactions to such behaviors.

In chapter 3, Charles Conrad and Bryan Taylor demonstrate that sexual harassment cannot be understood solely as a sociocultural phenomenon. They argue that organizations, and academic organizations in particular, are sites in which cultural assumptions sustaining sexual harassment are instantiated in action and discursively reproduced. Drawing from organizational theory and past research, Conrad and Taylor propose that harassment-prone organizational contexts are created and reproduced in complex interactions between dimensions of task/organizational structure, isolation of potential targets of

harassment, and organizational power relationships. These organizational contexts are illuminated as Conrad and Taylor ethnographically examine narratives
written by women who have been victims of sexual harassment. Themes identified in the women's presentations of their experiences suggest that in these
organizational contexts, sexual harassment incidences are not openly discussed
or taken seriously, victims of sexual harassment feel alone and vulnerable, and
victims are unlikely to speak out or be heard. Thus, through an "organizational
conspiracy of silence" perpetuated on interpersonal and institutional levels,
the sexist ideology and power asymmetries that underlie sexual harassment
are reproduced.

In chapter 4, Robin P. Clair draws from the work of Gramsci (1971) and
others to present a theory of hegemony and sexual harassment. After reviewing
and critiquing previous sexual harassment theorizing, she conceptualizes sexual
harassment as a political practice of oppression which is further reinforced by
the subjugated group's participation in their own domination. Clair draws from
women's narratives to illustrate her argument that when victims of sexual
harassment respond to and talk about their experiences, they often frame them
in ways that maintain rather than challenge the current system. Specifically,
Clair shows how trivialization of harassing behavior, denotative hesitancy, and
invoking the private domain are discursive frames used by victims that perpetuate hegemonic relations.

In chapter 5, Claudia L. Hale, Leda M. Cooks, and Sue DeWine demonstrate how, even when a woman dares to speak out publicly about sexual
harassment, her experiences may be reconstructed and discounted in ways
that sustain the status quo. Using dialectical criticism, Hale, Cooks, and
DeWine examine the questions asked and the statements made by members
of the Senate Judiciary Committee as they interrogated Professor Anita Hill
and Judge Clarence Thomas. The analysis reveals that the senators positioned
themselves as rational speakers of justice while portraying Hill as living in a
fantasy world; they positioned themselves as citizens of the democracy devoted
to fairness while construing Hill's actions as unfair both to Thomas and to
themselves; and they positioned themselves as protectors of truth concerning
the choices which were made while failing to understand the reality which
existed for Hill concerning the choices available. Each of these dialectics is
discussed in light of the avowed purpose for the hearings (an open-ended
inquiry into the "truth") as compared with what ultimately emerged ("the trial
of Anita Hill").

While Part II of this collection explores how discourses construct and legitimate oppressive ideologies which normalize and sustain sexual harassment,
Part III, "Discursive Activity Contesting Sexual Harassment," addresses the
capacity of discursive activities to empower marginalized groups. The diverse
essays and studies in this section explore the potential of discursive activities
to challenge and reconstruct understandings of sexual harassment in ways that
discourage the practice and free us to envision an alternative future. The

chapters explore how oppressive ideologies that have been reproduced in social life and individual consciousness might be reconstituted in discourse,
whether this be through women's collective storytelling, oral performance,
organizational communication and sense making, or shifts in ideological positioning.

In chapter 6, Janette Kenner Muir and Kathryn Mangus focus on storytelling as a powerful form of public discourse that has potential to reshape
understandings of sexual harassment and create possibilities for change. They
examine the Hill/Thomas hearings as they were interpreted by television viewers who watched the hearings on C-SPAN and called in to speak on the air.
The chapter begins by overviewing theoretical perspectives on the nature of
storytelling, and the role of women's storytelling in developing cultural meanings and shaping women's identities. Muir and Mangus then analyze the C-
SPAN call-in responses and identify themes in the callers' sexual harassment
stories. They find that although many women had experienced sexual harassment themselves and usually responded to the situation by avoiding the harasser, most callers viewed Hill's testimony as unbelievable. In contrast, when
the authors examine surveys and stories told after the hearings ended, they
find a substantial increase in the number of women who believed Anita Hill.
They also find that many more women, and African-American women in particular, are sharing their stories of sexual harassment. Muir and Mangus propose that these narratives have provided a collective voice for women that is
empowering, therapeutic, and may ultimately affect substantive policy actions.

In chapter 7, Della Pollock is concerned with finding ways to represent
sexual harassment that will counter its effects by replenishing, rather than
further delimiting, the eros of everyday, social life. Pollock's chapter narrates
her experience teaching "Oral History and Performance," a course that involves students in field and performance projects concerned with local histories of sexual harassment. She enacts the problems and advantages implicit in
sexual harassment in and as performance. In four subsections, she considers
the possibility of renewing the body of discourse surrounding harassment
through embodiment; the layers of performance reflected in one student's
account of a harassment experience; the regressive intrusion of dominant representations of harassment even over teaching about harassment; and the false
or weak liberalism expressed by mainstream harassment prevention videos. In
a concluding section, Pollock reviews the tendency of liberalism generally, and
the concept of "voice" specifically, to participate in the repression of sexuality
to which harassment is ultimately devoted. She suggests that a praxis of "performed difference" might be a more potent and effective response.

In chapter 8, Gary L. Kreps uses Weick's (1979) model of organizing as a
theoretical foundation for suggesting how sexual harassment might be more
effectively responded to and prevented in organizational contexts. Kreps views
sexual harassment as highly equivocal information situations that organizational actors respond to by engaging in symbolic interchanges that establish

sense-making systems. He argues that in present organizational life, actors often discursively trivialize sexual harassment, underestimate the equivocality of these situations, and respond to instances of harassment inappropriately. By applying the Weickian concepts of enactment, selection, and retention, Kreps suggests how situational communication rules can be developed by organization members to reconstruct understandings of sexual harassment, select appropriate strategies for responding, and institutionalize knowledge about how to handle sexual harassment in the future.

In chapter 9, Dana M. Kaland and Patricia Geist explore the ways employees think about and respond to real and hypothetical sexual harassment situations. Based on a naturalistic case study involving face-to-face interviews and narrative analysis, the authors propose a model that identifies four types of "ideological positioning." They argue that ideological positioning is embedded in the context in which harassment occurs, and that it frames victims' thinking about appropriate and available options for responding to sexual harassment. Ideological positioning is a dynamic construct in which shifting or repositioning takes place as women's perceptions of their own empowerment and of the severity of the harassment change. The analysis suggests that women choose to challenge dominant ideologies that perpetuate sexual harassment discursively when they feel empowered in the organizational system and when they judge the severity of the harassing behavior as warranting opposition.

Part IV of the collection, "Critical Reflections," contains one chapter by Karen A. Foss and Richard A. Rogers which reflects critically upon the volume, exposes some omissions and implicit assumptions, and suggests directions for further research. In their chapter, Foss and Rogers turn the discursive approach explored in this volume onto itself by critiquing this book as part of the discourse that constitutes sexual harassment. They argue that research practices in regard to sexual harassment, including most of the chapters in this collection, more often than not assume a strategic focus in their concern with definition, interest in organizational structures, and suggestions for the implementation of solutions from the top down. They contend that most of the suggested solutions presume agents who have access to certain resources (e.g., knowledge of legal definitions of sexual harassment) and particular levels of authority. Foss and Rogers propose that more research needs to be directed to a tactical focus—one that starts from the vantage point of those who experience the harassment and relies on personal experience, timing, and empowering interpretations of behavior to accomplish resistance. They emphasize the need for research that incorporates the tactical, bottom-up perspective, and that will take into consideration the local conditions and social positions of individual experiences with sexual harassment.

Understanding what we as researchers bring to our study begins the process of re-forming conceptual perspectives and exploring what other frames we might adopt is the next step. This book, in giving voice to discursive frameworks and encouraging debate among authors with differing ideas, invites and

models that process. Any changes in the concrete incidence of sexual harassment as well as persons' perceptions of it will depend, in large measure, on
enlarging how we think about the activity and ourselves. It is this kind of
rethinking and what it might lead to that this volume hopes to encourage.

NOTES

1. Movement toward the kind of egalitarian contexts that encourage open dialogue,
promote respect of differences, and foster expansive thinking might be facilitated in
several ways: (1) becoming more aware of our own prejudgments and biases, admitting
that all viewpoints are political and partial (Nielsen, 1990; Spender, 1985); (2) attempting to understand material and social conditions and perspectives of other groups (Ehrenreich, 1990), although this does not entail pretending to transcend our own
standpoints (Nielsen, 1990); (3) being curious, questioning, empathic, and open to
change through connecting with others' realities (McNamee, 1989; Nielsen, 1990); and
(4) establishing equal access to discursive forms and communication (Van Dijk, 1993).

2. For exceptions see Fain and Anderton, 1989; Rizzo and Brosnan, 1990; Tangri,
Burt and Johnson, 1982.

3. Recent studies of sexual harassment using a discursive approach include Clair
(1993a, 1993b); Strine (1992); and Taylor and Conrad (1992). Also, Rizzo and Brosnan
(1990) propose a critical theory framework for studying sexual harassment which focuses on discursive activities, and Burrell and Hearn (1989) describe a discursive approach as one of four major ways to conceptualize and study sexuality and gender.

4. I should point out that a feminist perspective on sexual harassment is itself
pluralistic. Feminists disagree, for example, about whether the prime means for opposing sexual harassment is large-scale sociological change, cumulative advances in the
legal system, change in organizational practices and structures, or the individual actions
of women in everyday life (e.g., Livingston 1982; Wise & Stanley, 1987).

Part I

A Discursive Approach: An Overview

1

Saying It Makes It So: The Discursive Construction of Sexual Harassment

Julia T. Wood

> There was a time when the facts that amounted to sexual harassment did not amount to sexual harassment. . . . The facts amounting to the harm did not socially 'exist.'
>
> —C. MacKinnon, 1987, pp. 105–106

To conceive sexual harassment as discursive activity is to argue that what it is understood to be and how it is practiced arise in discourses in circulation at any particular moment in a culture's life. As a constitutive force, discourse has social, political, and epistemological significance. Because discourse names, orders, and defines experience, it shapes what and how societies and individuals know. In addition, discourse is politically charged and potent: Serving particular interests within stratified social orders, discourses produce, reproduce, and/or contest ideologies and sustain relations of privilege and oppression. When alternative discourses exist, as with sexual harassment, meaning is problematized.

The significance of viewing human conduct as discursively constructed and sustained is neither self-evident nor agreed upon. Thus, in this chapter I sketch broad outlines of a discursive perspective by unraveling relationships among discourse, ideology, and subjective consciousness. In addition to focusing on assumptions, concerns, and implications of discursive theories of social life, I also directly engage this framework to analyze sexual harassment. Thus, into the fabric of my theoretical discussion I weave attention to sexual harassment as a specific experience that arises in discursive practices.

DISCOURSE AS CONSTITUTIVE

Once prominent conceptions of language as a transparent reflection of what *really* exists have been widely displaced by the view that language creates and sustains social life and, with that, power relations and individual identities. Writing in 1984, Dale Spender argued that naming is the fundamental symbolic act and, conversely, that not to name something negates it, makes it invisible, and denies that it exists. Because language defines human experience and even ways of knowing, it fundamentally frames what we understand to be the world and our activities within it. As Hennessy (1993) observes, individuals' "lives are shaped by ideology in the sense that their experience is never served up raw but . . . [is] only intelligible at all as a function of the ways of making sense of the world available in any historical moment" (p. 78).

Elsewhere (Wood, 1992, 1993d, e), I argue the history of sexual harassment dramatically illustrates how discourse constructs experience. While sexual harassment has always occurred, until recently it was not named and, thus, had no *social* existence. Compelling evidence that not naming silences victims comes from a recent study in which Brooks and Perot (1991) asked women faculty and graduate students if they had experienced thirty-one situations that meet the legal definition of sexual harassment. While up to 88.8 percent of respondents had suffered at least one, only 2.8 percent of graduate students and 5.6 percent of faculty answered "yes" to the direct question: Have you ever experienced sexual harassment?

Without a socially legitimated label, victims' struggles to understand what occurred took place outside the web of social-symbolic interaction in which meanings arise. Efforts to discuss sexual harassment were limited to the primitive and imprecise language of "and then he . . . and then he" (MacKinnon, 1987, p. 106), which fails to name sexual harassment as violation, wrong, or even a phenomenon that merits notice. Alternatively, victims could resort to the one discourse that is socially legitimated for describing sexual activities— that of romantic involvement. Yet, terms such as "pushy," "pass," "advance," and "went too far" egregiously misconstrue unwelcome violations that humiliate and invoke implied or explicit threats to professional standing (Wood, 1992, p. 353). As long as the only existing language for sexual conduct falsified the character of sexual harassment, victims were muted and reform was forestalled.

The injustice of having no name for personal injury fueled efforts to coin and situate within the general social discourse a term that captures the debasement, violation, and wrongness of sexual harassment.[1] The basic strategy was to name sexual harassment into public consciousness. Workshops, teach-ins, publications, and publicity about court rulings are specific examples of how naming transpired. Multimedia coverage of the Hill-Thomas hearings, Tailhook, and Senator Packwood's outrageous conduct further established sexual harassment in social vocabularies and associated it with serious wrongdoing.

Important as conferring social reality is, that alone does not explain why and how discourse constitutes social order. The ideological force of discourse is revealed in Foucault's insight that in discourse something *"is formed"* (1978, p. 18). What is formed are rules that organize and regulate social life to define "how things work" and who we are. Meanings for experience as well as subjective identity, then, are formed in social-symbolic interaction, which, in turn, is regulated by the discourses available. Because discourses are located within concrete structures and practices that reflect and sustain social order, simultaneously they are within material contexts and material praxes in their own right. Discourse's intimate bearing on ideology and consciousness accounts for its power to constitute social life and personal identity.

DISCOURSE, IDEOLOGY, AND CONSCIOUSNESS

Discourse and Ideology

Ideologies are fundamental and politically partisan forms of sense making that are embodied in discursive structures and practices to define "how things work" in particular historical-cultural settings. Discursive practices reproduce ideology by constantly reinscribing patterns of sense making that serve hegemonous interests. In constructing ideology, then, discourse establishes both interpretive frameworks and meanings of specific activities.

Exemplary of the ideological power of discursive activity is the history of sexual harassment. Until quite recently incidents of sexual harassment were unquestioned as part of "normal" life. They were not named as aberrations, but instead were treated as "how things work" in men's conduct toward women.[2] Viewing sexual harassment as usual was possible, perhaps even inevitable, because historically men held a monopoly on social power, including the power to name. From most men's perspective, sexual harassment was neither salient nor a problem. Unhampered by sexual harassment, men had no compelling reason to distinguish it from the flux of ordinary life by naming it (Wood, 1992).

Another perspective comes from victims whose accounts demonstrate that when they questioned or resisted sexual harassment, they—not the offenders and not the situation—were defined as abnormal: They were labeled prudes, hypersensitive, naive, and uninformed about norms of professional relationships ("Our Stories," 1992). In varied ways, victims were told their interpretations, their responses, and *they* were wrong. Further fostering their silence was the lack of alternative discourses that might ratify feelings of violation and judgments of wrongdoing.

This began to change when some victims did not accept prevailing definitions of "how things work" and refused to be silent.[3] Not only did some women object in moments of assault, but a number pursued formal and public redress by taking their grievances to court. Case law assumed a key role in, first, recognizing and, second, redefining sexual harassment. As a trickle of cases came forward in the 1960s and 1970s, rulings gradually began to specify what was to count as sexual harassment. Early recognition of blatant quid pro quo harassment was supplemented by acknowledgment that more subtle behaviors and intimidating and hostile work environments are sexually harassing. Thus, court opinions gradually etched out an alternative discourse which defined sexual harassment as sex discrimination and a prosecutable and punishable offense.

Because the judiciary is culturally powerful, its dictum that sexual harassment is wrong critically advanced victims' rights and social awareness. Discussing the significance of legal rulings in sculpting understandings of sexual harassment, MacKinnon (1987) noted "the sexually harassed have been given a name for their suffering. . . . They have been given a forum, legitimacy to speak, authority to make claims, and an avenue for possible relief. Before, what happened to them was all right. Now it is not" (pp. 103–104). Using words to establish what sexual harassment is, court rulings exemplify how discourse constructs, contests, and re-forms social meanings.

Discourse and Subject(ivity)

Conceiving of discourse as ideological inaugurates awareness of its role in constructing particular subject(ivitie)s. Summarizing the relationship between discourse and individual consciousness, Weedon (1987) wrote that "discourses represent political interests and in consequence are constantly vying for status and power. The site of this battle for power is the subjectivity of the individual" (p. 41). Language insinuates ideologies into individuals through discourses that constitute both conscious and unconscious understandings of the self in social relations.

Prominent in efforts to elucidate how discourse constructs subject(ivitie)s are post-structural theorists such as Foucault (1973, 1980a), Laclau and Mouffe (1985), Althusser (1977), and Kristeva (1982). While endorsing different and, to some extent, contradictory ontological assumptions, these theorists illuminate the role of human practices, especially discursive ones, in inscribing or resisting socially prescribed identities. Kristeva, for instance, insists that the symbolic order constructs social consciousness while the body, viewed as pre-symbolic, is the premiere site of resistance (see Moi, 1985).[4]

To explain how discourse constructs subject positions that uphold the prevailing social order, Foucault (1982) referred to language as "governance." By this he meant that discourses legitimated in any historical moment indoctrinate individuals to regulate themselves in ways that affirm and reproduce the prevailing social order. He argued discourse delineates available options for belief, conduct, and identity by representing as natural and right assumptions, codes of conduct, and hierarchical social relations that comprise and uphold hegemony. Existing order is reified as individuals embody it in everyday activities.

An emergent development in sociology illuminates further how discursive activities reproduce in individuals dominant ideologies which, in turn, incline them to engage in practices that fortify prevailing social organization. Challenging widespread belief that emotions are personal and spontaneous, the sociology of emotions (also called the sociology of feelings) suggests that "not only ideas, but emotions too are cultural artifacts" (Geertz, 1973, p. 81). This implies feelings are created through social-symbolic practices which prescribe what emotions are appropriate for whom in specific settings and/or under given conditions.

Sociologists of emotion contend others define for new members of a society how they should feel about particular events, situations, actions, and so forth. Regulating feelings is essential to social order since, as Shott (1979) noted, "certain types of emotions are so central to social control that society as we know it could not exist without them" (pp. 1317–1318). To the extent that individuals internalize cultural prescriptions for how they should feel in sundry situations, self-control serves social control and thereby reproduces resident ideology.

Without dismissing socially uncontaminated feelings, sociologists of emotion maintain that "a social framework modifies the actor's experience, interpretation, and expression of emotion" (Shott, 1979, p. 1320). This extends Foucault's insights into discourse as governance by asserting that a culture's discursive practices govern or regulate what individuals feel as well as what they think.

Particularly germane to understanding sexual harassment is the realization that certain emotions define and regulate moral conduct by stipulating normal and abnormal feelings about particular phenomena. For instance, we are supposed to feel shame if we steal, which should be compounded by embarrassment if we are caught; we are taught to feel pride when we succeed. Anticipatory guilt and shame deter socially discouraged behaviors, while pride promotes socially sanctioned ones. The experience of guilt or shame following transgressions punishes misconduct while post-act pride rewards good deeds. Both outcomes buttress social control and—yet more basic—social definitions of what is proper and deviant. Likewise, empathy is a feeling with considerable moral and social force since vicarious access to others' experiences allows actors to regulate their conduct by awareness of others' perspectives.

Understanding emotions as discursively constructed sheds light on why sexual harassment occurs. As Elizabeth Grauerholz points out in chapter 2, Western culture emphasizes sexuality as a linchpin of manhood. Males are taught to be sexually aggressive and to feel pride in sexual conquests that provide evidence of their masculine prowess (Gaylin, 1992; Wood, 1993b). Our culture also instructs men to gain and exercise power over others and, consequently, to feel proud when they do so (Wood, 1993b, d). Conversely, men are taught to feel shame when they are weak, passive, and/or sexually impotent. Finally, our culture defines men as superior in general and superior to women in particular (Brownmiller, 1993; French, 1992).

In combination, these teachings inform a coherent account of sexual harassment as something men are entitled to do to women (it is proper to enact power over inferiors) and for which they should feel pride (it certifies sexual prowess). Further, socially ensconced gender ideology invites reading victims' resistance, anger, or refusals as inappropriate (inferiors have no right to challenge superiors), as justification for escalating violation (not to persist is to be a wimp), and as cause for anger and retaliation (inferiors' impudence should be punished).

How do dominant social-discursive constructions of gender and feelings inform victims' experience of sexual harassment? Cultural prescriptions for femininity require attracting, pleasing, and deferring to men. Women are relentlessly exhorted to define themselves in relation to others, particularly men, and to measure self-worth by the ability to attract and hold men. By implication, women are urged to feel proud of gaining men's interest. Even if sexual attention is not wanted, women are inculcated to understand it certifies their worth, and they should not hurt, embarrass, or reject others, particularly men.

Prevailing discursive formations also define women in bipolar sexual terms: Madonna or whore. "Women of virtue" are taught to feel pride for having sexual standards, and women who are sexually assaulted are taught to feel shame and guilt, which reflects the related engendered teaching that they, not their aggressors, are at fault for sexual misconduct. When these aspects of socialization combine with the fundamental feminine imperatives to be deferential and nice, women subjected to unwanted sexual attention are virtually scripted either to tolerate it or to discourage it as amiably as possible so that assailants do not feel bad. In either case, victims are taught to feel responsible for both the problem and protecting harassers' egos.

Given a perpetrator taught to be proud of what he's doing—taught to link it to his manhood—and a victim taught to be tolerant, pleased, or ashamed of what is happening to her, sexual harassment is not only allowed, but underwritten by gender ideologies and the subjectivities they construct. This highlights the need to redefine "proper" feelings about sexual harassment. I will return to this point later.

If consciousness is discursively shaped, then the discourses legitimated in any particular historical moment limit what individuals experience and know of the world and themselves. Discourse constrains self-consciousness in its capacity to make available only certain subject positions while shrouding alternative ones. Women may be either whores or Madonnas; men may be either real men or wimps; and each is defined by sexuality. Women who receive uninvited sexual attention are either provocative and, thus, "deserve it," or they are prudes who do not recognize a compliment and hysterically overreact to "innocent" behaviors. Men who force sexual attention on others are either "Just being men"/studs so their assaults are excused/celebrated, or they are "going too far," which implies the basic direction of the activity is valid. Discourses that embody and reproduce this gender ideology create subject positions that encourage men to harass women sexually and women to tolerate abuse.

As I argued in my foregoing analysis, a primary reason sexual harassment was unregulated for so long is that it occurred within a cultural gender ideology that actively legitimates it. Gender ideology is so systematically and pervasively inscribed in social life that it appears natural, normal, and right. In circular fashion, once particular arbitrary understandings of selves and conduct are normalized, they are enacted in concrete moments and, thereby, the ideology underlying them is reproduced: As individuals participate in social life, using and being used by the discourses it privileges, they fortify or contest ideological frameworks embedded in linguistic practices.

Whose Standpoint?

Understanding discourse as constituting social life and subjective consciousness presupposes the existence of different positions within a power-stratified society. Were these not assumed, there would be no need to construct and buttress continually a particular ideology. Extending this tenet of discursive theories is standpoint logic, which calls attention to the epistemological significance of different positions within a society.

Developed by scholars such as Haraway (1988), Harding (1991), Hartsock (1983), and Smith (1987), standpoint theories claim that one's location has epistemological consequences, which is to say that a person's position in society shapes experience of the world, the self and, therefore, of what is known. Any position is socially produced largely through discourse, which upholds (or resists) culturally authorized ways of sense making. Standpoint logic's fundamental concern with how different and differentially valued positions are created invests it with a critical impulse to expose and contest structures and practices that oppress some groups and privilege others.

A specifically feminist standpoint entails thinking from the position of women's lives as they are shaped by material conditions and ideological frameworks that give rise to particular activities, interests, and motivations (Harding, 1991). Standpoint is a relational concept, not a synonym for women's experiences or lives. A standpoint is a position established by material and social-discursive circumstances within which one lives and through which one interprets (see Hennessy, 1993). While women's direct experience is a primary basis of feminist knowledge, that subjective reality is understood to be crafted by material conditions and discursive activities. This suggests that all phenomena—including oneself—are necessarily mediated by discourses available in a given time and place.[5] In sharpening insight into individuals as subjects-in-language, standpoint theory highlights the personal and political consequences of discourse.

Standpoint theory regards differences among women as cultivated by material and discursive conditions that assert race, sex, and class as criteria for assigning individuals to groups accorded unequal status and opportunity. In turn, different groups are assigned distinctive roles which involve members in disparate activities, which then act as further material constraints on members' perceptions, knowledge, and subjective consciousness. When individuals are assigned to groups whose identity and practices are specified, a culture reproduces in individuals the qualities used to define the group in the first place. In other words, persons are situated in circumstances designed to foster epistemological tendencies isomorphic with those originally used to define a group (e.g., mothering reproduces mothering, developing in relation to others reproduces relational orientation).

As I have said, discourse names phenomena, imbuing them with ideological significance. Yet naming does not occur in a vacuum, nor from an objective, Archimedian perspective; rather it partakes of a particular position within a social order. Within a culture, discourse and its derivative, ideology, are controlled by those in power. Accordingly, dominant groups use discourse to define what serves their interests as common sense, the natural order of things, right (Gramsci, 1971). Inscribed within social, moral, and political discourses are values and codes of conduct and identity that justify, uphold, and normalize hegemonous interests and the power relations upon which they depend.

Standpoint theory contributes to discursive conceptions of sexual harassment by directing us to ask from what perspective—from whose position in society—definitions of social life are crafted. The resoundingly androcentric bias of Western culture makes it unsurprising that legal concepts in general and sexual harassment in particular predominantly reflect masculine perspectives and experiences. What *is* surprising is that the distinctive validity of women's standpoint on sexual harassment has been acknowledged in even a minority of legal rulings.

The "reasonable woman standard," inaugurated in Judge Damon Keith's dissenting opinion in *Rabidue v. Osceola Refining Company* (1986), held that the conditions of women's and men's lives differ and may inform legitimately dissimilar interpretations of behavior, specifically what is intimidating and offensive (Fechner, 1990; Forell, 1993). A U.S. court of appeals held that the conventional standard of legal—"how would a reasonable man regard X situation"—was inappropriate in cases of sexual harassment. Ruling that pinups in public areas of a workplace that were not offensive to reasonable male workers could well be offensive "to reasonable women" in the company's employ, this case affirmed the reasonable woman standard for determining sexual harassment (Tiffs & VanOsdol, 1991).

According to MacKinnon (1987), "the legal claim for sexual harassment marks the first time in history . . . that women have defined women's injuries in law" (p. 105). MacKinnon's claim, however, is more wishful than factual since the reasonable woman standard is far from universally accepted in judicial proceedings (Fechner, 1990; Pollack, 1990). As this volume goes to press, different U.S. courts have invoked standards that vary radically in their recognition of sexual harassment as systemic, ideologically based, and perspectival.

The reasonable woman standard vies with the reasonable person standard, which acknowledges no difference between the standpoints of men and women. Both of these differ from the bases of majority judgment in *Rabidue*, which held that behavior that might be offensive to women was "an everyday occurrence . . . [that] is natural, acceptable, and part of the fabric of society's morality" (Pollack, 1990, p. 65). Most recently, the lower court ruling in *Harris v. Forklift Systems* found that only demonstrable "severe psychological harm" would hold legal status as sexual harassment, an opinion that suggests moderate psychological harm may be inflicted on others without penalty. These different standards used to define and judge behavior alleged to be sexually harassing reflect divergent ideologies swirling about in public life. In addition, because legal rulings shape ideology and public and personal consciousness, material consequences follow from which one(s) secures standing in legal and public understandings (Forell, 1993).

IMPLICATIONS OF A DISCURSIVE CONCEPTION OF SEXUAL HARASSMENT

As I have discussed it, a discursive understanding of human activity entails five major tenets:

1. Discourse is both situated within material and social practices that inform it and itself a material practice that constructs ideology and consciousness.

2. Discourse produces and reproduces ideologies and social organizations in particular historical-social locations.

3. Discourse constitutes subject(ivitie)s. The available positions of any self are delineated by discourses in circulation in any given moment, and these (in)form an individual's consciousness and her or his framework for interpreting experience. Thus, discourse and the standpoints it produces are epistemologically significant.

4. Because discourse constitutes ideologies and subjective consciousness, it governs self-control and social control by instilling in individuals the normalcy of social practices, structures, ideas, and feelings; individuals are then constituted to reproduce prevailing order.

5. Discourses are neither neutral nor universal; they always emanate from particular standpoints. For this reason, any discursive construction represents interests, experiences, and knowledge available from, and in the interests of, only certain positions within a society.

Societies, of course, must reproduce themselves in order to survive. As Habermas (1984) noted, societies reproduce themselves both materially (e.g., through exchange with the physical environment) and symbolically. In this chapter I have concentrated on the latter form of cultural reproduction, emphasizing how discourses construct and sustain ideologies both by insinuating them into concrete social structures and practices and by embedding them in subjective consciousness so that individuals' internalized self-control supports social control and, thus, prevailing power relations. As individuals are "talked into humanity" (Mead, 1934) they learn not only the significant symbols of a culture, but also the identities, values, and interpretive processes it privileges as right, normal, and natural.

Yet societies are not static. Ideologies that dominate in any moment may be challenged and transformed. Here, too, discourse is primary for it is through discursive activities that individuals and groups critique existing ideologies and author oppositional ones. In short, changing cultural understandings requires disrupting dominant discourses and the ideologies they embody. I now suggest how discursive understandings of sexual harassment might direct activities of activists and scholars working against it.

Activist Efforts for Change

Discursive perspectives on social life inform efforts to diminish sexual harassment, heighten its salience in public life, and empower those who might be victims. Activist work should be situated in sites where the symbolic reproduction of social life and, particularly, gender ideologies takes place: contexts where values, meanings, and feelings are normalized. Thus, families, schools, employee training programs, and courts are premiere locations for inserting discourses that name sexual harassment as violation, perpetrators as wrong, and victims' perspectives as the basis for assessing harm.

Inflected by standpoint logic, discursive frameworks assert that we act according to our beliefs about "how things work," and that those beliefs are produced and reproduced in discursive practices. Informed by this perspective, activists might adopt a dual strategy in which they contest discursive practices that uphold a hegemonous gender ideology and insert oppositional discourses into circulation. I have argued that ideologies that allow or foster sexual harassment rely centrally on traditional definitions of men as superior, powerful, and sexually aggressive and of women as subordinate, sexually accessible, and deferential. Educational strategies to reduce sexual harassment should denounce these gendered identities and propose alternate, nonoppressive views of men and women.

A related direction for intervention is implied by insights from sociologists of emotion. If how men and women are taught to feel about uninvited sexual advances perpetuates sexual harassment, then it seems advisable to teach people alternative feelings are appropriate. Specifically, it might be productive to assert that shame and guilt are the appropriate feelings for someone who imposes sexual attention or intimidation on people who do not welcome them. Relatedly, trainers and educators could empower potential victims by legitimating anger, resentment, and indignation and displacing guilt, shame, and toleration as "proper" responses to unwanted sexual attention.

Attention to empathy might also reduce sexual harassment. Potential victims, primarily women, might be encouraged to empathize *less* with perpetrators since not wanting to hurt, embarrass, or disappoint others serves to sustain a victim's oppression by inhibiting resistance and grievance. On the other hand, those who do or are likely to harass others sexually might be encouraged to have greater understanding of how it feels from a victim's standpoint. While some offenders know how deeply humiliating and injurious sexual harassment is, others may not. Many men's responses to both the Hill-Thomas hearings and to victims' accounts of harassment that were published in the *Journal of Applied Communication Research* ("Our Stories," 1992) revealed they had not understood the reality of sexual harassment from victims' perspectives. Encountering victims' own words, they finally did "get it." Perhaps having more victims tell their stories would further harassers' and potential harassers' understanding of victims' perspectives. Since emotions are central to self-control and consequently social control, defining as appropriate feelings that make sexual harassment less rewarding for harassers and less tolerable to victims could substantively change the positions of participants as well as what *is* actually experienced in situations that are or could become sexually harassing.

Another critical site for contesting conventional gender ideologies is the jurisprudential system. Perhaps the most visible and vigorous feminist presence in legal theorizing and practice today is MacKinnon, who has brought about substantial reforms in laws and bases of laws that affect women. Despite MacKinnon's work, however, Pollack's (1990) observation that "woman have named sexual harassment, but have lost control of the content of its definition" (p. 48) is unfortunately more true than not. Thus, a prime goal is establishing women's perspectives as the basis for judgments of sexual harassment. Women's ability to trust their own experience and men's need to acknowledge their perceptions would be greatly enhanced if courts consistently relied upon women's standpoint to define harm.

Research on Sexual Harassment as a Discursive Practice

A discursive understanding of social life also has implications for future research on sexual harassment. Most obviously, this perspective suggests fuller insight into what sexual harassment is and how and why it occurs depends centrally on understanding ideologies that inform its practice and how those are embodied in particular discursive practices. While some preliminary effort (Strine, 1992; Taylor & Conrad, 1992) has followed this route, considerably more research is needed. In this chapter I have argued that prevailing gender ideologies and the ways they position men and women allow/encourage sexual harassment. Future work should probe in greater depth what comprises current Western gender ideologies, how they legitimate sexual harassment, and how they are embodied in concrete interactions.

Relatedly, future scholarship should focus on the subject(ivitie)s of perpetrators, victims, and resisters of sexual harassment. Existing research (Malovich & Stake, 1990) indicates that the people most likely to tolerate sexual harassment are women with traditional sex role attitudes and high self-esteem about their femininity. Researchers might illuminate further how commitment to traditional sex roles and perceived success in enacting them invite women to tolerate unwanted sexual attention. Researchers should also note that we know little about the kinds of attitudes in men that cultivate or inhibit tendencies to sexually harass, which suggests a priority is research on men's attitudes and how they are discursively produced, reproduced, and altered.

These and other topics that emanate from a discursive conception of sexual harassment will be most instructive if they attend both to concrete practices of particularly situated actors and to larger social contexts, both material and symbolic, in which action occurs. Since knowledge of what *actually* occurs in the thought and action comprising sexual harassment is yet nascent, we need to discover the standpoints of specific actors as they are located in historical, material settings (Smith, 1987; Wood & Cox, 1993). The scene may then be enlarged by identifying social, material, and other conditions that shape individual experience. Finally, relying on concrete lives as entry points, scholars may trace how particular circumstances and resulting subjective consciousness are produced by discourses that normalize and sediment prevailing cultural ideologies in everyday thought and conduct.

This layered approach to research fuses recognition of an experiential, experiencing subject with understanding of all selves as constructed through social structures and practices that are embodied in particular discursive formations. This approach to scholarship is respectful of personal experience and subjects while it is simultaneously mindful that individuals are implicated in larger systems of social relations which prefigure everyday activities and consciousness. Concentrating on both concrete, lived experiences and discourses that inscribe social ideologies into particular moments enables us to situate embodied activities within broader horizons of cultural life.

SUMMARY

In this chapter I have argued that discourse, ideology, power relationships, and subjective consciousness are interlinked and that sexual harassment incarnates one instance of their connections. Sexual harassment depends on the existence of discourses that reproduce oppressive gender ideologies both in social structures and practices and in individual consciousness. While redressing violations of particular individuals is essential, if that is the only goal, we ensure the need for redress remains constant. Effort must also focus on structural change. Beyond protecting individual victims, researchers and activists need to address conditions, assumptions, and ideological relations that create inequality and, thus, susceptibility of women as a group to sexual abuses.

The central theme running through this chapter is that discursive practices profoundly affect human understanding and action. Conditions that legitimate and sometimes invite sexual harassment, as well as the ideology undergirding them, are produced and reproduced in social-discursive practices. Understanding cultural narratives as ideologies, both centered and marginal, exposes the potential of discourse to sustain prevailing social order, yet also highlights its power to foment change. For this reason, discursive theory imparts a distinctively critical edge to efforts to understand, critique, and alter conditions, identities, and practices that enable sexual harassment.

NOTES

1. Discourses within different spheres of cultural life interact continuously, so that what happens in courts, for instance, influences public opinion and institutional policies, and changes in social beliefs and business practices provoke shifts in legal perspectives and rulings. Naming sexual harassment into social consciousness required repeated interruptions of dominant discourses. Before sexual harassment could be named by the courts and the public sector, women had to name their oppression in general and sexual harassment in particular *to themselves.* Feminist consciousness raising sharpened women's insight into their collective situation in Western culture, which, in turn, impelled demands for changes in public structures and practices (see Pollack, 1990). Following this a series of rulings gradually gave legal standing to claims of sexual harassment: The 1964 Civil Rights Act defined sexual harassment as a form of sex discrimination prohibited in work settings; the Educational Amendments of 1972 extended this to educational contexts; the key case of *Meritor Savings Bank v. Vinson* enlarged the legal definition of sexual harassment to include hostile or intimidating environments in addition to quid pro quos.

2. Reports on sexual harassment concur that the vast majority of perpetrators are males and most victims are females. While some women may sexually harass and while some men may be victims, demographics argue the issue should be understood as one premised on ideologies of gender and power that authorize male aggression against females.

3. The question of why some individuals do not learn and/or accept dominant meanings of a culture merits considerable study. A discursive approach suggests women who resist sexual harassment and feel the perpetrators, not they, are wrong interact with discursive communities outside the mainstream. Hennessy (1993) discusses this as happening in the "cracks and seams" of a dominant ideology, and elsewhere (Wood, 1993a) I discuss social-symbolic influences on individuals' resistance to traditional sex roles.

4. Feminist theorists have issued some incisive criticisms of post-structuralism. Foucault is criticized for his dedication to local settings which limits his ability to illuminate connections among discursive constructions of "woman" and larger social hierarchies

and global relations (see Alcoff, 1990; Hartsock, 1990; Spivak, 1988). Geras (1987) sees Laclau and Mouffe's radical democracy mired in a particularized view of power as the struggle for equal rights by a subordinated group, which obscures critical economic and material facticities that allow one oppressed group to increase its power while ignoring or even contributing to the oppression of other groups. Kristeva is criticized (Fraser, 1990; Moi, 1985; Spivak, 1987, 1988; Wood, 1993c) for essentialist views of women as well as lack of attention to how historicity and politics shape identity, which incapacitate her ability to explain any *collective* resistance to discursive hegemony. The cutting edge of theorizing in this area is reconfiguring post-structuralist insights to map relationships between discursive practices and material (nondiscursive) conditions so that subjects are recognized as both embodied and constructed.

    5. I should not be misinterpreted as embracing radical contingency, nor as suggesting that discourse is more epistemologically real than are concrete conditions of life. Elsewhere (Wood & Cox, 1993) I have argued that while discursive practices may create ideological structures and practices, these take on a decisively material character as they become sedimented through repetitive everyday activities. To understand knowledge as situated (Haraway, 1988) requires recognizing that a mutually formative dialectic exists between materiality and symbolicity.

Part II

Discursive Activity Sustaining Sexual Harassment

2

Gender Socialization and Communication: The Inscription of Sexual Harassment in Social Life

Elizabeth Grauerholz

One of the most significant and robust findings revealed by studies of sexual harassment concerns gender. Gender differences exist with respect to the incidence of sexual harassment, the extent to which various behaviors are labeled as sexual harassment, and responses to sexual harassment. In addition, perpetrators are overwhelmingly male while victims are almost always female. (For a review of the literature on sexual harassment, see McKinney & Maroules, 1991).

The most powerful theory used to explain gender differences in sexual harassment experiences is feminist theory, which places power and gender at its core. Feminist theory maintains that sexual harassment, like all forms of violence against women, stems from males' greater power and status within society (MacKinnon, 1979). As McKinney and Maroules (1991, p. 35) note, "Whether formal or informal, organizational or diffuse, real or perceived, status differences between victims and offenders are the root of the problem of sexual harassment." Sexual harassment also represents a powerful means by which power differences are created and maintained. Sexual harassment effectively restricts women's movement in the world, making it more difficult for women to gain power and authority within the workplace and other institutions.

A sociocultural analysis such as this begs an important question: How does men's *institutional* power give rise to women's *personal* experiences of powerlessness? In other words, how do power differences that exist within the larger society impact common, everyday interactions between men and women? In this chapter, I explore this link between macro-structural phenomena and personal experiences. I argue that cultural power differences between men and women give rise to different communication styles and socialization experiences for males and females and that, in turn and in part, sexual harassment is an outcome of these differences. Although this discussion is intended to account for differences in men's and women's experiences, it is limited by existing research which focuses almost exclusively on white, middle-class women and men. My argument centers around the notions that white, middle-class women and men experience sexuality and power in different ways; consequently, these men and women bring different perceptions and expectations to cross-gender social interactions. Further, given the nature of some of these differences, it is not surprising that sexual harassment is prevalent.

I begin by reviewing briefly the nature of sexual harassment experiences. This discussion will provide the background necessary for understanding how gender, communication, and sexual harassment interact in social situations. Next, I explore several significant gender differences in socialization experiences which may be key to understanding how sexual harassment arises. Finally, I attempt to integrate these notions of gender, socialization, communication, and sexual harassment to derive a better understanding of why sexual harassment occurs.

THE SEXUAL HARASSMENT EXPERIENCE

Sexual harassment is widespread. Approximately 20 percent of men and 50 percent of women experience some form of sexual harassment, mostly from men, while in college or the workplace (McKinney & Maroules, 1991). These experiences can take a variety of forms:

Visual forms of harassment include leering, menacing staring and sexual gestures; verbal forms include whistles, use of innuendo and gossip, sexual joking, propositioning and explicitly threatening remarks; physical forms include unwanted proximity, touching, pinching, patting, deliberately brushing close, grabbing. (Kelly, 1988, p. 103)

Studies indicate that the most common type of sexual harassment is environmental (versus quid pro quo) and that such harassment may be nearly a daily occurrence in many women's lives (MacKinnon, 1979).

Thus, there is a variety of behaviors that may constitute sexual harassment, ranging from sexual comments to sexual assault, but not all these acts are commonly defined as sexual harassment. The most profound effect on definitions of sexual harassment is gender: Women are more likely than men to define various acts as sexual harassment and are less accepting of them (Kenig & Ryan, 1986; Powell, 1986).

Victims attempt to deal with sexual harassment in a number of ways (Gutek & Koss, 1993). The most common tactic is to ignore the problem, hoping it will go away, or attempt to avoid the abuser, although such tactics rarely are effective in stopping the harassment. Most victims believe that using assertive and direct strategies, such as telling the person to stop, is the most effective means of stopping the harassment. Another relatively effective option is to report the incident(s) to a supervisor or other authority, although few victims actually use this technique (Gutek, 1993). The pursuit of legal alternatives is even rarer.

In sum, environmental sexual harassment (sexual comments, undue attention, body language, propositions, etc.) is a relatively common experience for women and to a much lesser extent, men. While there is no question that women actually experience more sexual harassment than men, it appears that women "see" more sexual harassment and are more likely than men to label behaviors as sexual harassment. Finally, typical reactions to sexual harassment include avoiding the harasser and ignoring him. These aspects concerning the experience of sexual harassment will be referred to later in terms of how they relate to gender role socialization and to the occurrence of sexual harassment.

GENDER ROLE SOCIALIZATION

In order to understand the connection between gender socialization and sexual harassment, I focus here upon how gender socialization structures our understandings of power and sexuality. Although gender role socialization involves more extensive learning than this, these two variables are the most salient for understanding sexual harassment, since sex and power are at the root of sexual harassment.[1] In addition, special attention is given to discourse surrounding power and sexuality since it is through language that socialization is achieved (Mead, 1934).[2]

Gender socialization begins early in life. Soon after birth, boys and girls are handled and responded to differently (Rubin, Provenzano, & Luria, 1974; Stern & Karracker, 1989). Thus begins an extensive, lengthy, and sometimes difficult lesson about gender. By age two or three, children can readily identify themselves as male or female, have a stable gender identity, and have knowledge of gender stereotypes (Cowan & Hoffman, 1986; Money & Earhardt, 1972; Weinraub et al., 1984).

Not only do children learn what types of behaviors are appropriate to their gender, they also learn that power and privilege are not equally distributed in society (Weitzman, 1979). Hartley (1959) noted, nearly three and a half decades ago, that children perceive fathers as more punishing and controlling than mothers and to be the bosses in the home; and although her research is now dated, this lesson continues to be taught in a variety of ways in many American households. For instance, fathers may get the most comfortable chair in the house, larger and better portions of food at mealtime, a private space (desk, office, chair), and the seat at the head of the table (and often in the only chair with arms) (Charles & Kerr, 1987; Hartley, 1959). Male prerogative and privilege is further established in the nearly universal preference for male children (Steinbacher & Holmes, 1987). In conversations, girls are interrupted twice as often as boys by their parents, providing a clear message to girls that their opinions are not as important (Greif, 1979, cited in Weitzman, 1979). As a result, males and females inevitably come to experience power differently. Because this point is key to understanding how and why sexual harassment arises so often in male-female encounters, I explore the research on this topic in some depth here. As noted previously, this discussion is necessarily restricted to the experiences of white, middle-class individuals; the profound lack of research on race and class differences makes comparisons or generalizations risky (see chapter 10).

Not only have men and women historically had different amounts and types of power, there is also evidence that the desire to be powerful, or domineering, characterizes males more than females. This is not to suggest that women are less aware of power dynamics than men or that power characterizes women's relationships any less than men's. Given the fact that women traditionally have been subordinate to men, they must be cognizant of power dynamics; their survival may depend on it. Further, there is evidence that women can be powerful and influential, although their power may be less visible, less public, and the strategies used to exercise it less direct than men's (Falbo & Peplau, 1980; Grauerholz, 1985).

Thus, it is probably accurate to state that women and men are both concerned about power but in different ways. It has been suggested that women are more concerned with personal power (developing a sense of themselves and not being influenced by others) or with pro-social dominance (controlling others in order to promote social responsibility) than they are about interpersonal power (being able to influence others) or with egoistic dominance (controlling others for selfish ends) (Lips, 1981; Whiting & Edwards, 1973). Women are traditionally socialized to stress affiliation and egalitarian power, whereas men are socialized to stress competition and dominance. According to Hoffman et al. (1984, p. 809), "While females can be seen as being socialized to be able to relate with others, children included, men can be seen as learning to need to dominate, to need to be more powerful than others."

Research consistently shows that from an early age, females tend to be more affiliative, that is, concerned about other people, than males (Gilligan, Lyons, & Hanmer, 1990; Maccoby & Jacklin, 1974). Among children ages three to six, boys tend to engage in egoistic dominance whereas girls engage in more pro-social dominance (Whiting & Edwards, 1973). Maltz and Borker (1983) also found that within same-sex peer groups, boys are more concerned with dominance, girls with sustaining social relationships.

Such differences are further reflected in (and perhaps created by) the type of play activities in which boys and girls engage. Lever (1978) found that boys' play is more competitive, girls' more cooperative; boys tend to play in large groups, girls in smaller ones. Partly due to the difference in group size, boys' peer groups are more likely than girls' to be characterized by dominance hierarchies. These are created and sustained in part through the use of language. Thorne and Luria (1986) found that among boys, hierarchies are reaffirmed through the use of homophobic labels ("fag," "queer," etc.), which serve to alienate marginal children.

As adults, women's friendships continue to be characterized as more affiliative and men's as more competitive (Bernard, 1981; Pleck, 1980). A variety of studies have shown that when men and women encounter one another in social situations, men tend to be more competitive and domineering. For instance, Buss (1981) found that males rate agentic dominance (control over others for personal gain) as more desirable than communal dominance (control over others in order to strengthen group harmony or further group goals), although they used both types. Women, by contrast, rated communal dominance as more desirable.

As mentioned earlier, language is critical to socialization into social roles. Significantly, observers of communication styles and patterns between men and women have found that men tend to dominate conversations and interactions in a variety of ways, and that dominance is a theme in much verbal language of men.

Early studies by Thorne and Henley (1975) and Henley (1977) revealed the subtle ways in which verbal and nonverbal language subordinates women. Compared to women, men are less circumspect, use more familiar terms of address, disclose less, violate women's personal space more, touch more, and engage in less mutual eye contact—all of which are gestures of power and status. Some research shows that men talk more and interrupt more than women (Kollock, Blumstein, & Schwartz, 1985; Zimmerman & West, 1975).[3] Fishman (1978) also found that women do more "interactional work," that is, they work harder than men at keeping the conversation going by asking more questions to evoke responses and by providing well-timed responses. In conversations with children too, men speak more and use greater verbal space than women (Hoffman et al., 1984). According to Hoffman and his colleagues (p. 809) this reflects "a characteristic need for dominance and power in interpersonal interaction that is part of the male role."

Not only is dominance evident in the *way* men speak to women, but also in *what* is said. Bernard (1981, p. 376) suggests that "language is one way in which the misogyny of the male world . . . finds expression" (see also, Adams & Ware, 1989). Drawing upon past research, Bernard claims that the English language is hostile to women, sexually denigrating, subordinating, and inadequate for expressing women's sexual experiences. For instance, there are over two hundred terms in the English language to describe sexually promiscuous women but only about twenty for men. Also, there are more vernacular animal words to describe women (e.g., "bitch") versus men, there is a tendency for words that refer to women to become debased (e.g., "witch"), more insults are directed at women, women are usually "at the butt" of dirty jokes (which are usually originated by men), and words referring to men or male behavior often connote power, but those referring to female behavior often connote weakness (e.g., men yell, women scream).

Another way in which male dominance finds expression is in sexual relations, which are an outgrowth of gender socialization. MacCorquodale (1989, p. 103) explains:

> The strength of the childhood learning of gender roles results in gendered sexual scripts. Males are taught an achievement orientation. . . . The characteristics necessary for achievement promote a vision of the ideal man as active, physical, dominant, independent, unemotional, objective, forceful. When applied to sexuality, the normative prescription is that men should be the active initiators and pursuers in sexual situations and oriented toward the physical and power dimensions of relationships rather than the emotional aspects.

Stockard and Johnson (1992) suggest that growing up male involves learning about dominance and camaraderie and that this has important implications for males' sexual socialization. They note that in early adolescence, masturbation may become a competitive activity among boys, and later heterosexual prowess becomes the basis for this competition. According to Pleck (1980), women are used as symbols of men's success in their competition with other men. Most males come to believe that being a "real man" means having sex with many women and having no regard for them as individuals, in other words, seeing them as sexual objects to be manipulated for their own pleasure. Stockard and Johnson (p. 217) claim that "although men undoubtedly vary considerably in this respect, at least part of the explanation of why men are prone to consider women sex objects is that they become sexual in the context of competition with other males."

The linkage between sex and dominance permeates "normal," adult, heterosexual relations. To the extent that traditional gender roles dictate that men initiate, cajole, seduce, and continue to push their advantage despite protestations, and that women reject, resist, or acquiesce, it is difficult to distinguish such behaviors from sexual coercion. As Box (1983, p. 145) notes, "In sexual matters, the 'real' man must dominate his partner by charm, connivance, or cunning, and if these fail, by coercion."

This description of male-female sexual interactions implies a strong double standard, in which male sexual prowess is tolerated or encouraged but female sexual activity is restricted and negatively sanctioned. Although there is evidence that the double standard has declined in terms of attitudes and in terms of the proportion of men and women who have engaged in sexual intercourse, in many ways, this double standard persists and has important implications for the development of men's and women's sexual identity and how they respond in sexual situations (Grauerholz & Serpe, 1985). The double standard also finds expression in the ways in which males and females communicate about sexuality. Males' vocabulary for talking about sex is more varied and power oriented (Beneke, 1982; Metts and Cupach, 1989; Sanders & Robinson, 1979). By contrast, women are expected to be more silent about sexuality (Bernard, 1981).

In sum, dominance characterizes men's behavior more than women's. This concern for having power over others can be seen in everyday encounters in a variety of ways: in the language used to convey thoughts, in nonverbal behaviors, and especially in sexual relationships. The fact that men and women experience power and sexuality in such fundamentally different ways has important implications for understanding why and how sexual harassment arises in many cross-gender encounters, the point to which I now turn.

SOCIALIZATION OUTCOMES: THE INTERSECTION OF GENDER, COMMUNICATION, AND SEXUAL HARASSMENT

Socialization is the process by which individuals acquire cultural knowledge, including information about gender, power, and sexuality. According to symbolic interactionist theory, the way in which these cultural norms, expectations, and ideals are transmitted to each member of society is through symbolic systems, or language (Mead, 1934). That is, as children acquire language, or share the symbolic environment of those around them, they come to understand the meaning of objects (including themselves) and the expectations others have. As Stryker (1980, p. 56) notes, "The symbols that attach to the environment have meaning, are cues for behavior, and organize behavior."

Return for a moment to the question posed at the beginning of this chapter: How does men's institutional power give rise to women's personal experiences with sexual harassment? We have seen that institutional power is translated into the personal expression of power through language and communication— it is the critical link between the culture and the individual. Thus, if we wish to understand how men's power within the larger society is realized within everyday interactions, we must pay special attention to the communication and discourse surrounding male-female encounters. In this section, I attempt to link previously discussed notions of sexual harassment and gender role socialization to draw out this relationship more clearly.

Recall that the most common experiences with sexual harassment reported by women are such things as verbal comments, body language, and undue attention. It is important to recognize that such actions are precisely the types of behaviors that characterize men's interactions with women, as discussed earlier. Arliss (1991, p. 174) elaborates on this:

Keep in mind that women are approached more closely by others, touched more by others (particularly male others), and disclosed to more by others. Compared to men, women are called by their first names more often (as are subordinates), are called by pet names more often (as are children), are metaphorized more often as cuddly animals and edible objects, and are more often the object of sexual jokes.

Arliss goes on to suggest that "none of these communicative trends alone causes sexual harassment of women in any setting, but the combination of these communicative habits certainly establishes women as probable victims of unwelcome sexual innuendo" (p. 174). It also helps us to understand why some women perceive environmental harassment to be widespread.

If women are familiar with a more cooperative style of communication, they may also be made uncomfortable by the competitive nature of men's speech, in particular, the practice of "putting-down" others in order to increase their status. Ramazanoglu (1987, p. 64) describes the widespread use of such discursive practices within the academic environment where

skilled use of words and the voice are extremely effective means of silencing intellectual challenges and creating an atmosphere in which people are afraid to speak. . . . A violent academic situation is not so much an experience of fisticuffs and flying chairs as one of diminishing other human beings with the use of sarcasm, raised voices, jokes, veiled insults or the patronising put-down. . . . Academics are verbally highly skilled and can use verbiage to confuse and intimidate others; they are also powerful users of the voice to convey sarcasm, to interrupt, to prevent interruption and to override counter-arguments.

Although such practices may be more obvious in the university setting, women in virtually every line of work can encounter similar situations. This is not surprising given that men are socialized from an early age to be more competitive than cooperative in their communication with others. It is also no surprise that women commonly feel harassed—if not sexually harassed—in these situations. And it is also easy to understand how women may come to feel sexually harassed when one considers another aspect of language: that it tends to be hostile, subordinating, and sexually denigrating to women. Thus, as Arliss (1991, p. 175) notes,

For a woman entering a male-dominated workplace, she may feel victimized, offended, or just plain embarrassed by the expressions and jokes she hears. Her sense that she is a victim seems logical . . . [given] that sexual joking tends to be designed by men for male consumption and, as most humor, promotes group unity by making outsiders the "objects" of their laughter.

Another factor that may provide insight into how communication practices are related to sexual harassment is the responses of victims to harassment. As seen earlier, women typically use indirect strategies to deal with sexually unwanted advances. Such subtlety and indirectness is consistent with the traditional female role. Many women do not report the incident to others or use direct confrontation because, in addition to fearing that such tactics may backfire and harm themselves, many fear that to do so would hurt or create trouble for the harasser (Farley, 1978; Gutek, 1985). From the woman's perspective, subtlety is seen as a way to protect others' feelings and maintain a semblance of cooperation in the work setting, which is consistent with their affiliative role. Being sensitive to nonverbal cues, they may also believe that they are providing sufficient information to indicate disapproval. It is not uncommon to hear women say, "I just can't believe he didn't get the hint!" From a man's perspective, however, silence is likely to indicate acquiescence. His socialization experiences have taught him that unless he receives a direct "no," she means "go ahead." As Dziech and Weiner (1990, p. 84) note, "The offending individual interprets silence as assent or even encouragement to continue his behavior."[4]

Yet, even when a woman does respond directly and forcefully, there is no guarantee that this will stop the behavior. Hemming (1985) suggests that because men may confuse aggression and eroticism (see footnote 1), they may actually become sexually aroused when women respond with anger. Related to this is research that finds men are more likely than women to view interactions as sexual. Abbey (1982) found that men are likely to interpret women's friendliness as seductive or sexually inviting. Montgomery (cited in Metts and Cupach, 1989) also found that flirting often has different meanings for men and women. Whereas both men and women flirt sometimes to be friendly, men are more likely than women to flirt with sexual intent. It follows that some sexually harassing behaviors between men and women may arise from such miscommunication. Viewing an encounter through a sexual lens, men are likely to act according to a sexual script—making sexual comments, staring, touching, propositioning, and so on. Such behaviors will be viewed by women as inappropriate, at best, and sexual harassment, at worst. Compounding this, of course, is the fact that men are expected to be the initiators and women the gatekeepers in sexual encounters. Not only might men incorrectly interpret women's signals, they may assume that women's resistance is insincere (Metts and Cupach, 1989). Metts and Cupach (1989, p. 148) also suggest that "excessive or inflexible adherence to these roles or to interpersonal sexual scripts that have worked in the past may obscure the nuances of particular situations and partners."

Thus, gender socialization results in different communication styles, and such differences, when played out in the workplace or other environments, are likely to result in problematic interactions between men and women. Specifically, when men engage in competitive and domineering behaviors, and especially when these contain sexual overtones or sexual objectification, women are likely to feel uncomfortable and possibly violated.

Yet, if men are more focused on dominance and power than women, how do we come to understand the consistent research findings that suggest women "see" more sexual harassment and perceive identical behaviors as more sexually harassing than do men? One explanation is that women's heightened sensitivity to nonverbal behaviors (Henley, 1977) may cause them to tune in to the subtle, intimidating gestures that men simply do not see. However, differing perceptions and women's discomfort with men's behavior may have more to do with the fact that women must constantly negotiate their way in a world where violence against women is widespread, they must be alert to dangers even in seemingly safe places (e.g., the workplace, home, school, a party with friends), and they must do so in a society that affords men more resources than women. Bernard (1981, p. 386) explains that "the resources men bring with them, not only physical—larger size and louder voice—but also social—the support of their world—give them great initial advantage. They can make women feel uncomfortable or unsupported with even minimal gestures."

This may help to explain the confusion expressed by some men over what behaviors constitute sexual harassment or why women seem particularly "sensitive" to what they (men) perceive to be simply innocent, even complementary, behaviors. It may not be that men are so insensitive to social cues or choose to "play dumb" to the impact of their actions on women; rather, it may be that they have a completely different experience with power (or powerlessness). They may feel relatively powerless vis-à-vis particular others (e.g., a superior or a physically intimidating male) but not *all* other men. Women, on the other hand, have good reason to fear *all* men, including those with whom they are most intimate.[5] Women carry with them a different view of the world, a world in which misogyny and violence against women are prevalent. Thus, even "minimal gestures" may be viewed as potentially threatening. In fact, there is evidence that seemingly innocuous behaviors (e.g., a joke or petting) are regarded more by women as closely related to acts such as attempted rape or rape than by men. In research by Klein (cited in Rowe, 1985), men and women were given a list of behaviors (ranging from a wink to rape) and asked to evaluate the seriousness of each behavior. The range of seriousness for men was very wide, sometimes ranging from one to infinity. The range for women, however, was much narrower—about one to 100. Klein's research suggests that for many women, behaviors such as joking or touching are considered to be serious. Thus, a behavior that a man might consider to be innocuous, teasing, or even complimentary may be seen by a woman as hurtful, degrading, offensive, and potentially threatening.[6]

CONCLUSIONS AND IMPLICATIONS

This chapter has focused upon how gender differences within society are passed down into interpersonal relationships and shape encounters between women and men. Persons or groups in power (e.g., men) come to experience power in fundamentally different ways from those in relatively powerless positions (e.g., women). In white, middle-class American society, men are socialized to be competitive and domineering; women to be affiliative. These differences result in distinct communication styles for men and women. Sexual harassment can be seen as an outcome of these different communication styles. In particular, many forms of environmental harassment, including un-due attention, body language, and verbal comments, can be seen as expected outcomes of the different ways that women and men have been socialized and have learned to communicate. Quid pro quo harassment may also be seen as an outcome of such socialization, in that men may view working relationships as competitions, as "deals" to be negotiated (McKinney, 1993).

This is not to suggest that sexual harassment results from faulty commu-nication between the sexes. While miscommunication is undoubtedly involved in some incidences, I suggest that most sexual harassers are aware of their actions and intend them to be offensive or hostile. In fact, men are socialized to want to dominate others (male and female) and are skilled at doing this through the use of verbal and nonverbal language. The fact that some men attempt to establish dominance over women by degrading or abusing them sexually is most likely due to the fact that this is one of the most effective and devastating ways to achieve male dominance over women. Recall too that such behavior is entirely consistent with male socialization, which tolerates, if not encourages, treating women as sexual objects. By sexually harassing women, men can reaffirm their masculinity.

Several implications can be drawn from this analysis. It suggests that real change needs to occur in the way we socialize boys and girls. Unfortunately, there is little indication that early gender role socialization is changing radi-cally, and we cannot expect, nor do we want, victims to wait until it does. Fortunately, if language and communication is the key to socialization, as ar-gued here, social change can be promoted by altering the discourse surround-ing sexual harassment, as Wood argues in chapter 1. Not only must we continue to challenge traditional gender ideologies among children and adults, we must introduce new discourses concerning sexual harassment and gender relations.

NOTES

1. Most researchers recognize that sexual harassment has more to do with power than sex (MacKinnon, 1979), but it is important to recognize the sexual component as well. Although there is nothing sexually pleasurable for victims of sexual harassment, for harassers, there may indeed be an element of sexual titillation. In fact, the coercive element of these acts may make the sexual element more stimulating. Such a response is not unusual in a culture such as ours that routinely eroticizes sexual violence in popular culture, especially in pornography.

2. According to symbolic interactionist theory, language provides the basis of all social learning and for the development of a self-concept. Through the development of language and social interaction, infants acquire both the labels and meanings at-tached to symbols in their environment. Stryker (1964, pp. 104–141) explains:

Others supply us with a name, and they provide the meaning attached to that symbol. They categorize us in particular ways and on the basis of such categorization they expect some set of behaviors from us. On the basis of these expectations, they act with reference to us. The ways in which they act toward us define ourselves. We come to categorize ourselves as they categorize us and we come to act in ways implied in these categories and so, appropriate to their expectations.

3. The attempt by Kollock, Blumstein, and Schwartz (1985) to disentangle the effects of sex and power in conversations suggests that interruptions are linked to power differences, not sex. That is, powerful persons interrupt less powerful partners, regardless of their sex. Marche and Peterson (1993) have also shown that among peers (same sex and cross sex), males and females interrupt at the same rate. Thus, observed sex differences in communication styles seem to reflect the cultural power difference between men and women. In turn, these patterns of communication probably also reinforce power differences.

4. It should be noted that silence is rarely effective in stopping harassment. Farley (1978) reports that for women in her study who ignored harassment, in 75 percent of the cases, the harassment worsened, and about 25 percent of the women who ignored it were eventually penalized for not responding.

5. Research shows that husbands, family members, and other significant others are more likely to victimize women than are strangers (Russell, 1982).

6. Bingham (1993) suggests that men can/do become sensitive to such behaviors when it serves their interests, or perhaps when they perceive that they are the targets of harassment. A recent case in point is the controversy over gays in the military, in which some heterosexual men have expressed concern about gay men possibly making passes at them or ogling them in the shower. In situations such as these, men seem to perceive "minimal gestures" as serious and degrading, similar to how women feel in many situations with men.

3

The Context(s) of Sexual Harassment: Power, Silences, and Academe

Charles Conrad and Bryan Taylor

As the chapters in this book clearly indicate, the complexity of sexual harassment makes it an exceptionally challenging topic for research and theory. Cultural assumptions, including traditional sex roles and the relationship between sexuality and power, legal systems, performative processes, and social pressures which encourage the suppression of dissent of all kinds combine to form an almost bewildering maze. In this chapter we would like to complicate the picture further, by suggesting that harassment occurs in organizations and cannot be fully understood without also considering a number of organizational dynamics. In particular, we will argue that organizations are sites in which cultural assumptions are instantiated in action, and where cultural assumptions are reproduced through discourse. The incidence of harassment is related to a number of organizational factors, and the outcomes of harassment complaints are influenced by a group of organizational processes we will label the "organizational conspiracy of silence." Individual and institutional responses to harassment claims reproduce the contextual factors that facilitate harassment and the responses that help perpetuate it.

Our research base will be a series of narratives written by victims of sexual harassment and examined from the perspective[1] provided by contemporary organizational theory and past research on sexual harassment in organizations. From the outset we admit that all choices of interpretive frames, including the one we articulate in this chapter, are arbitrary and partial. We hope that the reading we offer will both be consonant with the texts being examined and will reveal opportunities for alternate readings.[2]

THE ORGANIZATIONAL CONTEXT OF SEXUAL HARASSMENT

Three interrelated aspects of formal organizations combine to create and reproduce harassment-prone situations: (1) certain dimensions of task and organizational structure; (2) the isolation of potential targets of harassment; and (3) organizational power relationships.

Task/organizational structure influences both harassment potential and the effectiveness of grievance procedures. Jobs that provide employees with no space exclusively under their control or require overtime work, business trips, or convention attendance increase the opportunity for harassment (Tangri, Burt, & Johnson, 1982). The vertical stratification of bureaucratic organizations allows upper-level persons (almost always males) to use their authority and control of organizational resources to extort sexual gratification from their subordinates (often female) (Tangri, Burt, & Johnson, 1982). When the structure also provides employees with high levels of autonomy (as in universities), opportunities for harassment are extensive (Dziech & Weiner, 1990).

Similarly, organizational structure influences the probability of targets' complaints being successfully resolved. The "loose, ambiguous, shifting, and poorly defined" authority relationships characteristic of universities makes it difficult for students or their advocates to take steps successfully against a faculty member (Baldridge, 1978). As a successful complainant pointed out to Farley (1978, p. 73):

The whole problem really is that we have no structure that's safe for the complainant to complain in. The normal grievance procedure is terrible, very simply because some faculty members are on the student grievance committee so that when the student does go to complain she can find that sitting on that very committee is either the person himself or his three best friends.

The "loosely coupled" structure of academic organizations (see, for instance, Orton & Weich, 1990) makes it highly unlikely that timely action will be taken in response to harassment complaints. In academic organizations delayed response is strategic because complaints tend to be dropped once a student leaves a harasser's class or the university. The structural configuration of universities has two effects: It significantly reduces the proportion of student victims who take formal action,[3] and it creates a complaint process that is so cumbersome that exhausted complainants often drop their complaints or accept "slaps on the wrist" as adequate punishment (Dziech & Weiner, 1990).[4]

Second, the extent to which women are isolated from one another either within a work group or across work groups influences the incidence of harassment (Tangri, Burt, & Johnson, 1982). In large universities undergraduates are so isolated from professors that they are unlikely to have ready access to support or advice from faculty members when harassment does occur (Benson

& Thompson, 1982). Although isolation may be less of a problem for graduate students, the mentoring arrangement which typifies graduate education combines with unequal power relationships to create a uniquely open opportunity for harassment. A harassment victim interviewed by Dziech and Weiner (1990, p. 149) observed:

[My adviser] just had too much authority over me. It was absolute. It was even more than the authority that a boss has over you in a job, it has parental aspects to it because this whole graduate experience is an apprenticeship system. You get attached to a guy [i.e., are assigned a major professor], they were all guys—there were only two women in the department and neither of them took graduate students—so there was no possibility of getting away from men.

When students do complain about harassment, they are isolated further. Myths of collegiality encourage faculty members to respond to complaints in ways that are "predictably supportive of their [accused] colleagues and unsympathetic to women complainants and their advocates" (Dziech & Weiner, 1990, p. 49). Dziech and Weiner's interviewee continued: "There was never the thought that you could go to one of them to help out against another. It was a solid block" (p. 149). Potential allies—affirmative action officers, ombudspersons, and sympathetic faculty—find it difficult to intervene on a student's behalf because they are "*de*valued—as colleagues, as professionals, and as people. Their motives are questioned, their long-established professionalism challenged, and their credibility diminished or lost" (Dziech & Weiner, 1990, p. xxix). So, they are reluctant to intervene, even when doing so is part of their job descriptions.

Finally, the incidence of harassment and the effectiveness of grievance procedures are influenced by organizational power relationships (see chapter 4). At one level the relationship between power and harassment is quite simple: When organizational power is roughly the same among men and women, harassment is rare, regardless of the type of organization or the culture in which the organization is located (Hemming, 1985).[5] Power also seems to explain who becomes a harasser and who becomes a target. The most common forms of sexual harassment are sexist jokes, innuendos, and comments from men who do not have formal power over the target woman (peers, clients, customers, and so on). But, the most extreme forms of harassment—sexual assault and quid pro quo negotiations—typically are initiated by men who have formal power over their targets (Gutek, 1985; Littler-Bishop, Seidler-Feller, & Opaluch, 1982; Loy & Stewart, 1984; Schneider, 1982; Tangri, Burt, & Johnson, 1982).

Although a wide range of motives lead to harassment, initiators who resort to extreme tactics seem to be frustrated, angry, or hostile to women in the workplace. Often the hostility stems from a desire not to compete with women (Carothers & Crull, 1984), and the goal of harassment is to force them out of traditionally male occupations (Gutek, 1985, 1989; O'Farrell & Harlan, 1982). The relatively high turnover rate among women in some male-dominated blue-collar jobs suggests that this strategy often is successful (DiTamaso, 1989; Gutek, 1985; Hemming, 1985; MacKinnon, 1979).[6] In other cases harassers are frustrated with their current position and/or advancement potential (Benson & Thompson, 1982, p. 240). For example, a frustrated professor may choose to exert his masculinity and manage his frustrations by "being openly abusive to them [women students], or he can turn to them for solace and ego-gratification" (Dziech & Weiner, 1990, p. 140).[7]

Women who are either particularly threatening to the established male power structure (for example, women "pioneers" in traditionally male occupations) or who are especially vulnerable (Gutek & Morasch, 1982; Hemming, 1985; Tangri, Burt, & Johnson, 1982) are likely targets of harassment. The former factor explains why a woman's educational level is positively correlated with the probability of her being sexually harassed (Hemming, 1982). The latter factor explains why targets in "pink collar" jobs tend to be young and economically vulnerable (for example, single heads of households who are highly dependent on their jobs [Crull, 1979; MacKinnon, 1979]). In academia the vulnerability often is psychological. College is a time of uncertainty and psychological vulnerability for almost all students, but the most likely targets of professor harassment are women who are nonassertive, experiencing stress, uncertain about their academic programs, loners, nontraditional students, members of minority groups, and/or in traditionally male fields (Dziech & Weiner, 1990). In short, the power relationship that exists between professors and students is even more asymmetrical than in most superior-subordinate relationships. When additional factors like vulnerability increase those power differences, harassment is especially likely (Benson & Thompson, 1982; Reilly et al., 1982, pp. 100–101).

Asymmetrical power relationships also influence the effectiveness of informal responses. Benson and Thompson (1982) found that overtly confronting a harasser often does get him to stop the behavior (twenty-one out of twenty-four cases), but only when the professor was untenured, the professor and student were in different academic fields, *and* the student had no aspirations for graduate school. When any one of these conditions was absent, confrontation was effective less than half of the time. Rizzo and Brosnan (1990) argued that the advice typically given students to communicate to a harasser in a direct and professional manner is unrealistically optimistic because it ignores organizational power relationships and the power/intimidation aspect of harassment, just as Bingham (1991) concluded that virtually all of the communication strategies available to victims are problematic in important ways.

A final dimension of organizational power relationships involves patterns of silence.[8] When professionals work relatively independent of one another and are similar in terms of their formal status (the kind of situation in which professors typically work), they tend to suppress discussion of a wide range of conflicts, including sexual harassment (Morrill, 1992; also see Martin, 1990). Even when administrators in colleges and universities do attempt to respond positively to students' complaints about harassment, "their efforts go unrecognized because their [the administrators'] obsessions with preserving privacy and maintaining their [public] images lead them to behave surreptitiously when grievances arise" (Dziech & Weiner, 1990, p. xxii). Universities usually conduct harassment investigations in private, often do not notify victims of the date and times of hearings or allow them to testify, and frequently fail to inform the victims of any actions taken against harassers. The rationale for maintaining secrecy typically is that the matter is a personnel action and the accused harasser deserves the protection of academic due process. But the code of silence serves primarily to protect the harasser's professional reputation and the university's public image. More important, it lulls people into complacency that harassment is not a problem, creates skepticism and mistrust of the system among students (which mitigates against victims filing complaints), and leads victims to believe that they are alone in experiencing harassment, thus encouraging them (and others) to blame themselves (Dziech & Weiner, 1990). Thus the circle is closed:

It is precisely this widespread confluence of authority relations, sexual interest and gender stratification which defines the problem of sexual harassment. There is, in other words, a *nexus to power and sexual prerogative* often enjoyed by men with formal authority over women. Men in such positions can engage in (or "get away with") overt sexual behaviors that would be rebuffed or avoided were the relationship not one of superior and subordinate. They can also discharge selectively the power and rewards of their positions as a means to obligate women sexually. As well as reward and punish women directly, men can manipulate and obscure their sexual intentions toward female subordinates. Women learn that the "official" attention of a male superior is often but a vehicle through which he can "press his pursuits" (Goffman, 1977). . . . [T]here is an intrinsic ambiguity between the *formal* definition of the male superior/female subordinate relationship and a *sexual* one, in which the gender of the woman can be made salient at the initiative of the man. (Benson and Thompson 1982, pp. 238–239; also see Balsamo, 1985)

It is this ideological and structural context that surrounds the case studies we will now examine.

READING SEXUAL HARASSMENT CASES

As indicated earlier, the details of these narratives are strikingly typical (and the experiences of harassed women strikingly "normal") when compared to those summarized in previous research, especially those from academic organizations (see, for example, Clair, 1993c; Dziech & Weiner, 1990; Farley, 1978).[9]

Harassment Episodes

Frequently the harassers were senior established faculty members who evidenced hostility to the presence of women in their domains—an adviser who asked:

"Why don't you go back to the South and marry a football player," bolted from the lips of the renown professor assigned to assist me in my transition from undergraduate to graduate school. . . . By my first academic appointment, I knew well "the place of women" in our discipline (7:1);

a department chair who

would loiter around my office door and inquire, always with a devious smile, "So what are *the women* up to now?" As the women's community grew and became more vocal on campus, he lashed out at me with sexist jokes, ridiculing women faculty. His taunting grew as he caught glimpses of my internal anger. Almost daily, he directed sexist comments to me, often at the expense of female students. "If that Amazon [woman] comes back," he announced, "be sure to let her in my class." Once, when I was advising a senior major, he stopped by my opened door, looked at me, and then turned and asked the student, "Are there any cute girls in your [sorority] house?" She blushed and turned to me. "You shouldn't say that!" I retorted. "Oh, I'm sorry. Are there any cute tarts? Are there any cute wenches?" he quipped. I yelled his name emphatically. "You know that's inappropriate." "I guess you think it's sexual harassment and you're writing it down," he responded as he smiled and walked away (7:3–4);

an ex-colleague

known for being patronizing to the women faculty, and who always commented on my appearance, suddenly strong-armed me when I jokingly reminded him of our newly set office accounting procedures for our copier, loudly proclaimed that he didn't need any controlling bitch telling him what to do (33:6);

or a chair who had just lost a vote on using gender neutral language in department discourse:

[He was] obviously very angry. The next time I came into the department office, he called me into his office to show me a pair of foam breasts that he had put on his phone as a shoulder rest. He didn't say anything, but the message was clear. I left his office without saying a word, seething but realizing that there was little I could do to stop his sexism until such time as I got tenure. He had the power and I didn't. (14:9)

But harassment in academic organizations, particularly when it involves students, often is more subtle. In some cases harassment came from men who espoused a pro-feminist ideology in their research and everyday conduct, making it especially difficult for a complainant to be perceived as being credible—

"he was teaching one of the courses I was taking and identified himself as a leftist, progressive professor" (6:2); or

when he first arrived, a male colleague and I had a long talk with him about the conservative character of the college, the relative lack of sophistication of the students, and his vulnerability to "student crushes." Projecting a kind of choirboy innocence, he responded . . . with a sensitive, "feminist" analysis of the dynamics of the situation. . . . The week he was charged, he had a full-page essay in the student newspaper, a "feminist" analysis of sexual harassment. (21:5, 14)[10]

Dziech and Weiner (1990) suggested that the typical modus operandi of faculty harassers is the "good student" come-on:

I loved the first course I took from this new, young professor. He focused massive attention on me, made me feel special, and bolstered my confidence. He became my informal advisor. (12:2)

Then he wanted to talk about the content of my paper—he seemed very interested in my experience and my insights. . . . This conversation was very satisfying to me. Then, one day during one of these "intellectual" discussions, the professor asked me when we were going to go away for the weekend. (10:4–5)

In the note Professor X asked me to come by his office late that afternoon to discuss a paper I'd written for him. . . . Naturally I was delighted by his interest in my work, and I rearranged my schedule to meet him in his office that afternoon. When I appeared he ushered me in, closed the door, and moved his chair from its usual position behind his desk to one beside me. He opened our meeting by telling me my ideas were good and he could help me refine them. As he talked, his right hand drifted first to my left arm and then to my leg. . . . He continued talking about my paper and my future in academe, all the while invading me bit by bit. The conversation closed with his telling me that we should plan on getting to know each other and working together closely. I wanted to work with him and agreed. We stood up and he embraced me and pressed a kiss on me. I recall backing up in surprise. (30:2–4)

The women who are chosen as targets describe themselves as vulnerable because of their naïveté about sexual politics:

when it [a get-together at a bar] broke up, a bunch of us were supposedly going to go to his [professor's] house to continue "the party." Then people started declining. . . . They seemed to be "in the know" with one another. . . . So I ended up at the professor's house with the understanding that others would come later (6:3);

he was fifty; I was twenty-one. He was a major professor in my area; I was a first year M.A. student. His position was secure; mine was nebulous and contingent on his support of me. He felt entitled; I felt dependent. He probably hasn't thought much about what happened; I've never forgotten (30:1);

or as being psychologically vulnerable because of being new to a program or unsure about their ability to succeed, as having recently experienced the end of an important interpersonal relationship, or as being economically vulnerable: "I was young, unworldly, liked my job, and had an unemployed husband" (33:3–4) or "I was under 30 and the single mother of a two year old" (13:1).

Targets' initial response to the harassment is to deny that it is occurring or that it is harassment (Salisbury et al., 1986):

At first I just stood there, still stunned and trying to go through all of these thoughts in my head—wondering why this was happening (6:3);

Periodically, John made comments about me that were of a sexual nature. . . . At the time, I was under no real stress and the comments seemed more like compliments than harassment (25:1);

At first, when I saw this man, his remarks about my physical appearance only seemed odd and inappropriate. But he quickly increased the level of harassment. On several occasions he called me into his office . . . to ask me if I was dating anyone. At first I just tried to ignore the questions, but he was persistent. . . . He then [after learning that I was not dating anyone] started telling me about movies he had seen, with scenes that inevitably had something to do with sex. When I ignored his innuendos, he finally got bolder and suggested that I might get more sections to teach the next semester if I was willing to go out with . . . married men. . . . By now there was no denying what was happening. (13:3–5)

Denial also was the typical response by people who learned of the harassment: "A few weeks later the first word reached me [a department chair]. From my own daughter! . . . My daughter does not lie, but I did not believe it" (21:6–7); "this felt like seduction, but he was my professor. . . . [I told a male] friend [who] laughed and said I was 'imagining things' and 'Richard' [fictional name for the professor] would never think of anything like that' " (16:4–5).

Once denial is no longer feasible, victims blame themselves:

I felt it was my own fault because I did not resist him [professor] and did not fight him off (6:4–5);

So I figured I must be wrong to feel his behavior was inappropriate, . . . exaggerating the significance of his "being friendly." . . . No matter what I said, he had a response that defined my [negative] feelings as inappropriate. . . . I accepted his view that I was a small town kid who suffered from an outdated sense of propriety (30:4, 7, 8);

and others blame them:

I've experienced a good deal of . . . accusations couched in subtle terms that I have succeeded in some areas of my life *because I am attractive* . . . etc. [emphasis ours] (1:1);

Once I did seek some confirmation about the effects of sexual harassment on my progress through graduate school, but it backfired. Two years ago I sought counseling when I had a severe case of "writers block." I thought the sessions might be a good time to talk about my experiences with sexual harassment. Unfortunately, my counselor, a woman, believed that there was no such thing as "sexual harassment," and to dwell on women's difficulties in the academy was futile." (8:13; also see 1:4)[11]

Many survivors report a loss of confidence in their intellectual abilities— "that episode weakened the confidence I had developed as an undergraduate that I, a female, could have a fulfilling and successful career in the academy" (8:7). Many felt so uncomfortable that they distanced themselves from both the harasser and male faculty members in general: "I know that for several years afterward I acted very strangely towards male professors in general" (8: 8); "Richard soon 'fell in love' with another young woman student. He remained my advisor but our professional relationship was now cool and distant and I was left with no mentor and great doubt about my abilities" (16:9).

Thus, responses by targets and by other members of their organizations serve to increase both their isolation and feelings of vulnerability. They, and any other targets who observe the outcomes of their complaints, become less likely to challenge harassment in the future and less likely to pursue effective sanctions against their harasser aggressively.

Silence and Silencing in Harassing Organizations

The effect of power inequalities is a recurring theme in these narratives. In general, harassers were either department chairmen harassing faculty members or professors harassing students.[12] Both harassers and targets understand this fact of organizational life: "At one point he dared me to complain to the head of the department, but said that he could make my job search 'difficult' in a few years. I believe he could easily do just that" (9:1). This observation is, of course, readily predicted by past research. But the concept of "silence," and the way in which silences at both the interpersonal and institutional levels contribute to power asymmetries, is a distinctive theme in these narratives.[13]

Silence in Harassing Interpersonal Interactions. When survivors do talk about their experiences, they often do so in terms of the threatening climate that has led them to remain silent, sometimes for years, and of the need for interpersonal and public support. One participant in this research noted that "the risk of making my stories known, even with the option of anonymity, seems very great to me. That the characters in the following scene might recognize themselves and enact retribution looms as a very real possibility" (15:1–2). In other narratives the threat of retribution was immediate, not anticipated:

Tensions remained high [between the author and her department chair] but rather than risk backlash and further harassment, I maintained my silence. Shortly before my tenure review, a newly appointed female colleague, teaching part-time, filed a grievance against the chair after he uttered a series of harassing remarks including one that she should have married him rather than her present husband. The female acting-provost counseled me about my precarious situation in offering supporting testimony. Out of fear, I chose silence. Out of frustration, my colleague abandoned her petition and resigned. Not to my surprise, but nonetheless painful, the department did not support me for tenure (7:7–8).

Silence leads victims to feel that they are alone, even when the same male harasses a series of women or a climate of harassment characterizes a department, circumstances that were repeatedly described in these narratives.[14] As circumstances change and victims become more secure they may begin to speak out:

While I remained silent and endured may [sic] other offensive remarks, I learned not to feel inferior and to name the thing for what it was—a political act of intimidation, an attempt to keep me in my place. Now that I have graduated, I no longer remain silent in the face of offensive remarks. I wish every speech department in the country had a feminist scholar who could empower female graduate students to name the oppression they undoubtedly also experience and to fight back. (31:11)

But, silence usually is a reasoned response by individual victims of harassment because of the very real power asymmetries they face; and power asymmetries are perpetuated largely through a conspiracy of silence at the institutional level.

The Institutional Conspiracy of Silence. Organizations and work groups silence discourse about sexual harassment both informally and formally. Informal silencing ranges from refusing to admit the existence or pervasiveness of the problem by academic organizations and by our disciplines (see narrative 8:12, above) to trivializing complaints about harassment to forming alliances to protect accused professors and isolating complainants—"the rumor mill has put on a second shift. I [chair] am gagged. The harasser and his supporters are not. Unlikely alliances have formed in his defense" (21:16)—to participating in activities that "set up" victims for harassment (as in the "in the know" party described in case 6).[15]

Formal silencing occurs primarily through the secrecy imposed on sexual harassment complaints within academic organizations (Dziech and Weiner, 1990):

I told an older man colleague whom I liked and trusted what had been happening. . . . He offered to talk to the Division Chair for me, but I was afraid that things would just get worse, so I asked him not to. Interestingly enough, the harassment episodes stopped shortly after that. It wasn't until years later that I learned that my friend had gone directly to the President of the college. . . . The President then sanctioned the Division Chair (13:6–7);

After several more complaints, this man was fired, but the ultimate irony is that as I understand it, the administration would never tell him why he had been terminated. (18:5)

Ombudspersons silence complainants when they violate promises of confidentiality—"at a meeting of women faculty I . . . asked specifically, for fear of reprisal, that my concerns not be publicly stated. The Affirmative Action Officer, a participant in that meeting, revealed my concerns an hour later in the presence of my chair [the harasser]" (7:5). Counseling centers allow repeat offenders to move from target to target with impunity by keeping their identities confidential (case 10), and formal gag orders on participants in successful complaints (case 21) all serve to (1) maintain a favorable public image of the institution, thus eliminating administrators' incentives to take effective action to solve the problem; (2) dissuade future victims from taking action; and thereby (3) perpetuate the perception that complainants are so atypical that the victim must in some way be responsible for the episode. "Slap on the wrist" punishments have similar effects:

The harasser, advised by an attorney, signed a statement admitting his guilt. He was allowed to return to the classroom on the conditions that (a) he have no further contact with the victim, (b) he do nothing to create an intimidating environment, and (c) he have no social contact with any students on or off campus for one year. He has already violated the last two terms, but the college has taken no action. (21:2)

Whether interpersonal or institutional, silencing of sexual harassment narratives serves to reproduce the sexist ideology and the power asymmetries that underlie the behavior.

CONCLUSION

In this chapter we have suggested that sexual harassment cannot be understood solely as a sociocultural phenomenon. Organizations differ in the extent to which they allow and sanction harassing behavior, and patterns of action within organizations reproduce the conditions that foster, suppress, or repress harassment. Our analysis contains a number of implications, some positive and some not. It suggests that, while substantive sociocultural change is necessary to confront the roots of sexual harassment, in the interim a number of steps can be taken to reduce its incidence and severity. But it also suggests that organizations are sufficiently fluid and adaptive to be able to offset the effects of surface-level changes. For example, recent court decisions that allow students to collect monetary damages from universities under Title IX may create incentives for administrators to take harassment more seriously, but they also may encourage them to rely even more heavily on the conspiracy of silence to suppress complaints. The latter option is readily available because new legal precedents do nothing to change the organizational structures and ideological assumptions that function to silence complaints. Neither social nor organizational change comes that easily.

NOTES

1. In January 1992 William Eadie, editor of the *Journal of Applied Communication Research (JACR)*, published a call for narratives about sexual harassment in the Speech Communication Association newsletter *Spectra*. The thirty-eight narratives that were submitted served as the basis of two articles published in that journal and are the data base for this chapter. Almost all of the cases involved harassment in academic organizations, leading us to focus in this essay on the distinctive characteristics of those settings. Although extreme forms of harassment like assault or quid pro quo demands made by supervisors are much less frequent than more subtle tactics, virtually all of the narratives examined in this study were extreme cases, for understandable reasons. Because there is wide agreement that extreme behaviors constitute harassment, and less agreement and more ambiguity whether less extreme behaviors or actions taken by coworkers or clients are harassing, it is not surprising that most of the cases submitted were of the former type—those instances *clearly* fit the call for stories of harassment. Otherwise the cases were typical of those included in research on harassment in academic organizations.

Using an ethnographic perspective we examined those narratives searching for patterns in the authors' presentations of their experiences. More detailed information about ethnographic approaches to the analysis of naturalistic narratives in general is available in Wood (1992) and about our individual research approach is presented in Taylor and Conrad (1992). In addition, a number of the narratives are published in toto in the special issue of the *Journal of Applied Communication Research* (1992, vol. 20, pp. 363–390) that includes these articles. Passages from the narratives are reprinted in this chapter and reproduced by permission of the publisher, copyright by the Speech Communication Association, July 1993.

2. Our reading of the narratives stimulated a second related-but-distinctive interpretation, one grounded in theories of organizational sexuality. For that reading see Taylor and Conrad (1992).

3. Two studies support this conclusion, a 1978–1979 study at M.I.T. and a 1987 survey of University of Illinois students (Dziech & Weiner, 1990, pp. xxi, 170).

4. Consequently, except in very rare cases, student targets should not rely solely on university hearing processes, but should also take outside action. The landmark *Meritor v. Vinson* U.S. Supreme Court decision allows plaintiffs to bypass internal grievance procedures (Paetzold & O'Leary-Kelly, 1993). Although the EEOC also is slow and ineffective, "a Title IX complaint can frighten the university into action" (Clarke, 1980, p. 45). In addition, the recent *Franklin v. Gwinnett County Public Schools* (112 S.C. 1028 [1992]) decision allows plaintiffs to collect monetary damages from educational institutions and harassers through Title IX actions and thus offset the legal, personal, and psychological costs that plaintiffs incur. On the surface this seems to be an especially important precedent, because one of the most important predictors

of the success of a sexual harassment complaint is the relative access to economic resources of the plaintiff and the defendant (Livingston, 1982). Being able to collect monetary damages provides additional incentives for victims to take legal action and makes it more likely that they will receive adequate legal assistance. Of course, relying on internal procedures provides neither of these advantages.

5. Although we will focus on organizational power relationships, we recognize that broader gender-related social/cultural power inequalities also are important factors. As Loy and Stewart conclude (1984, p. 31), "Power also is a component of cultural definitions of male and female sex role relationships. Because most women are in subordinate positions in work settings, culturally defined sex role expectations and workplace authority puts males in a cultural and organizational 'two up' position." But, we will argue, the immediate power structure of an organization can either exacerbate or mitigate the effects of cultural power asymmetries.

6. Farley (1979) argues that differences in the attrition rates of male and female graduate students also can largely be attributed to the effects of sexual harassment.

7. The latter observation is particularly important because professors seem to use more subtle forms of harassment than quid pro quo negotiation or assaults (Benson & Thompson, 1982, p. 243). Friendliness, extra attention, and unwarranted levels of help are used to lay the groundwork for sexual propositions and invitations.

8. In an essay that is notable in its theoretical rigor, Rizzo and Brosnan (1990) argue that sexual harassment and organizational responses to it can best be understood through Habermas's notion of "systematically distorted communication." Unfortunately, space limitations make it impossible for us to pursue this line of analysis here.

9. We will refer to segments of narratives by their number and the relevant paragraph (e.g., 2:6 is case number 2, paragraph 6). We are somewhat reticent to cite only parts because there is substantial evidence that women's narratives must be considered in toto in order to be fully understood (Roberts, 1981). All but three of the narratives we cite are printed in toto in the issue of the *Journal of Applied Communication Research* that includes Taylor and Conrad (1992).

10. Other harassers espoused "liberal" political values (see, for example, 7:2).

11. Survivors' self-blame may last for years:

I did try to deal with it the following semesters, but was unsuccessful. And as time went on, my shame and anger at myself settled in (6:6);

I felt embarrassed, degraded and devastated. I proceeded to class, but had a major crisis in self-esteem, feeling inadequate and self-conscious about my appearance (25:5; also see 27:9 and 31: 1);

I felt very betrayed. . . . His advances made me feel humiliated, like what a dupe I was. . . . My *anger* over having been trivialized over having my intellect take a back seat to my sexuality, has been the kernel of righteousness I've carried all these years (10.6);

Had I experienced a different kind of personal tragedy—such as a loss of eyesight, or hearing, or vision—there would be acknowledgement, recognition, perhaps some accommodation. . . . Yet, there is such profound absence of acknowledgement or recognition of sexual harassment in our field that I know that if I *ever* suggested that I had a particularly difficult beginning, one not, however, terribly dissimilar with other graduate women's experiences, that then I would be seen as *truly* out of my senses. (8:12)

12. Interestingly, some power asymmetries are situation-specific. Visiting professors are particularly immune from disciplinary action (33:6), and conventions provide a venue in which power imbalances are especially marked (33:7).

13. In an insightful and related essay, Robin Clair (1993c) has examined the ways in which the "sequestering" of sexual harassment narratives allow the dominant power structure of an organization to maintain itself.

14. Silence has a second interpersonal dimension when people whom victims seek out for advice counsel them to ignore or forget the incident or withhold valuable information about ways to deal with it.

15. In other cases the "setup" involved persons in a complex pattern of different kinds of silence and the conspirators included low-power persons:

Soon after the third of the unwelcome sexual advances happened, I confided in a senior doctoral student. Without my knowledge, he called a meeting of other doctoral students to address the sexual harassment problems in the department. Apparently, I was far from the first in-coming graduate student to be initiated into academic culture of the department via unwelcome sexual advances by male professors. (I later heard that it had been happening for several years, with the knowledge of most of the faculty). The doctoral student's own wife had been harassed at her workplace, and he thought the time was right for graduate students as a group to insist upon some disciplinary action. Unfortunately, although the three professors' names were not revealed, my anonymity was not preserved. Consequently, there was confusion about who was involved, and there was great speculation about what formal steps I might take. In a twilight-zone twist of events, the doctoral students did not go on to demand any action from the Chair of the Department. Instead, I was made the scapegoat. It seemed that there were several doctoral candidates who were being advised by a male professor with a long-standing reputation for making sexual advances toward graduate students. They believed that I might somehow make things uncomfortable for their advisor. They set out to convince everyone that I had brought this situation upon myself, and that I was blowing out of proportion some simple, friendly gestures. Ironically, their advisor was not one of the three professors who had made unwelcome sexual advances. (8: 3–5)

4

Hegemony and Harassment: A Discursive Practice

Robin P. Clair

Sexual harassment is a discursive political tool of oppression that has become entangled and enmeshed in distorted communication practices. The reality of its epidemic and pandemic proportions cannot be underestimated, questioned, or tolerated (Hanley, 1979), nor can its insidious nature and repercussions be dismissed. Yet, this is exactly what was done in the past and still continues at a variety of levels today. For example, the United States senators, who in 1991 dismissed claims of sexual harassment as unimportant to a decision of credibility regarding Supreme Court nominee Clarence Thomas, not only trivialized sexual harassment but sanctioned it as well. This patriarchal dismissal led concerned United States representatives (all female) to march to the Capitol, forcing the Senate to reevaluate its decision. Subsequently, America heard the voice of Anita Hill; the voice of female oppression.

As Conrad and Taylor point out in chapter 3, women's voices have long been and continue to be silenced on the subject of sexual harassment (also see Taylor & Conrad, 1992; Wood, 1992). Furthermore, this silence is indicative of oppression grounded in cultural assumptions about sexuality and sex roles and in the power relationships of formal organizations. Although it is true that women's voices have been silenced and that women are the primary targets of sexual harassment (Fain & Anderton, 1987), it is important to point out that men are sexually harassed also. This does not in any way undermine a feminist explanation of sexual harassment. To the contrary, recognizing that men, especially young men and minority men, also suffer under a patriarchal system supports the view that sexual harassment is a political tool of oppression that privileges the dominant ideology and marginalizes other views.

Sexual harassment is so "normalized" in our society that between 50 percent

(Loy & Stewart, 1984) and 75 percent (LaFontaine & Tredeau, 1986) of private-sector female workers report sexual harassment encounters. Although male harassment varies (Gutek, 1985) government statistics place it at approximately 15 percent (see USMSPB, 1981).

Sexual harassment is not only a pervasive problem; it is also a complex problem with serious ramifications. "The victims suffer a variety of negative (physical, emotional, and performative) consequences from their experiences with harassment" (McKinney & Maroules, 1991, p. 42). In some cases, the harassment is so severe as to result in post-traumatic stress disorder, leaving the survivor to deal with cold sweats and continuous nightmares (Castaneda, 1992). Many victims of sexual harassment are economically penalized by being transferred, fired, or forced to quit due to unbearable working conditions (Loy & Stewart, 1984; MacKinnon, 1979). Victims of sexual harassment often suffer physically, emotionally, and economically. Their suffering is carried into society; it does not stop with the individual who has been harassed.

When a pervasive and serious behavior like sexual harassment is tolerated and even rampant in society, it perpetuates an oppressive culture, which privileges a few and demeans many more people. "Sexual harassment is not 'personal': it is violence out of history" (Taylor & Conrad, 1992, p. 414). Unchallenged, this behavior sends a clear message that women occupy an inferior position in a male-dominated world (Strine, 1992). As such, *sexual harassment acts as a discursive practice*, establishing the privileged position of males, especially powerful white males. However, women are not the only ones to suffer due to patriarchal practices. Both men and women consent to a patriarchal system and, subsequently, fail to recognize how that system can "distort reality and destroy human potential, female and male" (Daly, 1973, p.7).

The purpose of this chapter is to review theoretical explanations of sexual harassment and to present hegemony as an additional means to understanding it. A theory of hegemony suggests that both dominant and subjugated individuals actively participate in the maintenance of the status quo. Thus, both women and men participate in the social construction of gender, and both may discursively frame sexual harassment in a way that perpetuates the current situation. This chapter addresses the role subjugated members play in their own domination through their use of framing devices. MacKinnon (1979) has offered numerous examples of how the dominant group contributes to the domination of women through the way they talk about sexual harassment. More recently, Clair (1993c) and Gutek (1985) offer examples of how the subjugated frame their experiences of sexual harassment. Before discussing how individual actors frame sexual harassment, I will present a brief overview of how theories frame it.

THEORETICAL EXPLANATIONS OF SEXUAL HARASSMENT

Considerable variation exists with respect to theoretical explanations of sexual harassment. Views range from a biological perspective of normal behavior to psychological explanations of abnormal social behavior (Hickson, Grierson, & Linder, 1991), from social exchange and habituation theories (Littler-Bishop, Seidler-Feller, and Opaluch, 1982) to organizational sex-role/sex-ratio explanations (Gutek & Cohen, 1987; Gutek & Morasch, 1982; see Kanter, 1977 for sex ratio).

The biological theory suggests that men are driven by testosterone, which makes them naturally sexually aggressive. It suggests that men cannot control these "natural urges." Current biological theories are rooted in aspects of Freudian theory and have been resurrected by anti-feminists (Cordes, 1993). To suggest that sexual harassment can be explained according to biological factors which are immutable paints a picture of fixed social relations. It condemns men and women to a life determined by hormonal fluctuations and fails to acknowledge the complex role that socialization plays in gender and power relationships (see Epstein, 1988; Grauerholz, chapter 2). In terms of sexual harassment, the idea that men are sexually aggressive and that women should just expect and accept this behavior reifies the age-old adage "boys will be boys" (Clair, 1993c; Cordes, 1993). Furthermore, the biological theory has been critiqued by several scholars who generally agree on its deficiency to account for sexual harassment (i.e., there is no evidence to support the notion that higher levels of testosterone lead to sexual aggression [Epstein, 1988]). (For more detailed critiques of biological theory in general see Epstein, 1988; Gutek, 1985; Tangri, Burt, & Johnson, 1982.)

Similar to yet distinct from biological theories of sexual harassment which reify male sexual aggression as the norm, psychological theories encourage the idea that sexual harassment is an "abnormal" (i.e., out of the norm) behavior and therefore is isolated to certain individuals. This view "particularizes" sexual harassment by limiting it to a few "sick" individuals. Psychological theories of this kind relieve organizations from accountability (Clair, 1993a), limit our understanding of complex issues, and reify patriarchy. Neither biological (i.e., hormonal, brain lateralization, etc.) nor psychopathological theories are acceptable explanations according to feminist philosophy or post-structuralist theories (Epstein, 1988); however, some psychological theories contribute to our understanding of sexual harassment.

Pryor (1987) provides "a partial profile of men who are more likely to sexually harass" (p. 288). Pryor's work is limited to the study of "attractive" females in heterosexual seduction situations within the college context, which suggests that the findings can be applied to only a small proportion of sexual harassment cases. Nevertheless, this work contributes to personality profiles as well as the notion that harassers are more likely to harass when their motives can be disguised (i.e., in ambiguous settings). Further contributions to the study of harasser profiles come from Zalk (1990) and Dziech and Weiner (1990), who also offer psychological portraits of heterosexual professors who engage in sexual intimacy with students. A psychoanalytic framework explains harassers as defining their "manhood" at the expense and exploitation of women. Zalk argues that harassers "are products of, and mirror, a sexist culture . . . [and] that culture also reflects the psychology of men" (p. 142). Although these studies define sexual harassment narrowly, they contribute to our understanding of specific forms of sexual harassment and suggest a link between macro- and micro-level explanations of harassment. As Zalk notes, although she believes it is unrealistic, "the transformation of societal structures is the ideal . . . for eliminating sexual harassment" (p. 170).

Social exchange theory coupled with habituation theory has also been offered as a theoretical explanation of sexual harassment and how women respond to it (Littler-Bishop, Seidler-Feller, & Opaluch, 1982). Littler-Bishop and colleagues report that "women tolerate harassment by high status males more than by low status males, perhaps because of potential gains" (p. 147) or fear of loss. Their results further indicate that the harassed women made distinctions based on status when the harasser touched them; yet, the women made no distinction based on status when the harasser made unwanted comments. In light of this finding the authors encourage habituation theory (i.e., some behaviors are so commonplace they are tolerated in similar ways no matter what the status of the harasser) be combined with social exchange theory to explain the results. Although this theory is informative, it leaves many questions unanswered. For example, the model does not explain why studies indicate that sexual harassment varies with type of work site.

Sex-role spillover and sex-ratio theories highlight the importance of work context and societal expectations for understanding sexual harassment (Gutek, 1985; Gutek & Cohen, 1987; Gutek & Morasch, 1982). Gutek and Morasch (1982) argue that sex roles, as defined by general societal standards and stereotypes, are carried into the workplace. Sometimes these stereotypes are consistent with the stereotype of the work performed (e.g., women are expected to be the nurturers in society and they are expected to be nurturing when they fill the work role of nurse). When the sex role is consistent with the work role as in the case of nurses, then sexual harassment seems to be a function of the job because the "job itself is sexualized" (p. 55). In the case of women entering traditionally male jobs, the sex-role spillover is termed a "role deviation"; and the harassment is considered a function of individuals breaking traditional gender norms. The theory's prediction that women in traditional and nontraditional jobs will be subjected to more harassment than women in integrated jobs has been supported (Gutek & Morasch, 1982; Gutek & Cohen, 1987).

Fain and Anderton (1987) argue that sex-ratio theory (i.e., the ratio of male to female workers impacting the frequency of sexual harassment) has ignored aspects of male domination other than numeric dominance. For example, even when males are the minority they tend to dominate leadership roles, suggesting that male dominance has been "institutionalized" and "legitimated" (see Israeli, 1983, as cited in Fain & Anderton, 1987). The authors examine whether work group composition (i.e., sex ratio), intraorganizational stratification (i.e., organizational status), or macro-level social stratification (i.e., general social status) best explains sexual harassment. Their findings do not support the sex-ratio theory; women in integrated and predominantly female work groups experience significantly more sexual harassment than in male-dominated groups, with the exception that male-dominated groups evidence more quid pro quo harassment. In contrast to the results for the sex-ratio theory, Fain and Anderton (1987) report that organizational status combined with general social status best explains occurrences of sexual harassment. With respect to hierarchal status, supervisors are less likely to be harassed than staff, and lower status workers are more likely to be harassed than higher status workers. However, macro-level diffuse status characteristics (i.e. education, race, marital status, and age) explained most of the variance. Women are more often sexually harassed than are men; women with some college or vocational training are more often sexually harassed than high school- or college-educated women; minority women are more frequently subjected to sexual harassment than white women; previously married women (i.e., divorced, widowed, and separated) report the most harassment, followed by single women and then married women; and age is inversely related to sexual harassment.

Fain and Anderton conclude that sexual harassment is best explained as a pervasive cultural system rooted in power inequities. According to the authors, one cannot promote intraorganizational theories to explain sexual harassment without giving serious attention to the cultural aspects that promote certain organization structures and processes. (See chapter 3 for further discussion of how organizational status combines with general social status characteristics to influence the incidence of sexual harassment.)

The theories reviewed in this chapter have demonstrated inadequacies; yet, each has helped elucidate some aspect of sexual harassment. In the following section, I explore the possibilities that a critical feminist perspective yields in explaining sexual harassment. By discussing hegemony and sexual harassment as a discursive practice, which is culturally grounded in the principles of patriarchy, I attempt to establish the powerful role that communication plays in the perpetuation of oppression. This approach, like others, is marked with limitations; however, it is my hope that the benefits incurred overshadow any deficiencies.

HEGEMONY AND HARASSMENT

As a discursive practice that perpetuates patriarchy, sexual harassment may best be explained by theories of hegemony.[1] Hegemony is the process by which groups of individuals come to participate in their own domination. Foundations for the conceptualization of hegemony are grounded in Marxist ideology and have been developed by Antonio Gramsci (1971). Gramsci is most famous for his consideration of how large European populations came to be controlled by fascists. Although his theory of hegemony is not fully developed, his work sheds light on the subject of social (Gitlin, 1980) and organizational control (Clegg & Dunkerley, 1980). Gramsci (p. 12) defines hegemony as

the "spontaneous" consent given by the great masses of the population to the general direction imposed on social life by the dominant fundamental group; this consent is "historically" caused by the prestige (and consequent confidence) which the dominant group enjoys because of its position and function in the world of production.

An important aspect of Gramsci's version of hegemony is that force by coercion and force by consent reinforce each other, and that domination through hegemony is constructed, not given. Gramsci (p. 12) defines coercion as

the apparatus of state coercive power which "legally" enforces discipline on those groups who do not "consent" either actively or passively. This apparatus is, however, constituted for the whole of society in anticipation of moments of crisis of command and direction when spontaneous consent has failed.

Hegemony is dependent upon the active consent of oppression and acceptance of privilege. The multiplicity of groups as well as the plurality of positions an individual can hold in society make hegemony a very complex concept.[2] The underlying premise of Gramsci's development of hegemony (i.e., consent by the oppressed groups) leads to the understanding that individuals discursively produce and reproduce the cultural order.

A hegemonic understanding of sexual harassment should not be confused with "blaming the victim." First, both victims and harassers play a role in the construction of society. Social actors are subjected to the principles of patriarchy through varied practices of socialization; as such, victims, harassers, and third parties are all likely to internalize the cultural ideology that supports sexual harassment. Victims who internalize the culture may frame sexual harassment in a way that is concurrent with and supportive of the status quo. However, even victims who do not internalize the cultural ideology may use the same strategies as those who do. These victims may use these strategies as a form of survival and sometimes as a form of resistance, although resistance may perpetuate the oppression. For example, numerous studies suggest that many women ignore sexual harassment. Some do this because they frame the harassment as trivial (internalizing a patriarchal principle), while others report using the same strategy as a form of resistance by suggesting that they do not want the harasser to know he has had an impact on them. Thus, a hegemonic explanation of sexual harassment views victims as contributing to their own domination, but it does not assign blame to them for doing so.

Several authors have elaborated the theory of hegemony by identifying discursive strategies social actors may employ to reproduce patriarchy. For example, although Daly (1973) does not employ the word hegemony explicitly, she advances a concern over a dynamic process of "cooptable reformism that nourishes the oppressive system" (p. 6). Women and men contribute to the current state of patriarchy through their discursive actions.

Giddens (1979) suggests that three ideological modes contribute to oppression: *universalization of dominant interests, disguising contradictions in the system,* and *reification.* In a recent study (Clair, 1993c), I transform these modes into discursive frames and use them to understand how stories of sexual harassment are sequestered. First, with respect to accepting the dominant interests as universal, victims of sexual harassment may perceive their own interests as secondary to the organization's (e.g., Although I'm the victim of sexual harassment, I should quit my job because that would be best for the company). Second, with regard to disguising contradictions in the system, victims might apply a simple misunderstanding frame to the behavior (e.g., I must have misunderstood his actions. He was probably only flirting with me). Finally, with regard to reification, victims may see sexual harassment as immutable (e.g., Some things can't be changed. Boys will be boys). The results of the study indicate that these three framing techniques were rarely employed by victims.

My research (Clair, 1993c) also suggests at least three additional framing techniques that might be used by the subjugated group: trivialization, denotative hesitancy, and public/private domain—public/private expression. In the following sections I illustrate these three framing devices with examples from in-depth interviews with working women (see Clair, 1993c, for a full description of the sample and interview procedures). I propose that victims of sexual harassment perpetuate the hegemonic relation through their use of these framing techniques.[3]

Trivialization

Trivialization is a discursive form that perpetuates patriarchy by not taking women "seriously." Women "are frequently told to turn their minds to *more serious questions*" (Daly, 1973, p. 81; emphasis added). This suggests that sexual harassment may be viewed as a minor annoyance and contributes to the silencing of victims. "Trivialization of sexual harassment has been a major means through which its invisibility has been enforced" (MacKinnon, 1979, p. 52). Both Daly and MacKinnon discuss trivialization of sexual harassment as a technique used by the dominant group (i.e., harassers and judges).

Victims may also trivialize sexual harassment by turning it into a joke or pretending that it is not a serious problem. For example, one woman explains: "Well, if it's subtle and it's jokingly, and it's not hurting me or my position, I'm okay with it. . . . But then it annoys you and you say something about it. You almost want to dish it back really bad."

Here sexual harassment is trivialized by the suggestion that the behavior is "subtle" and therefore does not hurt the woman or her position. Although the woman deems the behavior "okay," it infuriates her, and she is frustrated at being compelled to suffer the indignities of this behavior.

Some waitresses explain that sexual harassment is a common practice in the restaurant industry. Managers, cooks, and customers often sexually harass waitresses. One waitress says that her manager "used to come up to all the girls and put his arm around them and schmooze them. But he never really, I mean he never really, you know, never really tried anything." Once again sexual harassment is trivialized based upon the degree of unwanted behavior. Although the manager's actions could certainly be construed as sexually harassing, the waitress is willing to give his behavior the benefit of the doubt because other harassment that she might encounter could be much more intolerable. In other words, she puts up with some forms of harassment because they are less offensive than others.

Other women trivialize sexual harassment through their response to it rather than through their definition of its severity. For example, a medical technician reports that her boss "kept wanting to, I don't know, touch you. . . . I would joke with him about it and make light of it and just kind of blow him off." Several other women use similar tactics. One woman explains, "My former boss would come up behind me and rub against me. [Eventually] it got to be kind of a joke" in that she would watch for him and slip away when he got close. Another woman says when her boss would try to touch her she "sort of got up and walked away and made a joke of it." Another woman gives this rendition of how she handles sexual harassment: "Blow it off. Smile at them . . . and not let them know it gets to me."

Only one woman in the study reports contacting an organization that specifically deals with sexual harassment. Therefore, she does not trivialize the incident, at least not at first. She explains that after contacting the organization she realized she would need support from her coworkers, several of whom had been harassed by the same man, yet none would come forward. The woman reports that she gave up her complaint due to lack of support and later refers to the man's actions as "just touchy feely." Eventually, she says she "made a joke of it."

These stories indicate how victims of sexual harassment become complicit in their own oppression. By trivializing the harassment, these women perpetuate the hegemonic relation.

Denotative Hesitancy

Denotative hesitancy is a discursive practice that perpetuates patriarchy by not articulating the issues and interests of the subjugated group. Specifically, domination is achieved through the use of vocabulary. Feminist philosophers have pointed out that if the dominant group controls the language of society, then the subjugated group is unable to name their experience (Ardener, 1975; Clair, 1993c; Daly, 1975; MacKinnon, 1979; Spender, 1984; Wood, 1992; Wood, chapter 1). With denotative hesitancy, the subjugated group shows hesitancy in using terms that name and legitimate their experiences. (See Schiappa, in press and 1991 for reviews of denotative conformity, from which denotative hesitancy was derived.)

Denotative hesitancy surfaces in two ways. First, women reflect upon past experiences when sexual harassment was not discussed and no terms existed to explain this behavior. Second, they hesitate to call sexually harassing behavior "sexual harassment." Reflecting on the past, one woman explains: "And at that time, in the middle 70s, there was not this big thing about sexual harassment . . . it just wasn't the topic of the day. In other words, I would have been shown to be leading them on." Similarly a fifty-year-old sales representative recalls that the term "sexual harassment" did not exist when she first started working and therefore she couldn't be sure whether her experiences could be defined as such. Another woman who had recently encountered sexual harassment says, "I realize more that it's sexual harassment since it's come out more."

Established language plays a major role in validating the experiences women encounter, what action they might take, or what actions they might expect from society. However, women may also hesitate to use the term "sexual harassment" for reasons other than a lack of available language. For example, a telephone repair person said that what she encountered might be called sexual harassment: "It depends how you define it." She went on to say that one man "was blowing kisses and smacking his lips at me every time he saw me. He did it for about a year. . . . The thing is I don't have to be around them all the time. It's just in and out of the garage." She hesitates to label this man's behavior as sexual harassment. Since the term would label the behavior illegal, applying it might make it more difficult for a woman to tolerate, ignore, or trivialize her experience.

Excusing sexual harassment through denotative hesitancy perpetuates the hegemonic relation. Yet, declaring actions as sexual harassment and taking action in a legal way can be a frightening proposition. Women fear having their experiences trivialized by others, being ostracized by coworkers, being penalized for their actions with reduced salaries, transfers, or being fired. They fear that others will blame them, and/or they suffer guilt and anxiety about how others will judge them if their stories become public (Collins & Blodgett, 1981).

Private Domain

Public/private expression—public/private domain is a discursive practice based in Sennett's (1977) suggestion that there are basically two types of expression (i.e., private and public) which are used primarily in two types of domains (i.e., private and public). Private expression is spontaneous and emotional, while public expression is controlled and rational. The private domain is constituted by areas we consider personal (e.g., the home or, more specifically, the bedroom), while the public domain is open to public view. Mac-Kinnon (1979) argues that although sexual harassment takes place in the public domain, it is usually deemed a private experience. By privatizing sexual harassment, organizations reduce their accountability and isolate "women's reactions to an experience which is common and shared" (p. 87).

One way to frame harassment in a privatizing style is to bring in the personal life of the harasser. For example, a nurse describes a physician she worked with who was "pretty handsy" and had sexually harassed several nurses: "He came up to me a couple of days ago and said he gets turned on by pregnant women [the respondent was pregnant at the time]. I told him I felt sorry for him. . . . It was really an injustice to his wife." In this situation the nurse fails to articulate that the sexually harassing behavior is an injustice to her; rather she personalizes the behavior, drawing on the man's marital status and claims that the injustice is being done to his wife. This discursive strategy promotes hegemony by privileging the wife's status above that of the nurse. Furthermore, it fails to make the organization accountable for the actions of an individual, even though the nurse is aware of the doctor's past violations with other nurses.

Other women say that they would remind a man of his marital status by inviting him to bring his wife along when he suggested a meeting elsewhere. Once again this strategy frames the harassment in a personal way. It suggests that the women can handle sexual harassment by simply reminding the man that his personal obligations constrain his "rights" to harass sexually. This discursive frame encourages the hegemonic relation, as the women offer partial consent to harassment by suggesting that other sexual relationships should constrain the man's behavior, rather than their own rights to justice and respect.

Another way of invoking the private domain is for the victim of harassment to call upon her own personal life to deflect the harassment, as the following story reflects: "I had an operator . . . who would constantly ask me for sex. Every morning he would be waiting to ask me for sex; and, he would always tell me he'd pay me, that he'd give me his check. Whatever it took for me to have sex with him. I brought my boyfriend on the job and he stopped [respondent laughed]."

When victims of sexual harassment rely on their personal attachment to other men (e.g., a boyfriend, husband, brother, etc.), they hegemonically reinforce the patriarchal practice of privatizing sexual harassment. It becomes the concern of individual males to protect or fight over the possession of a female. This strategy reinforces male dominance over women and keeps sexual harassment at an individual level, relieving the organization and society of its responsibility.

These framing techniques are also excellent exemplars of how resistance is oppressive in some circumstances. These victims may assert that they have effectively handled the situation, yet they have done so by relying on other oppressive principles.

CONCLUSION

Sexual harassment is a discursive practice that degrades women and controls them in numerous ways (physically, emotionally, economically, politically, and culturally). Theories proposed thus far to explain sexual harassment have been helpful; yet, they have also been unable to deal with the myriad sexual harassment events and their wider cultural implications.

Theories, like victim's responses, may overtly or subtly contribute to the hegemonic relation. For example, theories that focus narrowly on quid pro quo harassment fail to address the majority of sexual harassment (i.e., hostile environment). Specifically, Pryor's (1987) work, although well intentioned, focuses on the "seduction" scenario. Although this form of sexual harassment does indeed exist and needs to be addressed, framing sexual harassment as seduction rather than misogynistic behavior can lead to assumptions that suggest harassers are victims of their own biological/psychological sexual drive, demonstrate a perverse need for power, or are incompetent romantics. None of these assumptions explains the pervasiveness of gender discrimination through sexual harassment. Furthermore, this type of theorizing reduces and limits the explanation of sexual harassment to the individual level of analysis.

Within this chapter I have suggested that hegemony may best explain how sexual harassment acts as a discursive tool of oppression which the victims help perpetuate through their own discursive practices. Specifically, examples of how women trivialize sexual harassment, fail to label it as "sexual harassment," and invoke the private domain are three ways that women reproduce the status quo. By framing sexual harassment in a way that perpetuates domination rather than challenges it, women reinforce the hegemonic relation.

Not all women consent to their oppression through discursive strategies. A few report using meta-communicative strategies (i.e., rather than reacting to the harassment, they communicate about the sexual harassment; see Clair, McGoun, & Spirek, 1993). For example, one female surgeon refused to accept this degrading behavior as "valid." She and a sales representative both called sexually harassing behavior, "sexual harassment." These two women and one other said that sexual harassment simply cannot be tolerated. They did not call upon their personal life or the personal life of the harasser to stop the behavior. They relied on their freedom to voice their concerns about intolerable and unacceptable behavior. These are examples of discursive practices that challenge the status quo. These forms of discursive resistance help to shatter the "silence" of sexual harassment and break the hold of hegemony.

Although meta-communicative strategies may be more productive than trivializing, hesitating denotatively, or privatizing sexual harassment, it is crucial to remember that women are not singularly responsible for perpetuating the hegemonic relation and are rarely harassers themselves. Resistance to oppression must be countered from myriad sources. As Gramsci (1971) points out, hegemony is inextricably linked with coercion. Thus, both the hidden and overt threat of violence toward women must cease. All individuals play a role in the perpetuation of the status quo. One need not be labeled a "harasser" or a "victim" to participate in an oppressive system. Resistance must come from all of us.

NOTES

I would like to thank Betsy Campbell, Katie Namen, Cindy Rauser, Annie Streepy, Kelly Thompson, and Mike McGoun for their assistance on data collection and transcriptions described in this chapter. I also wish to thank Timothy J. Hack and especially Shereen Bingham for excellent editorial comments.

1. It is beyond the scope of this chapter to detail the complex phenomenon of hegemony completely. However, it is important to point out that at least four forms of hegemony exist, which may not be mutually exclusive nor exhaustive: consent, strategy, privilege, and abandonment (Clair, 1993b).

2. This brief overview presents the early foundations of hegemony. A more elaborate theory is available in Laclau and Mouffe (1985), who discuss the plurality of subject positions and call for a radical democracy.

3. All of the stories discussed in this chapter were collected prior to the Clarence Thomas hearings. Quotations of women's experiences with sexual harassment are excerpted from Clair, 1993c.

5

Anita Hill on Trial: A Dialectical Analysis of a Persuasive Interrogation

Claudia L. Hale, Leda M. Cooks, and Sue DeWine

In the fall of 1991, Anita F. Hill, professor of law at the University of Oklahoma, was invited to participate in the information-seeking activities of the Senate Judiciary Committee. The committee's charge was to offer a recommendation concerning the nomination of Judge Clarence Thomas to the United States Supreme Court. In describing what was to occur, *The New York Times* predicted that the "cross-examination intended to discern the truth in the diametrically opposed stories of two intelligent, articulate, self-made lawyers, is likely to be excruciating and embarrassing, and could well lead to a muddled outcome" (Dowd, 1991, p. A1). Senator Joseph Biden (Democrat, Delaware), who chaired the committee, said:

> I must start off with a presumption of giving the person accused the benefit of the doubt. I must seek the truth and I must ask straightforward and tough questions and in my heart I know if *that woman* is telling the truth it will be *almost unfair* to her. On the other hand, if I don't ask legitimate questions, then I am doing a *great injustice* to someone who might be totally innocent. (Krauss, 1991, p. A18; emphasis added)

Our objective is to offer a critical examination of the Judiciary Committee's "truth-seeking" efforts. Our analysis focuses specifically on the questions and comments committee members posed to Professor Hill and Judge Thomas. We attempt to identify the key characteristics that contribute to our belief that the confirmation hearings were less about information seeking than they were protection of the patriarchal structure and the status quo. Through the questions asked and, more particularly, the comments offered by the senators, the hearings were, in fact, efforts at persuasion and at providing justifications for the committee's actions not only during but prior to Anita Hill's testimony.

Our analysis relies on discourse analytic methodology and, more specifically, dialectical criticism. Dialectical criticism is well suited to an examination of the Thomas-Hill hearings because this form of analysis commands that attention be devoted both to what was spoken and to what was not spoken as the senators engaged in their questioning and orations. A dialectical analysis is especially appropriate for our purposes because of its emphasis on language or discourse *as strategy*. Through examining the hearing transcripts[1] (as well as relevant videotapes), we sought to uncover the ways in which the very information-seeking activities of the members of the Judiciary Committee function as argument in support of our perception that, ultimately, the hearings served as the *Trial of Anita Hill*.

DIALECTICAL CRITICISM AND THE THOMAS-HILL HEARINGS

Dialectical criticism finds its roots in Marxist critiques of structure and the strategies of omission (or neglect), immanence (or context), and transcendence (or creativity). Marxist criticism has tended to examine the "present absent" in discourse, that is, that which, through omission, speaks the unspeakable. This approach to criticism also examines the context within which the omission occurs and the creativity (or lack of creativity) that, in its own way, has enabled the omission.

As an analytic framework, Marxist criticism dictates an exploration of what is not said. That is, Marxist criticism attends to the code of opposition that establishes a dialectic between what is made present (and natural) by questions asked and statements made versus what is concealed in that very presence. The omission of arguments from a line of questioning, as occurred in the hearings, seems natural. After all, inventing new ways of questioning any of the witnesses would have been time consuming and not within the structural boundaries of the hearing process.

Arguments against changing the normative structure are precisely what Marxist critics point to as the "naturalizing" function of ideology. For its part, ideology obviates the need to make any argument for changing structure or for reading the code of oppositions and omissions in language. Instead, ideology functions like a "linguistic legislature which defines what is available for public discussion and what is not" (Thompson, 1984, p. 85).

Marxist criticism also attends to the context within which the omission occurs and the creativity (or lack of creativity) revealed in that omission. The meaning of any linguistic event is tied to context. This tie between language and context allows the speaker to create an immanent presence in the discourse, corresponding to tradition and to the hegemonic function of ideology. At the same time, the linguistic event and the terms used to describe it carry meanings that come both before and after the event. These meanings make the location of speaker and audience political.

According to Grossberg (1979), the strategy of transcendence corresponds to ideas of freedom and to the human use of creativity in order to escape the boundaries that language (and, by extension, society) imposes. Any rhetorical criticism of the Thomas-Hill hearings must locate itself first in context in order to examine the possibilities for and constraints against transcendence. An examination of the hearings as context necessitates viewing speaker and audience, fashioned through their location in space and time, as primary in the immanence-transcendence dialectic. The hearings provide an exemplar of constraints against creativity (realized freedom) through the invocation of tradition as the seeking of truth, justice, and rationality (idealized freedom). The Judiciary Committee invoked these themes throughout the hearings—obscuring the absent (sexual harassment and the oppression of women) by "tapping values rooted in the political and economic priorities a society has already established" (Hart, 1991, p. 404).

That the senators would be (or should have been) interested in truth does not render the opposing code invisible or implausible. Invoking the values of truth and justice merely prevents an audience from arguing for and realizing changes that are necessary for transcendence or, in the case of the Thomas-Hill hearings, changes that are necessary for women to gain a voice in the dialectic.

For Grossberg (1979), immanence should be weighed over transcendence as the primary domain of rhetorical and communication scholarship. Emphasizing immanence highlights the constraints of tradition, bringing into focus the seemingly inescapable traps of hegemony in discussions of truth and fairness. The idea of truth as separate from the spoken presence, of that which must be sought, is fundamental to the Platonic tradition. Yet, by privileging truth-in-absence (that which must be found), the hearings and other such inquiries position themselves as means for uncovering that which otherwise cannot be known. The context of the hearings, as defined by Senator Biden, was that of a *fact-finding* mission. Thus, if there are facts "out there" to be found, the method for discovering them is positioned as the real "truth" in the process. The systematization of method becomes the structure through which truth will somehow appear.

The absence of a language with which to articulate women's experience is the focus of many feminists who, through their writing, attempt to deconstruct androcentric language (Allen & Baber, 1992; Daly, 1983). However, the notion that there is no such thing as *spoken* truth for women, while intriguing, does not facilitate critique of everyday events and activities that oppress women. Our attempt in this chapter is to look at the ways (male) languaging of evidence/experience operates as a basis for comparison and understanding one woman's experience of sexual harassment. Dialectical analysis places emphasis on the spoken as the means for uncovering that for which the structure of language cannot account. The structure of the hearings, as described in the opening remarks made by the senators, sanctioned their approach to seeking truth by way of three operant ideologies: rationality, fairness and choice. Specifically, during the initial moments of the hearings, each of the senators who spoke framed the hearings in a manner that privileged the senators themselves as *rational* speakers of justice, citizens of the democracy devoted to *fairness*, and protectors (controllers) of the process for uncovering the truth concerning the *choices* that had been made (particularly the choices made by Anita Hill, but also those made by the committee, itself).

Dialectic of Rationality v. Irrationality (or Truth v. Fantasy)

Radical feminists, such as Dworkin (1987) and MacKinnon (1987), have criticized the legal system for setting up a process that positions women and women's experiences as irrational. Patriarchy dictates the search for a truth that is "out there," a positivist philosophy of an accessible and single reality for all. The systematic process for finding truth becomes the only "logical" means of establishing precedents for fairness. Senator Leahy gave voice to this dilemma when questioning Judge Thomas: "One of you is not telling the truth or is there any possibility that the both of you were seeing the same thing, both of you were seeing the robbery but seeing it entirely differently. Which is it?" (Day 2, Part 2, p. 17).

Within the American system of justice, precedents for fairness are derived through a combination of context and theory which result in a logic of process. This logic is revealed in the oft-cited argument that the process, if properly executed, will result in "truth" being revealed. Thus, accused and accuser alike are urged to "trust the system." Unfortunately for Anita Hill, the combination of conditions that brought her concerns before the Judiciary Committee did not fit within the rational framework of the patriarchal judicial system. The committee found itself faced with the challenge of finding an appropriate mechanism for handling an accusation emerging from one woman's experience of powerlessness. The response to this challenge was a continuing demand that Hill make rational that which, for the male senators, stood as totally irrational.

The context in which sexual harassment typically occurs is the public (male) space of the workplace, a space in which women have traditionally been displayed as decorations or intruders rather than worthy participants. The problem facing the senate committee was to find a way of determining "truth." The theory that commonly guides such efforts situates truth as an objective reality existing apart from those who experience it. Truth can be discovered and validated, but only through the experiences and accomplishments of those in power, *not* through the experiences of the powerless. The notion that truth can somehow be established through a different logic or rationality is not plausible.

In his opening statement, Senator Biden asserted that truth could be discerned only by "not allow[ing] questions on matters that are totally irrelevant to our investigation of the professional relationship of Judge Thomas and any woman who has been employed by him" (Day 1, Part 1, p. 2). Through this statement, as well as other pronouncements, Biden framed the hearings in the context not of establishing the truth of Anita Hill's claims but, rather, of the extent to which her statement reflected or spoke to truth as established by Clarence Thomas.

Senator Thurmond stated that the hearings were a reality only "because Judge Thomas [had] requested an opportunity to refute these allegations and restore his good name" (Day 1, Part 1, p. 2). Thurmond then framed Hill's statement as manipulative, citing her "friendly contact" with Thomas during and after their formal working relationship, and Thurmond wrongly accused Hill of "[choosing] to publicize her allegations the day before the full Senate would have voted to confirm Judge Thomas" (Day 1, Part 1, p. 3). These statements paint the picture of a woman who must be lying—if only because she didn't handle the alleged harassment in a "logical" (i.e., rational) manner. At least for Thurmond, "truth" had to lie outside of Hill's allegations, because her claims were not in line with reality as he experienced it.

Implied throughout the questioning by Specter, Hatch, Simpson, and others was the "illogical" relationship between Thomas and Hill which existed for over ten years after their formal association had ended. After all, what woman in her right mind would maintain a cordial professional relationship with a man who had harassed her. Continuing attempts were made to establish the (il)legitimacy of Hill's claims by gathering evidence of her irrational behavior in continuing to treat Thomas in a gracious manner. From the beginning, Hill had little room to defend her right to object to the terrorism she had experienced. Instead, she found herself in the unenviable position of defending the logic—or rationality—of (1) her judgement in moving from the Department of Education to the Equal Employment Opportunity Commission (EEOC), (2) her decision to maintain a cordial professional relationship after the formal employment tie had ended, and (3) her "decision" to bring her experiences to the attention of the committee.

In the first day of the hearings, Senator Heflin played a significant role in establishing the alleged harassment as a fantasy, fabricated by Hill because of unfulfilled sexual desires. Heflin might have been playing "devil's advocate," trying to provide an opportunity for Hill to refute various motives that had been attributed to her. However, the impact of Heflin's questions was to invoke and give implicit, if not explicit, credence to the traditional image of the irrational woman: "Are you a scorned woman? . . . Are you a zealot civil rights believer that progress will be turned back if Clarence Thomas goes on the court? . . . Do you have a martyr complex? . . . Do you see that coming out of this you can be a hero in the civil rights movement?" (Day 1, Part 3, p. 14).

Heflin noted that Hill had studied psychology as an undergraduate. He then raised the issue of fantasy, asking, "What are the traits of fantasy that you studied?" (Day 1, Part 3, p. 14). While this question allowed Hill to refute allegations that she was suffering from delusions (she responded by noting "there is no indication that I'm an individual who is not in touch with reality"), the fact that the issue was raised gave credence to the fantasy accusation. Heflin's line of questioning also meant that his hearing time (not only with Hill but later with Thomas) was spent exploring Hill's character and motivations rather than critically examining Thomas's actions or the reception Hill might have expected to receive had she complained about the harassment at the time of its occurrence.

Senator Specter pressed Hill about her inability to recall the events preceding the hearings. Specter asserted that, if Hill could recall with clarity and detail the circumstances that led her to question Thomas's nomination to the Supreme Court, surely she should be capable of recalling events of the month prior to the hearings. Specter's questioning positioned the clarity with which Hill described the harassment incidents against the seeming irrationality of her inability to relate details of her FBI interview. Specter repeatedly attacked the "seriousness" of Hill's charges, not in terms of validating her experiences and the problems she faced in dealing with sexual harassment but against the possibility that she might damage Thomas's reputation and cause him to withdraw from the nomination process.

Specter: I can understand why you would say that these comments—alleged comments—would stand out in your mind. . . . But when you talk about the withdrawal of a Supreme Court nominee, you're talking about something that is very vivid—stark, and you're talking about something that occurred within the past four or five weeks.

Hill: Well, Senator, I would suggest to you that for me these are more than mere allegations. . . . These comments are the truth to me. . . . I may not respond to it in the same way that you do. (Day 1, Part 2, p. 15)

The dialectic of rationality-irrationality, while seemingly constant in terms of the meanings given to the logic of "neutered" memory (e.g., the memory associated with the chronological ordering of events), is constantly shifting and realigning itself to position the dominant order as the only way by which rational experience can be validated. Thus, in the case of the question (challenge) posed by Specter, the "rational" order of events had already been determined through male experience, leaving little room for the validation of female memory and female ways of going through the world. Sexual harassment itself was not considered a worthy problem for consideration and remedial action but, instead, a spur in the saddle of the nomination process and an obstacle in the way of one man's rise to prominence and power.

Ultimately, the question of rationality-irrationality centered around Professor Hill's decisions not to report the harassment when she was at the Department of Education and to "follow" Judge Thomas from Education to EEOC. Senator Specter pursued the first of these issues when he asked: "What went on through your mind? I know that you decided not to make a complaint, but did you give that any consideration, and if so how could you allow this kind of reprehensible conduct to go on right in the headquarters without doing something about it?" (Day 1, Part 2, p. 16).

What was not addressed in the hearings (and is typically acknowledged only in formal discussions of women's powerlessness in a patriarchal society) is the lack of choice women have for dealing with issues involving their own sexuality and, thus, the rationality of "nonaction." Women have traditionally been invalidated by the legal system and subjected to ridicule when they have tried to protest that invalidation. In the Judiciary Committee hearings, the nature of harassment, how harassment is experienced by women, and the ways that harassment threatens women's advancement in the work force was not confronted because sexual harassment was secondary to the larger issue of the nomination of a black man, Clarence Thomas, to the Supreme Court.

Thomas helped the committee avoid the issue of sexual harassment by providing an alternate focus. In his opening statement, he purposefully invoked the specter of racism when he said, "I will not provide the rope for my own lynching" (Day 1, Part 1, p. 5). Following Hill's testimony, Thomas returned to the hearing room. He again raised the lynch mob analogy, stating:

Thomas: [A]s far as I'm concerned, it is a high-tech lynching for uppity blacks who in any way deign to think for themselves, to do for themselves, to have different ideas, and it is a message that unless you kowtow to an old order, this is what will happen to you. You will be lynched, destroyed, caricatured by a committee of the U.S. Senate rather than hung from a tree. (Day 1, Part 4, p. 1)

Since the hearings, a number of commentators have noted the lack of historic context within Thomas's claim, specifically that there are no records of a black man ever having been lynched for violations of a *black* woman (e.g., Davis, 1992; Freedman, 1992). Nonetheless, through his statements, Thomas successfully framed (i.e., "rationalized") the hearings in the context of racial discrimination as opposed to sexual harassment.

We probably should not be surprised that the focus on racial discrimination proved powerful. Many commentators have suggested that, at least with respect to the Democratic senators, their long-standing identification with a liberal agenda made it virtually impossible to question Thomas's claim of racism. A different (albeit compatible) explanation emerges when we examine the perspective of the perpetrator as compared with that of the victim. As King (1992, p. 66) explains:

[M]any black men who have suffered as victims of race discrimination are unable to see the sex discrimination women complain about because as perpetrators of that sex discrimination, they can only view sex discrimination from the perpetrator perspective—as a series of acts inflicted on the victim by the perpetrator, whereas they may clearly be able to view race discrimination from their perspective as victims—as the objective conditions of life and the consciousness associated with those objective conditions.

While the King statement speaks specifically to barriers facing black men, we can readily generalize to any group. To the extent that a problem (in this case, sexual harassment) exists outside an individual's realm of experience, then rationalizing the behavior of those who must actually confront that problem can prove not only challenging but impossible.

The shift in focus (to racial discrimination) was not the only dynamic permitting the senators to avoid the issue of sexual harassment. Professor Hill contributed to the process through her inability to rationalize her behavior in a way that the all-male Judiciary Committee could understand. Even she was forced to admit that the chasm between her sense-making (i.e., rationalized action) at the time of the harassment and the senators' retrospective sense-making (i.e., ability to rationalize) would probably never be traversed:

Simpson: [I]f what you say this man said to you occurred . . . why in God's name would you ever speak to a man like that the rest of your life?

Hill: That's a very good question. And I'm sure that I cannot answer that to your satisfaction. That is one of the things that I have tried to do today. I have suggested that I was afraid of retaliation. I was afraid of damage to my professional life. And I believe that you have to understand that . . . this kind of response is not atypical. And I can't explain. It takes an expert in psychology to explain how that can happen. But it can happen, because it happened to me. (Day 1, Part 3, p. 39)

Dialectic of Fair v. Unfair

Many black feminist scholars (e.g., Collins, 1990; hooks, 1990; King, 1992) have pointed to the rationality of the white, male system of justice as working to create fairness only for those who fit within the paradigm. For many African-American women, whose lives and experiences speak to a much different set of truths than those the senators hoped to uncover, the legal process itself becomes irrelevant. Yet, the senators, convinced that the hearing process would reveal the truth, thought that fairness could be achieved by simply examining Hill's allegations in light of the importance of Thomas's nomination to the Supreme Court.

Senator Biden invoked the concept of fairness during his opening statement, establishing his belief that "fairness is the primary responsibility of this committee" (Day 1, Part 1, p. 2). He then offered two different conceptualizations of fairness. In the case of Professor Hill, Biden noted that fairness meant "understanding what a victim of sexual harassment goes through, why victims often do not report such crimes, why they often believe that they should not or cannot leave their jobs" (Day 1, Part 1, p. 2). With respect to Judge Thomas, fairness meant being given "a full and fair opportunity to confront these charges against him, to respond fully, to tell us his side of the story, and to be given the benefit of the doubt" (Day 1, Part 1, p. 2).

From that point on, fairness for Anita Hill disappeared as a major point of concern. Instead, fairness for Clarence Thomas assumed preeminence, as exemplified in the first day's closing statement by Senator Orrin Hatch: "[T]he accuser, under our system of jurisprudence and under any system of fairness, should have to prove the case" (Day 1, Part 4, p. 14). Within the next few minutes, Senator Simpson echoed that sentiment:

Simpson: [T]his is a quote from our Chairman this morning, "Fairness also means that Judge Thomas must be given a full and fair opportunity to confront these charges. . . ."Now that's what we're doing here, and if there is any doubt, it goes to Clarence Thomas. It does not go to Professor Hill. (Day 1, Part 4, p. 14)

There was no responding voice reminding the senators of any need to treat Anita Hill with fairness. No one assumed responsibility for talking about the stress, self-doubt, and fears experienced by victims of sexual harassment, or the need to provide a forum that would hear the voice of one woman as she spoke about harassment.

As far as Anita Hill was concerned, she had dared to speak that which should have remained unspoken. She had complained about her treatment in a patriarchal society. Not only did she have responsibility for proving the validity of her claims but for defending her actions. Hill became responsible for arguing that *she* was acting fairly toward *both* Thomas *and* the senators. Interestingly, one line of argument that emerged was that, *if the harassment had occurred*, the only action that would be understandable (i.e., both rational and fair) at this point would be continued silence. Specter exemplified this belief when he asked Hill: "In the context of the federal law limiting a sexual harassment claim to six months because of the grave difficulty of someone defending themselves in this context, what is your view of the fairness of asking Judge Thomas to reply eight, nine, ten years after the fact? (Day 1, Part 3, p. 10). In other words, *assuming* we grant the harassment claim as true, Hill is, nonetheless, the unfair actor for raising the issue now as opposed to maintaining the course of silence she chose at the time of the events.

Perhaps it would have been reasonable to anticipate that fairness would not only be an issue which involved Hill and Thomas but would, ultimately, involve the committee members in disputes with each other. Minutes after Judge Thomas's opening statement, the first of several disputes erupted. The focus of virtually all of these disputes was on the rules for conducting the hearings and, more specifically, the questions that could or could not be asked of whomever was testifying. The initial dispute occurred when Senator Biden, who was about to question Thomas (who had elected to speak first in the proceedings), reminded committee members that they were to limit the focus of their questions to issues *other than* the allegations raised by Hill. This restriction was due to a request by Hill that she be allowed to share her story for herself (rather than having her story—or a version of her story—conveyed via the questions and orations of the committee members). Senator Hatch immediately took exception to any restrictions:

Hatch: I am not going to sit here and tolerate her [Hill] and her attorneys telling you, or me, or anybody else that now that she's made these statements in writing with what is, if the Judge is telling the truth and I believe he is, scurrilous allegations, that that statement can't be used, especially in this proceeding. It's a matter of fairness. (Day 1, Part 1, p. 6)

Throughout the hearings, Hatch continued to pursue similar "matter(s) of fairness." With each dispute, fairness to Anita Hill emerged as less and less important. Instead, fairness to Clarence Thomas, a "fair" exercise of the process, and even fairness to the senators, themselves, took center stage:

Biden: There is one simple reason why I would not like to go forward now [in questioning Hill about John Doggett], and quite frankly, it is not totally as a consequence of whether or not we're being fair to the witness [Hill], which I think would be somewhat unfair to her now. It's simply that I don't know enough to know. I want to be able to question contemporaneously the witness on this issue.

Leahy: Mr. Chairman, [my opinion] merely echoes what you have said . . . we've worked out ground rules that you and Senator Thurmond and the rest of the committee have agreed to. . . . This would go outside them.

Hatch: Well, Mr. Chairman, I don't [know about?] these ground rules. I haven't heard this, that you can't ask a witness questions. (Day 1, Part 3, p. 18)

The final procedural dispute concerned a line of questions intended for Judge Thomas but focusing on statements made by Anita Hill to the FBI. As with the other disputes, Senator Hatch argued that he was not a party to any agreement and that it would not be fair to Thomas if he (Hatch) edited his line of questioning in any way:

Biden: It's incredible to me that you would walk in here and read from an FBI report when we all know it is against the Committee rules to read from FBI reports.

Hatch: Senator, listen. I've refused to accept a process where someone on this committee releases [Hill's] statement and materials from the FBI report, for all the world to see and the newspapers to print and the media to show, that are tremendously damaging to the Judge . . . because somebody in a sleazy way broke the rules. . . . I used the FBI report under very fair circumstances. (Day 2, Part 3, p. 2)

In comparison with the protests voiced by Senator Hatch, none of the senators objected when a witness (Angela Wright) who might have leant credence to Hill's claims was subjected in absentia to ridicule, and her willingness to testify was called into question. Specifically, Senator Hatch stated that: "Last night we were trying to obtain all the knowledge we could from this *so called* Angela Wright. Well she gave so much testimony and then refused to talk after that" (Day 1, Part 3, p. 23; emphasis added). As opposed to the impression created by Hatch's statement, not only was Angela Wright willing to testify, but according to one source, there was yet another witness prepared to corroborate her statements (Edwards, 1992).

One other realization of the concept of "fair" should be explored. Throughout their questioning of *both* Hill and Thomas, Senators Leahy and DeConcini frequently employed reflective probes, that is, they restated what they believed the witness had just said and then asked whether their restatement or paraphrase was accurate. For example, Leahy and Hill engaged in the following exchange:

Leahy: Now you said you made it clear to him [Thomas] on the discussions of pornography and all that you didn't like what he was saying. Is that a fair statement of your—

Hill: Uh-huh. Yes, it is. (Day 1, Part 3, p. 5)

Senator Hatch employed a similar approach when questioning Judge Thomas. By contrast, Senator Specter, in his questioning of Anita Hill, continually privileged his interpretation of her statements over her objections to those privileged interpretations:

Specter: But when you make a statement in August of 1991, and say that, "Judicial experience aside, the Clarence Thomas of that period would have made a better judge on the Supreme Court, because he was more open minded" . . . you are saying that at one stage of his career he would have made an adequate Supreme Court Justice.

Hill: Well, I am not sure that that's what I am saying at all. I am sure that what I was trying to give to that reporter was my assessment of him [Thomas], objectively, without considering the personal information that I had.

Specter: Well, let's take it the way you have just re-explained it. . . . How could you conclude in any respect that he would be appropriate for the Court even if you say that was without considering the personal information, if you had all of this personal information?

Hill: I did not say that he would be appropriate for the Court, Senator. I said that he would make a better judge. I didn't say that I would consider him the best person for the Supreme Court.

Specter: Well, when you say he would have made a better judge at one point, are you saying that there is not an explicit recommendation or statement that as you said earlier on the basis of his intellect, aside from the personal information, which you decided not to share, that he would have been a better Supreme Court Justice? (Day 1, Part 3, pp. 7–8)

This line of questioning lasted for several minutes, with Specter continuing to express doubt about and lack of understanding with respect to Hill's position.

This type of privileging occurred only during Senator Specter's examination of Anita Hill. At no time did any of the senators engage in a similar privileging while examining Clarence Thomas, and there was only one objection voiced:

Specter: Well, if your answer now turns on process, all I can say is that it would have been much shorter had you said at the outset that Mr. Brudney [told you] that if you came forward Judge Thomas might withdraw. That is the essence as to what occurred.

Hill: No, it is not. I think we differ on our interpretation of what I said.

Specter: Well, what am I missing here, Professor Hill?

Kennedy: Mr. Chairman, could we let the witness speak in her own words rather than having words put in her mouth?

Specter: Mr. Chairman, I object to that. I object to that vociferously. I'm asking questions here. If Senator Kennedy has anything to say, let him participate in this hearing. (Day 1, Part 3, p. 33)

Dialectic of Choice v. Circumstance

From the opening moments of the hearings, choice emerged as a problematic issue. Two foci to the dialectic developed. One concerned the choices available to the committee with respect to how Professor Hill's allegations should be handled. The second concerned the choices available to Professor Hill, both in bringing forth her allegations and in her relationship with Judge Thomas.

With respect to the committee's own actions, the argument that emerged concerned lack of choice (i.e., the committee had adopted the only reasonable course of action given the circumstances). As they commented on their handling of Hill's allegations, quite clearly members of the Judiciary Committee believed themselves to be on the defensive. They tried either to rationalize or to criticize the events that ultimately led to the hearings. Biden assumed the defensive, asking, "How can you expect us to have forced Professor Hill, against her will, into the blinding light which you see here today?" (Day 1, Part 1, p. 1). Senator Simon even implored Professor Hill to provide the committee with guidance:

Simon: How do we deal with a charge that someone makes that is a substantial charge, but that person says, "I don't want my name used publicly," or even "I don't want the charge made publicly." We should not simply ignore it.

On the other hand, how are you fair to a nominee? This is the struggle that this committee has gone through and the Senate is going through. (Day 1, Part 3, p. 39)

Throughout the hearings, the picture that emerged was one of a senate committee that, due to lack of choice, had been forced to acknowledge and explore the possibility publicly that a Supreme Court nominee was guilty of sexual harassment. Committee members rallied against the unknown individual whose actions in leaking an FBI report had resulted in the public revelation of Hill's allegations. Time and again, the claim was made that the committee had no options other than to (1) initially ignore the allegation and, now, (2) conduct a formal, public investigation.

However, while the committee members could easily understand their situation as one of lack of choice, they had far greater difficulty in understanding the circumstances that had confronted Anita Hill. The picture that emerged, as product of both text and subtext, was that of a woman who was free to choose from multiple alternatives (restricted only by her own creativity). Since the actions she chose (especially her actions in maintaining a professional relationship with Judge Thomas) did not make sense within the context of an abusive environment, the allegations she was bringing forward must not be true.

Senators Biden and Thurmond, in particular, offered differing claims concerning whether circumstances had forced Hill to come forward or she had acted purposefully in timing her revelations. For her part, Hill argued that "it would have been more comfortable to remain silent. I took no initiative to inform anyone" (Day 1, Part 2, p. 4). However, despite her claim and support from selected senators, this issue would not die. The Republican senators in particular needed to identify a motive for this "scurrilous allegation" (Hatch, Day 1, Part 1, p. 6) made about "an individual of great character and accomplishment" (Thurmond, Day 1, Part 1, p. 3). Defining Hill's actions as purposeful and a matter of personal choice was essential to the claim that it was Thomas, rather than Hill, who was the victim of abuse.

Interestingly, the senators never questioned each other with respect to their contradictory assertions. Throughout the hearings, they used their time to establish arguments rather than seek information. Their "preambles" (preorations) and assertions (orations) established frameworks that went without question or criticism, at least within the public forum of the hearings themselves.

As they searched for motives, the senators repeatedly turned to Hill's decision to move with Thomas from Education to EEOC. According to the expressed logic, if Thomas had engaged in the egregious behavior described by Hill, how could she possibly bring herself to maintain their relationship? Hill attempted to address this decision in her opening statement when she noted: "When Judge Thomas was made chair of the EEOC, I needed to face the question of whether to go with him. I was asked to do so, and I did. The work itself was interesting, and at that time it appeared that the sexual overtures which had so troubled me had ended. I also faced the realistic fact that I had no alternative" (Day 1, Part 2, p. 2). Throughout the hearings, Hill continued to insist that she believed she had no acceptable career alternative except to follow Thomas to EEOC. Her claims were, however, impossible for many of the senators to understand. At one point Senator Kennedy attempted to defend Hill against the claim that she had other job offers: "[A] senator is saying, well, don't you know that Mr. Singleton, who happens to be one of Clarence Thomas's best friends, had a job just out there, and why didn't you take it, and the fact you didn't take it must reflect something. And I think all of us know what is trying to be reflected" (Day 1, Part 3, p. 22). Unfortunately, Kennedy failed to make specific the conclusion he had drawn, returning instead to the more concrete issue of the procedures the committee should be following. Moments later, Senator Specter again raised questions concerning Hill's decision to move to EEOC and the other choices available to her.

During his testimony, Thomas reinforced the notion that Hill had made a strategic and purposeful choice among multiple alternatives, as if that reality would exonerate him from her accusations and justify any actions he might have taken: "[T]here is—would have been no reason for me to have said that she could not remain at the Department of Education. . . . It seems more likely to me that someone of her intellect and her capabilities would know what her classification was and would certainly find out when there is a question of whether or not you are going to have a job in a transitional period" (Day 2, Part 2, pp. 11–12). Interestingly, Thomas was careful to reinforce Hill's image as a bright, capable person who surely should have known what her alternatives were and been able to pursue a professional relationship away from him (albeit with his help).

The fact that Hill had chosen not to criticize Thomas publicly at other points in time was an issue for the committee. At one point, Hill explained that: "During the time that I was at Oral Roberts University, I realized that Charles Kothe, who was the founding Dean of that school, had very high regards for Clarence Thomas. I did not risk talking in disparaging ways about Clarence" (Day 1, Part 2, p. 10). Later, Senator Leahy asked Hill to speculate about what would have happened had she come forward with her allegations at an earlier point in time:

Hill: I can speculate that had I come forward immediately after I left the EEOC, I can speculate that I would have lost my job at Oral Roberts. (Day 1, Part 3, p. 4)

Minutes after that, Hill repeated her description of the constraints she believed existed and encouraged her silence: "I felt my job could be taken away or it could be at least threatened that I wasn't going to be able to work, that this person who had some power in the new administration would make it difficult for me in terms of other positions" (Day 1, Part 3, p. 6).

Time and again, Professor Hill tried to establish a sense of reality that existed for her and her understanding of the options available. However, the questions asked and orations offered by the senators continued to reveal an inability to appreciate Hill's sense of reality. Ultimately, the senators found it very easy to rationalize the constraints impacting their own actions but impossible to appreciate the constraints impacting Anita Hill.

CONCLUSION

In his opening statement, Senator Biden asserted: "The committee is not here to put Judge Thomas or Professor Hill on trial. I hope my colleagues will keep in mind that the best way to do our job is to ask questions that are nonjudgmental and open-ended" (Day 1, Part 1, p. 2). Unfortunately, what emerged over the next seventy-two hours was not the "nonjudgmental, open-ended" inquiry Senator Biden requested. Someone was put on trial, but that person was not Judge Clarence Thomas, nor was it the conditions that not only permit but foster sexual harassment as "acceptable" conduct. Through the questions asked and the statements made, the Judiciary Committee created a defendant in and reinforced the victim status of Professor Anita Hill.

Certainly one of the factors in the transformation of the hearings from their intended mission (i.e., information seeking) into their realized mission (i.e., a "truth-seeking" trial) had to be the fact that the majority of the senators were trained as lawyers and brought an advocate's (and an adversarial) perspective to the proceedings. The perspective of advocate naturalized the search for a winner and a loser. From the advocate's perspective, only one party could be speaking the "truth"; only one person's description of reality could be confirmed as "accurate."

Within minutes after Senator Biden called the first session to order, the statements made and questions asked revealed the person whose reality was to be questioned, the person who was to be on trial. That person was Anita Hill. Her motives were to be challenged and debated, not the motives or actions of Clarence Thomas. Through the continuing focus on her actions as well as her inability to rationalize those actions in an "acceptable" (to the senators) fashion, Hill was placed on the defensive and was effectively disempowered.

From the point of view of the white, male senators, Hill had choices available to her, and she chose to follow Thomas when, if her accusations were valid, a strong person would have pursued a different course of action. Hill was defined (by the senators) in the context of educated lawyer and, thus, empowered, rather than in the context of black woman and, thus, disempowered. As King (1992) observes and others echo (e.g., Bunch, 1986; Gordon, 1991), the problem extant in examining the choices available to any individual is in our ability (or inability) to appreciate his/her reality and the constraints he/she believes frame the environment. Instead, the natural tendency is to apply our own standards and to reference what we would have done, how we would have acted. This ignores the fact that it is one thing to be able to see a choice, and another thing to believe you have the power to pursue that choice. Mobility, as an option, is clearly available to members of the dominant culture but much less accessible to others.

If Anita Hill failed in any respect, it was that she was not able to convey to the senators the constraints that impacted not only the choices available to her but her ability to act on those choices. This failure, however, was not hers alone. Members of the dominant culture see only choices and possibilities. However, boundaries (i.e., constraints against choice), both visible and invisible, force people to realize they are at the "margins." In large measure, the failure in the Thomas-Hill hearings was the inability and seeming unwillingness of individuals who are not constrained to appreciate the challenges faced by those who are.

What does this experience teach us about sexual harassment and how it is discursively sustained within our culture? This question is difficult to answer because the response depends so much on where one is situated within society (i.e., member of the dominant culture or on the margins) and on whether the hearings serve to reinforce a sense of powerlessness or provide a newfound sense of power.

With respect to the participants, as of this analysis Clarence Thomas has made only one public appearance; thus, the experience for him has resulted in an apparent effort to withdraw from public view. By contrast, Anita Hill has been placed in the position (wanted or not) of national spokesperson with respect to sexual harassment. During the year after the hearings, Senator Specter found himself in a successful but difficult reelection campaign against an opponent (Lynn Yeakel) who said she chose to run because of the hearings. Specter subsequently indicated that he understood the hearings "struck a chord" with women across the country. In 1992 more women were elected to the United States Senate than ever before; yet, the numbers are still embarrassingly low. More women have filed sexual harassment claims (an increase of approximately 60 percent during the first half of 1992; Blumenfeld, 1992). Yet, there have been strident criticisms of the EEOC, including a statement by Kim Keller, a NOW spokesperson, that "filing a claim in the nearest waste receptacle is about as effective as filing it with the EEOC" (cited in Blumenfeld, 1992).

For a broader approach to the question of what we have learned, perhaps the best response would be one borrowed from Taylor and Conrad (1992). As part of their analysis of sexual harassment narratives submitted for a special issue of the *Journal of Applied Communication Research*, they described three objectives: (1) to move readers to reflect, (2) to educate, and (3) to transform oppressive structures. Through this project, we find ourselves *reflecting* on the realities of power imposed upon women. Our *education* emerges in the silence women select in response to that power. Unfortunately, then, the product of our analysis provides persuasive evidence as to the power of patriarchical discourse to *sustain*, rather than *transform*, discriminatory and marginalizing practices. As the Thomas-Hill hearings and the narratives analyzed by Taylor and Conrad demonstrate, those who come forward must be willing to risk accusations of living in a fantasy world, with their actions construed as unfair to the accused harasser and their choices micro-analyzed by those who fail to appreciate that *reality* can be understood and experienced in different ways.

Changing the social structures and the discursive practices that sustain sexual harassment will not be simple matters for legislative injunction. Ultimately, those in the dominant culture of our society must understand that the options available to them are not the same options available to those in the minority or on the margins of the culture. We must continue to provide avenues for those without power to protest actions by those in power when those actions are inappropriate, threatening, obnoxious, and/or create an unhealthy work environment. However, the ability to give voice to a complaint is not enough. We must all continue to sensitize ourselves to perspectives different from our own and exert the additional effort required of understanding, as opposed to judging, the lived experiences of others.

NOTE

1. Transcripts of the testimony from the Judiciary Committee hearing for the confirmation of Justice Clarence Thomas were transcribed by the Federal News Service and obtained from the Purdue University Public Affairs Video Archives, West Lafayette, Indiana.

Part III

Discursive Activity Contesting Sexual Harassment

6

Talk About Sexual Harassment: Women's Stories on a Woman's Story

*Janette Kenner Muir
and Kathryn Mangus*

Anita Hill's voice is part of our process now. It thunders in the chorus of voices—voices that have been raised at great personal risk, with courage, in ever-widening circles of reclaimed power. . . . We tell our stories and we tell a collective one—of minds and bodies damaged by abuse, of unredressed grievances, or a travesty that will no longer give in to silence.
—Margaret Randall, 1992, p. 22

The testimony of Anita Hill before the Senate Judiciary Committee will long be remembered as an important turning point for women concerning the issue of sexual harassment. Speaking before fourteen white men, Hill told the story of how Clarence Thomas, a respected conservative black justice, had repeatedly made sexual advances, requested dates, and engaged in verbal sexual abuse. The incredulous jury grilled her for hours, asking her to conjure up suppressed memories and anxieties, challenging her motivations to come forward so late in the process, and trading their own stories about pornography and appropriate behavior toward women (see chapter 5).

As the drama unfolded before millions of television viewers, and more questions than answers prevailed, women talked. They talked about their own experiences with sexual harassment, they talked about definitions of harassment, and they talked about the prevalence of sexism in American society. It is in the telling of these stories that we are beginning to come to grips with the intricacies of the issue, with the difficulties in knowing how to handle sexual harassment experiences, and with the anxieties that continue to linger long after the experience is over. In essence, we are learning how to tell our stories, and as each story is told, it is added to the collective voice which, in turn, will ultimately have an impact on public discourse and policy actions.

This chapter considers the power of storytelling as public discourse to reconstruct understandings of sexual harassment and to reshape the identities of women who have been sexually harassed. The chapter studies the nature of talk about sexual harassment to examine reactions to Anita Hill's story, and to explore the power of stories women tell in response to her testimony. Discussion first focuses on the nature of storytelling in our society and its particular importance for women. We then turn to a description of stories told during the weekend of the committee hearings by looking at C-SPAN call-in programs and, in particular, calls made by women. We further consider the polling results and storytelling that has transpired since Hill's testimony to see how our understandings about sexual harassment have evolved. In looking at these narratives, focus is on the major themes that emerge in the telling of the story, and the subsequent actions that resulted. Finally, discussion centers on the significance of narratives in empowering women and ultimately affecting substantive policy actions.

While both men and women participated in the call-in programs and told their stories of sexual harassment, we have chosen to look specifically at women for two reasons. First, Anita Hill was an African-American woman who told her story to a jury of white males. This unique public event draws special attention to the act of storytelling as a woman's only recourse in dealing with a powerless situation. We believe that there is a unique form of storytelling inherent in women's narratives and in women's responses to Hill's story. Second, and more importantly, sexual harassment is experienced predominantly by women, and Hill's testimony had the greatest impact on this gender during the subsequent year. By examining the collective telling of women's stories we may come to understand better how to respond as a society to these collaborative voices.

UNDERSTANDING WOMEN'S NARRATIVES

For as long as humans have existed on this earth so has the capacity for storytelling. Even before organized educational systems and the written word, stories, the narratives of a culture, guided children and adults in acceptable behaviors and community codes. Through storytelling, we have learned what values are important for a culture and what rules should be upheld. Stories help humans to come to grips with who they are, how they view the world, and the moral grounding that guides them (Rybacki & Rybacki, 1991; Rowland, 1987).

The Nature of Storytelling

A story is a narrative, a kind of discourse organized around "the passage of time in some 'world' " (Polyanyi, 1985, p. 10), a symbolic explanation of the action of certain characters which can provide order and meaning for an audience (Rybacki & Rybacki, 1991). Attempting to argue for a narrative paradigm that encompasses all human communication, Fisher contends communication is essentially storytelling (1985; 1987). While other scholars argue that this all-encompassing definition delimits the power of narrative theory (Rowland, 1987; Warnick, 1987), they do agree that narratives provide powerful ways to make arguments and shape worldviews.

A narrative describes at least two events with focus on the characters, actions, and settings which evolve over time. Through identifying what takes place in a story, and how it takes place, the critic can then evaluate the various aspects of the story with regard to its truthfulness and coherence.[1] Fisher (1985) identifies two major evaluative elements useful for assessing the quality of the story. Narrative probability considers how well the story hangs together, and narrative fidelity appraises the "truth qualities" of the story, the soundness of its reasoning or values compared to the audience's personal notions of reality (pp. 349–350).

An important aspect of narrative, Gronbeck (1983) argues, is that it implies preexisting knowledge. He observes that while the focus is on the telling or unfolding of a story, it is founded on something pre-known, and it is the calling up of previous knowledge, rather than the actual telling of the story, that can make a narrative so significant (p. 233). For example, we might listen to a reading of *Cinderella* and judge it not by the talent of the particular storyteller but, more importantly, react to the story based on the previous knowledge we have with regard to unequal social relations and domination. Based on our understanding of social relations and how patriarchal society perpetuates the story of man as woman's salvation, *Cinderella* conjures up unpleasant experiences for the listener who has this prior knowledge. Another way of considering the understanding one brings to a narrative is when an individual might grapple with some knowledge of her past that has been suppressed, and when this experience is finally evoked through storytelling, a cathartic effect may occur. At the same time, the purging of a long forgotten memory may be empowering because she has finally come to acknowledge, and deal with, an unpleasant event in her life. Stories as a means of therapy have considerable power and have played an important role in helping individuals cope with social circumstances (Smith and Morris, 1992).

Stories can take on a variety of forms and represent many different genres. Kenneth Burke (1968) talks about the nature of conventional form in storytelling which creates expectancies for the listener of the story, guiding how we anticipate the story to unfold. "It was a dark and stormy night" or "once upon a time" sets the scene and creates an appetite for what we might expect to find in the story. Generic conventions also guide how stories unfold. Horror stories and disaster stories have certain substantive and stylistic characteristics and organizing principles which reflect the conventions of the particular genre. It is in the formal and generic constraints of the story that listeners often make judgments, especially if the story does not conform to their conventional notions of how a story should unfold. Clarence Thomas's story of a hardworking African-American man, working his way up from poverty to a Supreme Court nomination, is a conventional Horatio Alger story. The storyline is a believable one, fulfilling the expectations that many listeners have about the value of hard work.[2] In turn, by listening to the story, the audience interprets and incorporates it into their own particular worldviews.

Women and Storytelling

The stories women tell to one another have long had an important place in the development of cultures and the understanding of world experiences. From the ancient medicine women who laid out the spiritual mores of the community to our grandmothers who instill a sense of history within the family structure, women have told stories to one another. Foss and Foss (1991) describe Tamara Burk's ongoing research which observes several unique characteristics inherent in women's stories. The stories that women tell often begin with a complicating action, go in various time orders to explain it, and may be more commonplace than remarkable (p. 90). So where some theorists would argue that narrative is a more linear construct (see Chatman, 1978; Ricoeur, 1980; Polanyi, 1985), moving temporally from one event to another, this characteristic suggests a different manner in which the action takes place. A woman might use several examples to support the main idea of a story, go backward in time, or predict future action based on recurrent themes.

Another unique characteristic Burk suggests is the collaborative nature of women's stories, the ways in which the narrative unfolds as women participate in the story (p. 90). Tannen's (1990) work on differences in men's and women's talk substantiates this collaborative nature. Defining stories as "accounts of personal experiences that people exchange in conversation," she argues that "the ways that women and men talk about events in their lives reflect and create their different worlds" (p. 176). Citing Barbara Johnstone's work with conversational narratives, Tannen identifies important differences in the ways men and women view storytelling:

Men live in a world where they see power as coming from an individual acting in opposition to others and to natural forces. For them, life is a contest in which they are constantly tested and must perform, in order to avoid the risk of failure. For women . . . the community is the source of power. If men see life in terms of a contest, a struggle against nature and other men, for women life is a struggle against the danger of being cut off from their community. (p. 178)

In a study of conversations among second graders, Tannen observed that the brief stories told by second grade girls are typical of the ways stories are collaboratively linked together, based on shared experiences. There was clear evidence of rapport as the second graders exchanged matching complaints about their little brothers and supported each other's stories (p. 254).

The rapport-building, supportive nature of little girls' stories that Tannen found is similar to patterns found in women's talk. Burk provides an example in Foss and Foss (1991) of family storytelling which includes a session among herself, her mother, and her grandmother. It is interesting to note the chaining out of the story line as the women collaborate on a particular theme. What begins as talk about a pregnancy concludes with a discussion of breast cancer. In between, the women have discussed religion, family members, abuse, divorce, and numerous other topics (pp. 91–119). The order of events and talk among the family members is a dramatic and complex collaborative account, a sharing and building of experiences often unique to women's stories.

Storytelling has been known to have particularly powerful effects for African-American women. Quoting novelists such as Paule Marshall, Augusta Baker, and Vertamae Smart-Grosvenor, Nancie Caraway (1991) identifies stories as "the symbolic yeast of African-American militancy and political awareness" (p. 36). Marshall notes: "Storytelling, the power of language, was like money, it was legal tender, a symbol of wealth. . . . And the self-articulated political project for these women is keeping the word alive. . . . You must believe that what we say is possible and that there's nothing that can impede a black person. . . . You *must* believe in the storyteller" (in Caraway, pp. 36–37).

Two of the most well-known contemporary African-American storytellers, Alice Walker and Toni Morrison, draw on memories to tell their stories. Commenting in an interview about *The Temple of My Familiar* (1989), Walker notes that it was a "novel of memory," an attempt to construct her own history (Brennan, 1989, p. 13). Morrison's *Beloved* (1987) represents the suppression of slave memories for contemporary African-Americans, and the story of horror that slaves experienced. She notes that her book is "about something that the characters don't want to remember. I don't want to remember, black people don't want to remember, white people don't want to remember" (1989, p. 120). Through their puissant narratives, these African-American authors evoke powerful memories for their readers and symbolize the experiences of African-American women in American society.

In sum, women's stories tend to be collaborative, temporally varied, defining experiences. It is the sharing of the stories that makes narrative a powerful element in women's identities.

Stories of Sexual Harassment

In the *Journal of Applied Communication Research* (1992), Julia Wood defines sexual harassment as "a range of personal experiences, each of which is embedded in particular historical, social and institutional contexts" (p. 356). Efforts to understand the issue, she explains, should be informed by attending to the actual experiences of harassers as well as to the conditions that have influenced their behaviors. By listening to the accounts of those who have been harassed, researchers, in turn, may inductively derive conceptual frameworks which may be pragmatically useful to understanding sexual harassment (p. 356).

Through sharing accounts of their experiences with sexual harassment, women can obviously benefit. First, as the stories are told we may come to understand the complexities of the issue better. By naming the action that has made a woman uncomfortable, defining the terms that denote such an experience, we may come closer to establishing a vocabulary that can capture the essence of the sexual harassment experience. Additionally, since a narrative is universally defined as a series of events, we can see that it is not merely an isolated event that leads a woman to claim sexual harassment, but rather, it is a pattern of behavior on the part of the harasser that leads a woman to discomfort and a sense of powerlessness. A male coworker might ask a woman out for a date and her response may be no. Most people would not consider this simple request an example of harassment. However, if the coworker continues to make the same request and the woman feels unduly pressured, then most would agree that sexual harassment is occurring. Thus, it is in the chain of events, the unfolding of a story, that patterns develop. In turn, these patterns provide clear grounds for action should the woman decide to give her account of the experience.

Second, there is a great catharsis inherent in the telling of the story. The most notable result of the Hill-Thomas hearings was that many women and men began to speak out, telling their own stories about being sexually harassed. Stories tend to bind a culture, and the telling of stories dealing with sexual abuse tend to bind women together, in turn creating a cathartic effect based on these shared experiences. The catharsis that comes with the telling of the story has an empowering effect on the storyteller. By conjuring up the suppressed experience, speaking out after a long silence, the survivor gives voice to her pain and frustration and begins to confront the patterns that led to her oppression. By coming to terms with her experiences and articulating them to those who will listen, she can begin to understand her reasons for suppressing the experience and her inability to take previous action. By telling the story, the survivor gains power over her own psyche.

As Anita Hill shared her narrative, women throughout the country were inspired to share their stories. Although Hill's story had this initial positive effect, it was not until later that other benefits (e.g., binding women together) could be seen.

ANALYZING C-SPAN CALL-IN RESPONSES

When Anita Hill first told her story to the Senate Judiciary Committee, polls indicated that the majority of the American public did not believe her testimony (Duke, 1992, p. A10). Polls, however, cannot capture the reasoning behind these results—that is, they do not allow for any explanation of a woman's particular reaction to the entire event. As evidenced by the 1992 presidential campaign, call-in programs have become increasingly important as ways to get immediate public reaction to a particular event. Radio talk shows, "Larry King Live," and, most recently, morning news shows are all vehicles for public participation and provide a unique forum for reaction to events.

C-SPAN, the cable-satellite public affairs network, has presented live viewer call-in programs since 1980. The philosophy of the network is to show viewers the process of government and allow them to draw their own conclusions about the action taking place. Consonant with this philosophy, call-in programs are a staple of the network. They are scheduled for every weekday, and during special events lines are opened to get viewer reactions to what has taken place (Muir, 1992). Callers are frequently given the opportunity to speak directly with their representatives, and many political actors and legislators have appeared on call-ins to answer questions and talk directly to the audience about issues. Though the network is able to handle only approximately fifteen calls per hour, C-SPAN managed to field over 17,600 calls in 1991 (Range, 1992).

In line with C-SPAN's commitment to show Congress and the Senate in action, the network aired all of the Thomas confirmation hearings and the following hearings with Anita Hill. Open phones were provided during the various breaks in the hearings and after their completion. Phone lines were also available before and after the Senate debate and confirmation vote for Thomas. This was a heavy viewer weekend for the network, with many people tuning in who had never done so before.[3]

In an effort to analyze the responses to the Hill-Thomas hearings, 126 calls between October 11 and 15, 1991, were coded. This time period included responses to Thomas's testimony as well as the final Senate confirmation vote. Calls were coded for content with regard to location, sex, race (if identified), and who the caller believed was telling the truth. Narrative content and form was evaluated by coding caller responses to the testimony and individual stories about sexual harassment. Stories were coded with regard to the particular event or events that occurred, the cause or effect of the harassment, whether or not the story was shared with others, and the final action taken.

Half the coded calls came from women. Of this number, 41 percent of white females claimed that they believed Clarence Thomas, 17 percent indicated that they believed Anita Hill. Of the African-American women who shared their opinions about the hearings, all believed Thomas was telling the truth. Three major findings resulted from the analysis and will be addressed in the following ways: (1) reactions to Anita Hill's story; (2) sexual harassment narratives; and (3) the impact of women interviewers.

Reactions to Anita Hill's Story

Many of the women who reached the network critiqued Hill's story for its truthfulness and coherence with their individual worldviews. Focusing on one or two elements of the story line, many found her testimony unbelievable and argued that she had ulterior motives in coming forward so late in Thomas's confirmation process.

First, several callers reduced Hill to a scorned woman, an opportunist who would probably become famous for her story. They claimed that she was jealous because Thomas did not respond to her advances, finally marrying a white woman, and that Hill had a problem distinguishing reality from fantasy. This response is typical when women come forward with charges of sexual harassment, as was also seen in the subsequent William Kennedy Smith and Mike Tyson rape trials. In both cases, the women who made the charges were questioned with regard to their credibility and their motives for making such claims. Frequently the victim is blamed, with many finding her story to be implausible. This type of response "minoritizes" the issue, seeing sexual harassment as something out of the ordinary, a rare occurrence conducted by an unusual person (Mantilla, 1992, p. 1). Since harassment is an atypical occurrence, the minoritizing view concludes, then the accuser must not be telling the truth or has some ulterior motive in coming forward. In the case of Clarence Thomas, the notion that a person who was otherwise self-disciplined and hard-working could at times express a "malicious and salacious" side cast doubt on Hill's accusations (p. 1).

A second criticism of Hill was based on the time frame. Many callers questioned why she waited so long to come forward and puzzled over the possibility that someone could remember the minute details of events that took place over ten years prior to her testimony. Some concluded that Hill was the product of zealous feminist groups, that she was guided by special interests— particularly pro-choice groups, and that the only reason she came forward after so long was to help the women's movement. The women who identified this particular issue also adamantly claimed that women's organizations did not represent their perspectives.

A final criticism women made was that Hill followed Thomas to the EEOC. This was difficult for many of the callers to understand, and many thus dismissed her testimony, challenging its coherence. For the majority of women callers who commented on her believability (41 percent), Hill's story did not ring true; her story did not satisfy their ideas of narrative fidelity. It is interesting to note the parallels between the callers' responses and the senators' questions as identified by Hale, Cooks, and DeWine in chapter 5. Hence, the perceptions of many callers seemed in line with the senators' arguments.

The most significant finding to come out of this discussion was the way women critiqued the fidelity of Hill's story. As the calls were coded, we were struck by how often one part of Hills story would be chosen and then evaluated against the caller's own version of reality. One caller claimed that Hill looked too poised throughout the hearings, that her behavior was inconsistent with the way she handled her preceding press conference. Another caller reacted to Hill's hesitancy when asked about knowing the man from Texas who had substantiated Thomas's story. Frequently, a pattern existed of picking out one aspect that either supported or negated the individual's feelings about sexual harassment. This ties back to the notion of the representative anecdote in the sense that we frequently tend to focus on one particular example in a story to assess how truthful it is compared to our particular notions of reality. Thus, the example serves as a synecdochic fragment, a representation of the entire narrative.

Sexual Harassment Narratives

Over 25 percent of the women who called in to express their opinions about Anita Hill's testimony claimed that they had experienced sexual harassment to some degree during their lifetime. Given the constraints of a telephone call, their stories are brief, yet compelling, because they provide some understanding of the complexities of the sexual harassment issue and the actions women take in dealing with their experiences.

Representative anecdotes. In order to give voice to the power of storytelling in this context, two brief stories are included.

Caller A: I, myself, have been a victim of sexual harassment and I totally understand why someone would wait to come forward. I'm in the process of waiting for charges to be investigated and have tried to continue to have working relationships with some of the people involved since I work in a male-dominated field. I feel sorry for both parties. Males obviously have low self-esteem, and females who are single parents have to decide whether or not to come forward.

Caller B: I can remember being seventeen years old and working in a store, and the employer commented about my breasts and what he wanted to do sexually. Because his family was rich and he was well respected, people said nobody would believe me and they didn't. And they didn't believe Anita Hill. If people had talked about the issue of sexual harassment before [the hearings] would not have happened.

Other stories included discussions of experiences with coworkers and a broad range of incidents from verbal suggestions to physical abuse.

Responses to sexual harassment. One relevant theme that came out in the discussion was the notion that sexual harassment is a fact of life and that women should just learn how to deal with it. Most of the callers who made this observation used it as a rationale for why they did not come forward and publicly tell their own stories. Since sexual harassment happens all the time, they reasoned, why make an issue of it, especially when one's job could be affected in the process. Generally, the action taken was avoidance behavior. They either quit their jobs or avoided the harasser as much as they were able. For some survivors of sexual harassment, Hill's choice to continue her job made rational sense.

Mantilla (1992) argues that the commonality view of sexual harassment is a universalizing one. It holds that sexual harassment is a frequent occurrence, a matter of degree which occurs against the backdrop of routine objectification of women (p. 1). Women who experience persistent oppression may look at sexual harassment in the context of their other experiences. Each event is evaluated from a cost-benefit perspective where the cost of sexual harassment is weighed against the benefits of keeping their jobs, and it is considered in relationship to other forms of objectification, such as rape or incest (p. 6). Robin Clair (chapter 4) argues that when victims choose not to make an issue of the incidents, they contribute to their own domination and the continuation of sexual harassment. Yet, at the same time, the commonality of the occurrence may mitigate any decisive action on the part of the victim and may seem insignificant when compared to greater forms of oppression.

It was interesting to note the actions women did take in response to their harassers. While most engaged in avoidance behavior, others decided to lodge formal complaints. Most of the callers who described their experiences found employers to be nonresponsive, and only a small number met with any level of success. One dominant theme was that nobody would believe the victim when she did come forward. One caller claimed that when she told higher authorities in her workplace that she had been molested and sexually harassed, the only action taken was to put her on probation. Another caller noted that when she finally decided to come forward, she was fired from her job.

Fortunately, some women who had been abused were successful in coming forward and telling their stories. While the process was long and exhausting, some found positive results by winning law suits or by seeing their oppressors dismissed from their positions.

Women Interviewers

One point worth noting about the call-ins is that women were more likely to tell stories on the open phones to a female moderator. Most of the moderators were men; the results were more questions asked and fewer and shorter stories. When Susan Swain, C-SPAN's senior vice president, operated the phone lines, the stories women told seemed to be fuller and more detailed. This would suggest that when dealing with sexual harassment complaints within the workplace, women will be more apt to talk with other women than with men. While this may seem like an obvious point, it is frequently the case that a man will be in charge of dealing with sexual harassment complaints and not realize the impact that his gender may have on the woman's willingness to come forward. Even the most sensitive and caring man may run into difficulties with women feeling comfortable enough to share their experiences, and familiarity may not make it any easier to share their stories.

During the hearings the majority of those polled believed Thomas was telling the truth and that Hill's testimony lacked credibility. Even with the reaction toward Hill, however, people began to share their own stories of sexual harassment either to substantiate the choices Hill made or to argue against her actions. Hence, the most significant feature to come out of the hearings was the dialogue that engaged many people. Women and men started to talk to each other about their actions. Most importantly, women began to speak out more forcefully and tell their stories.

THE AFTERMATH

In the months following the Hill-Thomas hearings, more women began to tell their stories and express outrage over the callous nature of the Senate Judiciary Committee. Some women decided to run for political office, others acted through the voting process, and eventually Anita Hill was vindicated. Where many women had remained silent, too fearful to confront the objectification felt in the workplace, they were now speaking out and telling their stories. Editorials, letters to editors, and numerous magazine articles talked about the changing nature of the workplace. Men reported that they were becoming more sensitive to their own actions, and women talked about feeling empowered and determined to report on-the-job sexual pressures (Jordan and Buckley, 1991, p. A1).

The increasing frequency of narratives about sexual harassment has substantially contributed to shaping the standards people use to evaluate the stories. As the narratives are shared, the same story is told over and over again and thus becomes a standard for acceptance by shaping the ground of preknowledge regarding sexual harassment. Hence, our understanding of the issue is changed by the intensity and frequency of the stories being told. In this sense, Fisher's concept of narrative fidelity has evolved because of the stories told by women after the Hill-Thomas hearings. This is especially evident in shifting public opinion.

In 1992 *Working Woman* magazine conducted a survey to find out readers' reactions to sexual harassment issues and Anita Hill's story. The survey was a follow-up to a similar one conducted in 1988 which questioned human resources directors from *Fortune* 1,000 companies. Participants were asked questions regarding their stands on sexual harassment, their experiences in the workplace, what should be done, and their reactions to the Hill-Thomas controversy.

The reactions to the *Working Woman* survey were overwhelming. In addition to more than 9,000 responses, the magazine received hundreds of letters detailing painful, personal experiences (Sandroff, 1992, p. 47). The survey results were compared to the responses of the human resource executives. While most companies concluded that the system generally works, many readers insisted that filing a complaint could still result in "career suicide," and were so angry that they intended to make the Thomas confirmation a voting issue in the 1992 election (p. 48). In response to the Hill-Thomas hearings, 59 percent believed Hill was telling the truth, while only 38 percent of the corporate executives believed the same. Most importantly, 40 percent of the respondents said the confrontation had brought the issue out in the open, leading women to trade "war stories" about sexual harassment. The collective voice concluded that the old prey on the young, the powerful on the less powerful. Women in managerial and professional positions, as well as those who work in male-dominated professions, are most likely to experience harassment. Sixty percent of *Working Woman* readers reported that they had been victimized (p. 48).

The National Association for Female Executives (NAFE) conducted a similar survey of 1,300 members and found that 53 percent had experienced sexual harassment in the workplace or knew of someone else who had been sexual harassed; of those who had been harassed, only 36 percent reported the incident (Howard, Stuart, & Crisp, 1992, p. 8).

One of the most recent polls conducted regarding the Hill-Thomas hearings was the *Washington Post*–ABC News poll (Morin, 1992). In this survey, 85 percent of men and women said sexual harassment is a problem in the workplace and that the public, over time, has come to believe Anita Hill. The biggest change noted in the survey is that more people, men and women, are willing to share their stories (p. A22).

As a result of women and men sharing their experiences, many companies have instituted sexual harassment policies. One of the most important documents created in response to the issue is *Sexual Harassment: Research & Resources* (Siegel, 1992), a publication developed by the National Council for Research on Women. This study was a direct result of the Hill-Thomas hearings, which directly attests to the impact Hill's story has had on American women. Within this document several important aspects of sexual harassment are identified.

First, through the stories women have told, there appears to be differences in what women see as sexual harassment in the workplace. Part of the problem with multiple definitions is that for so long there had been no words to describe this experience (MacKinnon, 1979, p. 27). For older women, in particular, sexual harassment was just a part of life that had to be endured. With the outpouring of women's stories, we are closer to defining the term clearly, but differences continue to exist in how people view the issue.

Second, more research is needed to understand sexual harassment better, especially from the standpoint of the victim. By listening to various stories, we can learn a great deal about why women wait to come forward, or why they choose to remain silent. The study notes that little formal research has been done to understand how victims respond to and cope with sexual harassment (p. 11). Through more analysis of the stories women tell, we may gain a better understanding of the way women respond to their individual experiences.

Another important aspect of the sharing of stories is the discovery that women encounter sexual harassment at very young ages. Many of the C-SPAN callers who admitted to being harassed also indicated that they were young when the harassment had occurred. As young women become more educated about sexual abuse, we learn that a great deal of harassment takes place in the school system (Siegel, 1992, p. 15). *Working Woman* indicated in its 1992 survey that almost 30 percent of the sexual harassment incidents reported occurred among eighteen- to twenty-four-year-old women (p. 48), those who often feel the least empowered to act against the undesirable behavior.

Other forums have been provided for women to tell their stories. For example, in *Sexual Harassment: Women Speak Out* (1992), editors Sumrall and Taylor have compiled an anthology of seventy-seven women's sexual harassment stories. The editors conclude that the Hill-Thomas hearings have forever changed women's character, empowering them to speak out, name names, and fight back (p. viii).

In the time since Anita Hill's testimony, more African-American women are telling their stories of sexual harassment and discovering that their experiences are particularly compelling because they serve as a confluence of both racist and sexist viewpoints. Gillespie (1992) talks about the silencing of African-American women within their culture and the larger society:

We don't talk about the man who whispered nasty words in our ears when we were ten, the job we lost because we wouldn't, or maybe because we did and were fired just the same. We rarely/almost never speak aloud, much less to each other, all the things we were taught to "swallow," as the sister who testified in support of Anita Hill said in that hearing room. The burdens borne, the price paid to be a "strong black woman." (p. 42)

This silencing may explain why many African-American women reacted negatively to Hill's testimony. Hill spoke out against a successful African-American male, hence she violated what many considered to be just the way of life.

Yet African-American women are now speaking out and telling their stories. In a retrospective at Georgetown University on the anniversary of the hearings, Anita Hill talked about the many women who had written to her and shared their experiences. These narratives, she claimed, were important for introducing the issue of sexual harassment into the culture and for legitimizing African-American concerns. Now, thousands of black women across the country are speaking up and telling their personal stories of sexual harassment (Norment, 1992, p. 119).

All of these stories have contributed to a collaborative voice which is both therapeutic and empowering. The rapport-building, supportive nature of these narratives has assured women that they are not alone, that they are not objects, and that they are part of a collective consciousness. Through the sharing of stories, women come to realize that many share the same problems and confront the same frustrations in deciding how to deal with sexual harassment.

Anita Hill's willingness to speak out has impacted on many women since that October weekend in 1991. Her testimony set the tone for other gender confrontations during the ensuing year, such as the Navy Tailhook scandal, the rape trials of Smith and Tyson, and the controversy over Senator Robert Packwood (Blumenfeld, 1992, p. E5). Each woman who brings charges has a story to tell, and it is this collective voice that may, ultimately, have an impact on society. As Susan Faludi observes, Anita Hill finally allowed women to take themselves seriously, and once they did "it opened the floodgates to all the rage" (quoted in Blumenfeld, 1992, p. E5).

With the emergence of this outrage and the talk that women and men engage in, definitions of sexual harassment have been broadened, allowing for greater moral grounding. As discussions about sexual harassment become more socially acceptable, more powerful reasoning exists for social action. Women overcome their reticence to speak out and, in turn, provide a stronger basis for their own existence and for reshaping their identity.

Much of the change in talk about sexual harassment has come about through education and public forums. Through women coming together, building collaborative stories, we are much closer to a better understanding of sexual harassment. Education, it seems, can play a vital role in dealing with sexual harassment by creating awareness of the issue's significance (Anita Hill, quoted in Duke, 1992, p. A10). Through listening to the stories that individuals are willing to tell, others can learn about the nature of sexual harassment, perhaps recognize its occurrence in their own lives, and pass their story on to someone else.

In the same sense that narrative form creates an appetite to be satisfied, shared narrative experience can create solutions for common problems. Individually, women may feel powerless, but as a collective whole, the sharing of experience can sustain a significant cultural evolution. This, above all else, is the hope of Anita Hill's story.

Robin Morgan (1992) eloquently summarizes the empowerment that comes with the sharing of women's experiences and the impact that this sharing may have on our society. She writes:

We have worked for a quarter of a century to name our pain and rage aloud—and now it is spoken. It should come as no surprise that what is at last heard will at first be disbelieved. They will try to deny it, denounce it, defuse it, rename it. They will call it "postfeminism," or the Gaia principle, or the Aquarian Age. They can call it anything they wish, but they can never again ignore it. It is a woman in Oklahoma and in Florida, in Burma and South Africa, in Montreal and Rio, naming herself. It is the surfacing to the depths onto the shore, of the private into the public, of the hidden and despised into the light. It is momentum against inertia. It is the energy of action. It is the earth erupting. It is the people speaking. (p. 1)

NOTES

1. There have been a variety of essays that attempt to define the nature of narratives and lay out methodological analyses. For example, Lewis (1987) focuses on Fisher's

narrative paradigm and develops a methodology for assessing Ronald Reagan's rhetoric during his terms as president of the United States. More relevant for this essay is Strine's (1992) critique of women's sexual harassment stories from a post-structuralist view. Given that there is no one correct way of conducting narrative criticism, the critic can develop her methodology with an eye toward her goals, interests, and artifacts being studied.

2. Much work on the actual testimony of both Clarence Thomas and Anita Hill has been conducted since the hearings. Young and Muir (1992) analyze the stories told by each individual and draw conclusions as to why many Americans doubted Hill's credibility. They argue that Thomas's story occupied all of the narrative ground, that it was the story of an African-American male's American dream (pulling one's self up by one's bootstraps), and that for most audiences, the dream was in line with their notions of narrative fidelity, leaving no room for Hill's countervailing position because it directly conflicted with this idealized success story.

3. Discussions regarding the significance of call-ins and the nature of the C-SPAN audience have been published elsewhere (see, for example, Muir, 1992; 1993). It is important to note that C-SPAN viewers tend to be those who participate in the political process. In 1990, for example, viewers were questioned about their voting behavior, and it was discovered that over 90 percent of the viewers questioned had participated in the 1990 election ("Survey: More Young Viewers Are Tuning in C-SPAN," 1991).

7

(Un)Becoming "Voices": Representing Sexual Harassment in Performance

Della Pollock

I am not a monolithic being.

—Anita Hill, 1992

We need a politics that is expressive, evocative, and that speaks to desire—to the desire for social meaning and connectedness, and that speaks in a nonrational way to sexual desire as well, in an affirming way. This is a quality of politics, rather than a specific content.

—Peter Gabel, 1992

I want to tell some stories about teaching a new course in Oral History and Performance at the University of North Carolina, Chapel Hill.[1] I want to represent the course in a way that reflects its commitments to narrative as a possible site of social and sexual agency, to perform in story the very power of women's desire my students, co-instructor, and I saw consistently repressed within the discourses of sexual harassment. But at the same time I need to acknowledge that I can't—at least not in a way that fulfills Western narrative expectations for a unified agent who heroically overcomes whatever problems or obstacles lie in his way. I can't settle myself into the role of a narrative "I" when "I" am implicated as both a spectator and a star, a subject and an object, a hero and his "other," in the stories I wish to recount. I can't fulfill my desire for a seamless counter-narrative without ignoring one of the keenest lessons of the course: the duplicity and ambivalence of desire itself.

I am left then with what Teresa de Lauretis calls "narrativity" as opposed to narrative, or the uneasy "working through" of the kinds of desire evoked in narrative forms.[2] In other words, I take this chapter to be a narrative performance, a reflexive enactment of contradictions expressed variously throughout the course—in oral histories, in performances of those histories, and in the "history" of interaction among the course participants. The course invited us "to perform [the] figures of movement and closure, image and gaze" that characterize narrative and so to make the ways in which narrative resolves desire in meaning a subject of critique (de Lauretis, 1984, p. 156). As a result, the performance work in the class—and the performances that seemed to surround it—were, for instance, consistently more ambivalent, ambiguous, and complex than the video "skits" presented by the university's sexual harassment prevention team. I will have more to say about these presentations later, but for now, it is important to recognize that sexual harassment as we know it unfolds in the form of performance. It is itself a rite of gender coding related in stories and made familiar and manageable largely through "official" video dramas. In this light, I have come to think that oral history performance may be a more suitable way to speak of and against harassment, especially insofar as it renews the "narrativity" of oral history and engages the body on its own behalf.[3]

In this chapter, then, I am less concerned with how to teach the Oral History and Performance course or with its particular achievement than I am with the problem of representing women's sexuality generally and sexual harassment specifically.[4] Among other things, the course has challenged me to write differently, to try to embrace in writing the irreducibly contingent, contextual, imaginative, interactive, and, indeed, erotic dimensions of performances of histories that were themselves layered in performance. This chapter is consequently rangy and episodic in structure, evocative and interrogative in style. It revolves around the problems posed by three "scenes" of harassment: a workshop performance of an oral history of harassment; a student's story of being harassed by a male professor; and my own performance as a teacher in a classroom centrally concerned with sexual harassment.

BECOMING BODIES

I'll begin by describing one of the first performances in the course during the first semester it was taught. The students had just completed their fieldwork projects and presentations. We were all feeling angry, overwhelmed, even depressed by the apparent omnipresence of harassment in our immediate community. Harassment seemed to be everywhere: tracking us, shaping us, making us feel vulnerable, suspect, and suspicious, reminding us to be nice and make do. On the day we were scheduled to do a preparatory performance workshop, the students seemed especially sluggish—weighed down by indignation and disbelief.

I divided them into small groups and asked them to improvise a performance based on one page of an interview transcript and ten minutes of brainstorming. The last performance was especially striking: One woman sat on another's back, caressing and massaging the back of the woman lying down, while the woman lying down tried to write the story of harassment reported in the interview. At first looking like no more than supportive encouragement to the writer, the stroking became aggressive, faster, more frenetic. It extended to arms, hips, legs, and belly. The prone woman's clothes and hair became disheveled, her face red with embarassment, anger, and surprise. She was trapped in a hip lock, turned at an odd angle from the audience. She persisted in trying to write, trying to speak, but found her voice increasingly lost to this sudden, strange mix of sex and violence. The more menacing the massage became, the more impossible it was for her to describe the feelings of violation reported by the interviewee and now rising within her. Polly, the woman lying down, described her experience in this way:

Although I have not ever experienced sex, an abortion, a miscarriage, or a real dangerous threat of sexual harassment, I feel as if the best way I can possibly achieve any empathy for or understanding of the experiences (good or bad) of other women is through performance. This thought became crystallized for me in this class when our group did the "mini-performance," and I completely underwent some of the pain, humiliation, and confusion surrounding many of the issues we have discussed. As my face grew hotter and redder, I became angry, not at Ellen (who was "harassing" me), but at all men and women who cruelly and intentionally harass others. I have never understood, nor do I understand now, motivation for such actions; however, after this experience in which I felt so violated and uncomfortable, I especially cannot. Therefore, I believe that this performance in class was truly an example of the possible "textual economy" of a performance, when a person "gives up" or trades a sense of pleasure for a feeling of power.[5]

As Polly describes it, the performance was empowering. The intense vulnerability she felt in the performance, displaced as it was from an actual experience of harassment or abuse, translated not into weakness but into what Bertolt Brecht would call "great" anger: a passionate, critical consciousness of injustice demanding large-scale change.[6] Polly understood her experience as part of an open matrix of sexuality that included sex, abortion, miscarriage, and sexual harassment. Her emergent anger was general: "I became angry, not at Ellen (who was "harassing" me), but at all men and women who cruelly and intentionally harass others." For Polly, at least, the performance politicized the personal. The personal here—the interviewee's story intensified in the performers' felt experience—was a point of purchase on the politics of sexuality. Rather than reducing the harassment reported to the interviewee and/or performers' particular experiences, the performance opened up a vista of shared concern that remained nonetheless grounded in feeling, sensation, and interaction.

As Polly notes, this process entailed the surrender of some kinds of pleasure (the satisfaction we take in what Polly elsewhere calls "happy end" stories—

stories that end heroically or even just *end*; the security we feel in remaining at an analytical distance). But it clearly offered us others. Indeed, we all left the class reeling, this time not with angst but with an almost giddy sense of power *and* pleasure. As we spilled out into the hall and offices, we kept asking each other, What happened here? Where had we been? None of us expected the three-minute performance to penetrate the sheer gloss of demonstration. None of us anticipated the performance subsuming, as if with carnivorous delight, the past it was meant to re-present. This was no longer about something that happened to someone else somewhere else. The performance redoubled the threatening immediacy of harassment and so made it strangely thrilling. This was what happens in sexual harassment, and it was happening *now*.

If nothing else, this performance made us take the metaphor of violation seriously. As a crowd of the mostly converted, we thought we knew what violation meant. We used it all the time and got the usual nodding response. But the meaning of violation, the violence implicit in sexual harassment, and perhaps most significantly (although apparently unintentionally), the brutal, buried violence *among women* around the issue of harassment, had become attenuated even for us. The word had become something of a cliché, a sign without substance, a sterile and complacent trace of experience, so disembodied as to be at risk of betraying the body's real pain.

In this performance, the body told its own story with unremitting force— but not without some irony. The performance repeated and intensified some of the core dynamics of sexual harassment: that subtle process of trust turned inside out, of the body twisted in paroxysms of submission, arousal, and assault. But this was plainly a performance, and the massage itself was plainly a metaphor of harassment. Indeed, we were at least in part watching the body at *play*, renewing the body of discourse about sexual harassment with vitality, strength, imagination, and possibility. As Susan Suleiman (1990) says of play generally: "To play is to affirm an 'I,' an autonomous subjectivity that exercises control over a world of possibilities; at the same time, and contrarily, it is in playing that the 'I' can experience itself in its most fluid and boundaryless state" (p. 179). In this playful evocation of a transcript (to which the performance bore almost no direct resemblance), the performers liberated themselves as creative agents even as they lost themselves to the terrifying roles represented. They made visible and concrete the power of the body to write and to *right* itself, to trace out the story that had been inscribed in its very sinews and to remake itself in irony, image, and action.[7] The terror represented in this performance was then qualified by pleasure in the act of representation, by pleasure in the uncontainable power of women's bodies to resist by representation the sadistic and voyeuristic delights men—and women—take in them.

AN UNBECOMING HISTORY

Around the middle of the fall of 1992, just as the students in the Oral History and Performance course were beginning their field studies of sexual harassment in the university community, an undergraduate student came to see me. In the context of talking about her honors project, she told me a story much like the one on which the "massage performance" was based. Amy was a triple major in speech communication, English, and education.[8] She had been a student of mine in an advanced graduate/undergraduate criticism course two years before. As a sophomore, she outran most of the graduate students in preparation, determination, and interest.

Amy seemed worn out. She began by explaining the difficulty she was having in doing both student teaching at a local high school and thesis research, and asked whether she might not postpone the thesis work until the second semester. She was apologetic, anxious about what I'd think of her, and generally embarrassed about having to back out of anything. I guess I was glad—even warmed—to see her show such an old-fashioned sense of duty and responsibility. But I was pained, too, to see her so afraid to let me down. I saw myself in her—trembling at the edge of disappointing a favorite teacher—and trembled to think I could instill that kind of fear.

Before I could say much, another story erupted. I don't recall how—what the segue was, or motive. Her face pale, her neck and chest flushing, her normally active hands still, she told me about being dressed down by her adviser in the education department in front of her supervising teacher during an early morning review session at the high school. She watched herself as she spoke, apparently bewildered and depressed by what she saw: a girl in a classroom being yelled at by a trusted adviser, protesting his insinuations, finally crying, and suffering his mockery of her tears. Amy's face became a grotesque mask as she imitated him imitating her, saying maybe she couldn't handle this, maybe she shouldn't be in the program at all. I don't remember all the details of his tirade. What I remember most clearly is her account of the make-up session out in the hall. She began by making herself even more vulnerable to him, by reasserting her trust in him: She was probably overreacting, she offered, because of her experiences with an abusive boyfriend. He enthusiastically rejoined that he had a hard time with powerful women. Then, on the grounds of this new intimacy, he proceeded to extract absolution from her. He asked (unbelievably), "Could I have a hug?" And Amy, as if puppeted by laws of courtesy, nurture, and submission, and astonished by her automatic response, provided the necessary hug.

Was this sexual harassment? It certainly was a gendered abuse of power. It traded on sexual histories and tested sexual boundaries (the "hug" imposed a kind of sexual discipline; looking like no more than a New Age handshake, it said: You are still a woman and you still have to touch me). It involved threats to Amy's career and certainly impeded her academic progress. (Her supervising teacher subsequently gave her a low score on "ability to get along with superiors.") But was this sexual harassment? It probably couldn't be prosecuted as such. The sexuality here could not be reduced to inappropriate advances or nasty comments. And to the very extent that it exceeded legal definitions of what was "sexual" in "sexual harassment," I began to wonder whether the rhetoric of "sexual harassment" didn't teach such reductiveness, whether it didn't promote a debased notion of sexuality.

Amy's situation *was* sexual—in ways that seem to surpass our current languages of gender and sexuality. It entailed the dynamics of trust, the attractions of intimacy, the erotics of power, the power of play, desire for affiliation and succor, touch, pleasure, passion, risk, personal and social histories of all of these, and just about everything else—good or bad—that's sexy about life generally. As I listened to Amy—and watched her watch another self walk through a ritual humiliation—I wanted to help her as much as I wanted to "save" sexuality from this abuse, to retrieve it from the cruel and jealous stepmother in the old Cinderella story, who was determined to cut off her own daughters' heels if it meant securing the power of the king. Here was a young woman, full of passionate enthusiasm for teaching, basically incapable of disingenuity, suddenly divided against herself—distrusting her own instincts, seeing herself slip from being a subject into being an object in another's (and now her own) sexual/gendered memory.[9]

Several performances converged on Amy's subjectivity here. First, she was infantilized—bullied into a spectacle of weakness and femininity while (as I imagine it) the classroom teacher looked on from behind her desk, imperious, stunned, vicariously shamed.[10] Second, her adviser "played" her. He mimicked her anguish. In his fun house performance of her, she became but a trace of herself, a spectator to the signs of her subjectivity (her facial expressions and gestures) now deliriously, sadistically emptied out, trivialized, meaningless. The performers then escaped the classroom stage and entered a more liminal space: the hallway. Here, in the "betwixt-and-between" world of banging lockers and young romance, they seemed to take off their masks, to reveal themselves as people separate from their "official" classroom roles.[11] But here also, precisely because this stage looked "off-stage," gender roles so naturalized as to look "real" got free play. In this emotional recess, the teacher and student, the initiator and initiand, actually completed the gender drama (boy meets girl, boy abuses girl, girl forgives boy) they began earlier. And insofar as they did so in a spirit of being "real," they made *seem* real—they "reified"—the subject positions that enabled the classroom scene in the first place: They refreshed the very social structure they thought they'd left behind.

And then there is Amy's story. This was apparently only the second of many times she was to tell it (upon my advice, she spoke with an associate dean, who in turn advised professional mediation; as she later told me, she also subsequently spoke with other faculty, friends, and family members). Was this an instance of "coming to voice"?[12] Was it a performance of narrative agency, an exercise in overcoming silence and silencing through story? I guess I'd have to say it was one of the first in a long line of rehearsals toward agency. "Coming to voice" is not equivalent merely to speaking out—or to assuming the conventionally masculine position of the narrator-agent. It is not enough to break the silence, to speak the unspoken, to name the unnamed. As bell hooks argues, "coming to voice" must be understood as a transformative act, and, to be transformative, personal narratives must contextualize and theorize their content. They must adopt a political perspective that resists reduction to the "personal."[13] In this light, "voice" cannot be understood—as it too often is— as an unproblematic category of expression, as something *there*, whole and perfect, ready and waiting, the origin and destination of a journey through speech. This journey is circular and so, ultimately, regressive. It begins and ends with the self for whom the experience reported is personal. Insofar as this notion of "voice" suggests that the speaking subject thus comes in/to her "self" in the act of speaking out about her experience, it reduces the possibility for change to self-realization. It moreover immunizes speech against critique, suggesting as it does that the words spoken are secondary to the act of speaking; that speech is the direct, unmediated expression of experience; and that speech "belongs," irreducibly, to the speaker whose "self" is reflected in it (leading to what seem to me unfortunately defensive claims on "my story" and patronizing refusals to touch, much less dispute "her story").

Rather than something given or arrived at, narrative "voice" is made in acts of telling to and with an audience. It is the fluid effect of an "other-oriented" conversation, the function of an explicit or implicit dialogue in which the narrator is a central but collaborating participant.[14] In this light, "voice" is always already social rather than personal in the sense of individual or primarily related to some kind of "raw experience." It is mediated by contact, layered by the scenes and other "voices" through which it passes. It is thus, moreover, in a constant relation of transformation—unstable, contested, as mobile as the words through which the speaking subject knows and creates her "self." From this performative perspective, Amy's "mediation" began long before I called the dean. And I have had to ask: Who was I in the scene of our conversation anyway? How did the performance of my role shape the tone, content, and meaning of what she told me?

Was I the female teacher (like the classroom teacher in Amy's story), sitting imperiously and stunned behind her big desk? Another advisor, entrusted with the power to "survey" Amy's professional and personal life? A mother who could and should hug away the pain? I did hold Amy for a moment as she left my office and, as I did, felt my body tense and withdraw, felt my desire to comfort and cleanse suddenly inhibited. I had to ask, Was I a confessor? Was she asking for forgiveness from me? Was it possible, whether intentional or not, that she was making me into the mother-confessor she'd been for him? Or was I, by the very fact of my position, making her excuse herself to me?

Was there a sexual component to this hug, whether disciplinary or desiring? And what were the implications of my power to forgive?

In their essay on the discourse of survivors of sexual abuse, Linda Alcoff and Laura Gray explore the power of the confessor especially to "recuperate" potentially transgressive discourses to the dominant discourse, to defuse survivor speech even while appearing to welcome it. Following Foucault, Alcoff and Gray argue that the confessional mode invites in order to contain threatening speech. They identify five "dangers" of such confessional structures as TV talk shows and Senate judiciary hearings:

1. Survivor speech may become a media commodity whose use value is related primarily to its sensationalism and drama, to its capacity to titillate and to arouse.

2. The confessional mode may focus attention on the victim and her emotional/psychological state and away from the perpetrator and social conditions, thus reifying the survivor's role as victim and reducing the relevance of feeling to social change.

3. It may relocate authority in the confessor/mediator/therapist/judge who is presumed to draw dispassionately on the resources of "abstract knowledge" rather than "personal experience."

4. It may consequently further discredit so-called "subjective" knowledge by perpetuating a binary opposition between "raw experience" and theory, body and mind, subjective and objective perspectives.

5. Confession may be coerced. Enthusiasm for speaking out, whether as a political or therapeutic tactic, may put pressure on survivors to disclose what they may wish to withhold. (Alcoff and Gray, 1993, pp. 270–281)

I did send Amy to the "experts." I even called the dean for her while she was in my office. I also traded bits of my own "secrets," heightening—I suspect—the aura of taboo talk surrounding our conversation. But I don't think I was Sally Jessy Raphael to Amy's women-who-get-harassed or Orrin Hatch to Amy's Anita Hill. Surely, it would diminish the magnitude of these inquisitions to suggest that I was. It would moreover obscure the extent to which the power of the auditor is not always or purely hegemonic. In the end, Alcoff and Gray encourage survivors of sexual abuse "not to confess, but to witness," "to create new discursive forms and spaces in which to gain autonomy" (1993, p. 287). They place the burden of resistance on the narrators of sexual histories who will face what Alcoff and Gray see as inevitable efforts at recuperation.

I take Alcoff and Gray to be more cautionary than explanatory of my situation. While listening to Amy I could not, any more than could Amy, entirely relinquish the recuperative position of mother-confessor to which I was hailed. But I simultaneously occupied several other, often contradictory positions and remained, as a spectator, also capable of bearing witness—not to Amy's confrontation with her adviser, but to Amy's account of it.

This brings us to my performance of Amy's story in this chapter.[15] I realize that I have cast myself as something of a Prince Charming in the story I told earlier ("I wanted to help her as much as I wanted to 'save' sexuality from this abuse, to retrieve it from the cruel and jealous stepmother in the old Cinderella story, who was determined to cut off her own daughters' heels if it meant securing the power of the king"). Amy appears as the ideal student, the "good" student and good girl (is she Cinderella here?). At the time, I didn't know any other Amy. Whether this was the only persona she presented to me or the only one I could or would see, I don't know. The question is: In the performance of "her story," do I confess or bear witness? Do I appropriate her story to a fairy-tale patriarchy in which I am suddenly the hero-savior, or do I make a space for her body to talk and for women's sexuality generally to be heard? I'd like to think that I've appropriated the Cinderella story to what I took to be Amy's interests and made its deep images resonate with contemporary issues rather than, for instance, freezing Amy and all her story represents in an archetypal, ahistorical pattern of abuse. I don't know. I really can't say how the story falls out. Like so many stories of harassment (or stories of stories), I have to leave its interpretation for my reader/spectator to perform.

PERFORMED BY HARASSMENT

Amy's harassment was very much a part of her teacher-training program. It was a lesson in hierarchy and a lesson in gender. It was also a lesson that, as a university professor, I'd never had to learn—at least not directly. However, problems in teaching the Oral History and Performance course, and, in particular, my interactions with the sole white male in one class, have led me to wonder just how much of this lesson I have both absorbed and taught.

Bill was a returning graduate student.[16] He was approaching fifty and was one of three men in a class of twelve and the only white male. (Interestingly, there was only one white male in the course each time it was taught.) On the first day of class, Bill expressed anxiety about his relatively unique position—and surprise at the feminist and feminized orientation of the class. The rest of us, sitting in a small circle in the middle of a large room, laughed and provided the discursive equivalent of a group hug: We rehearsed familiar platitudes—we're all here to learn, these are problems for women and men—and made smug gestures at inclusion. The tables were suddenly turned—women and black males were in the majority—and we were going to show the patriarchs how to do it.

At least that was my view, unarticulated as it was at the time. As the class proceeded, animosities developed between Bill and other students—a feminist graduate student, a black campus revolutionary. Bill became increasingly bitter. He started sitting further and further away from the group, often with his back half-turned to us, his lips pressed in smirking anger at our sometimes inept attempts to formulate the intersections of oral history, women's sexuality, and performance. He chided me after class one day for violating what he took

to be the terms of my discipline: "This is more of a sociology than a performance class," he explained. Two or three times, he offered the liberal-
conservative benediction on all social problems: It [whatever] is just like racism
or poverty or discrimination of all kinds; it's too bad but what are you going
to do about it? He started our discussion of sexual harassment (which he
insisted on calling "sexual pestering") and Carole Vance's landmark essay,
"Pleasure and Danger: Toward a Politics of Sexuality," by asking—a skeptical
smile playing at the corners of his mouth: "Do all women live 'in terror' of
sexual assault?" and then cautioned us—following his own example—not to
go into bars with motorcycles parked out front.

I don't wish to make Bill a strawman to be burned in effigy at the next
"Take Back the Night" rally. And yet I do. I am filled with a kind of anger
toward him I couldn't and wouldn't feel during the course. To the contrary:
I rather primly pursued peace. When the black militant student in the class
started talking about a racial war on campus, Bill interrupted. In a suddenly
thick Southern drawl, he patronized and vaguely threatened James: "I hope
you mean a psychological war, James. . . . I hope that's what you mean."[17] My
answer to James's tensing fists and Bill's dismissive glare: politically correct
conflict management. "Let's be sensitive to each others' point of view," I
offered—and immediately stalled the conversation. In this case, "sensitivity"
meant silence. It meant inserting a buffer between James and Bill that protected their differences from engagement and conflict. And how did I follow
this triumph? I spoke to Bill after class. I cozied up to him, white person to
white person, younger woman to older man, teacher to student. I appealed
to his power, to what I believed must be his ultimately good sense, and to
what surely was his need for the redemptive force of my attention: "Talk to
James," I said. "Just sit him down and tell him he has to listen to you for ten
minutes." As I recall, I suggested that he then listen to James for a similar
period. But whatever happened next washes out in my memory as I stare, in
shocked dismay, at my own arrogance. Who was this that so completely mar-
tyred James to Bill's interest? Why was I—as I seemed to be, making up,
"making nice," even making love to Bill? Where did these words come from?
I felt ventriloquised, performed. I watched myself appeasing Bill in much the
same way Amy had watched herself hugging her adviser. As if at once helpless
on the sidelines and a key player in the game, I ingratiated myself to a perspective I hated—and have been kicking myself ever since.

But there was more going on here than playing patsy to the white guy.
James was a football player, something like a defensive back: He was relatively
short, lithe, quick. He had an all-or-nothing smile that occasionally, suddenly
broke out against his otherwise cautious demeanor. He was an earnest student,
apologetic for his lapses due to extracurricular commitments but never deferential. I had to prove myself to him—even as I curried Bill's favor. I had
to show my credentials, to make it clear that I was not an "infiltrator" who
would use insider information against his activist efforts. I had to get him to

trust me. I wanted him to trust me. I found him more attractive than I like to admit.

So why admit it now? Because it shades the racial and gender politics that surfaced in my relationship with Bill with sexual politics, with erotic possibility diverted through and straining against the protocols of "appropriate" student/ teacher relations. Indeed, eros was leaking out everywhere in the class, in various forms—in conflict, disclosure, community, humor, "carnival" trans- gressions: in interviews fraught with disagreement and concern; in a heated, testy argument over whether a student was justified in calling her treatment on the college debate circuit "harassment"; in another student's emotional collapse in the middle of presenting her study of harassment in the campus African-American community; in poems and reports of conversations with friends and parents that seemed to float in and out of the classroom space; in performances that tested our willingness to touch and to be touched—and turned Anita Hill's testimony before the Senate Judiciary Committee into fly- ing rolls of toilet paper; in a male student's insistent interruption of my intro- duction to Emily Martin's Marxist analysis of childbirth in *The Woman in the Body*: "was this what it was like for you? I mean, *really*?"—and my mostly direct, often awkward, hour-long response.

The class was not orgiastic. It was messy. It participated in what Miriam Camitta calls "the eroticizing of the scientific enterprise" by licensing feeling, desire, and play in the production of knowledge (1990, p. 27). In so doing it blurred the boundaries between academic and "real" life, between what Ste- phen Tyler, calls "transcendent" and "evocative" ways of knowing (1987, pp. 199–218) or what Jane Tompkins calls more simply the "out there" and the "in here." As Tompkins (1990, p. 658) says of the graduate seminar on emotion she describes in "Pedagogy of the Distressed": "I wanted never to lose sight of the fleshly, desiring selves who were engaged in discussing he- gemony or ideology or whatever it happened to be; I wanted to get the ideas that were 'out there,' the knowledge that was piled up impersonally on shelves, in relation with the people who were producing and consuming it. I wanted to get 'out there' and 'in here' together."[18]

I'd like to think, like Tompkins, that the course thus enacted "that very unalienated condition which the revolution presumably exists to usher in" (1990, p. 653). And I do believe I glimpsed utopia in some of the students' work. But the main lesson I learned from Bill is that when you open this door, everything comes rushing in. On the one hand, the course encouraged stu- dents to practice the kind of unalienated sexuality whose absence in our daily lives it otherwise mourned. In subject and method, it at least allowed for the integrated exercise of mind and body that is at the root of sexual agency. On the other hand, it showed just how firm is the grip of deep cultural scripts on even the most reflexive attempts at counter-representation. In my interactions with Bill, I behaved like the classic victim of harassment—even while leading discussion on harassment! I flew from conflict and a sense of powerlessness toward the conventionally gendered role of mother-temptress-teacher: I would seduce Bill into consciousness, I would nurture his better self. And I was seduced by failure: The harder I tried, the more recalcitrant he became, and the harder I tried. As a result, I found myself enervated, my other students neglected, and significant racial and sexual issues denied. It was only in conversation with a couple of the female graduate students in the class at the beginning of the next semester that I realized that I had been had—by Bill and by my own worst instincts—and that my anger began to surface.

REMEDIAL "VOICES"

All three of these "scenes" of harassment raise questions about teaching: What is entailed in teaching about harassment? How does teaching recapitulate the dynamics of harassment? And how might the classroom become a site of resisting the deep scripts that enable harassment and continue to control its avowed correctives? These scenes thus bring us back to the organizing problem of this essay and the course: the power of dominant representations of harassment to secure regressive patterns of gender relations.

While harassment itself (whether direct or indirect, large or small scale) punishes women into submission and self-doubt, the representation of harassment in legal and prevention discourses often, ironically, renews the punishment it is meant to redress—and I don't mean merely in the sense that it exposes women to public humiliation and retaliation; it certainly does that. It somewhat more insidiously carries on the work of harassment by reproducing stereotypes, encouraging false clarity, and exoticizing the sexual "secret." The result is rationalized sexuality; sexuality made orderly and manageable; gender purified of its threatening "low other": sex, sexuality, eros;[19] gender-ized sexuality; sexuality cut up and cut out to fit the norms of the workplace—norms that borrow on Puritanism not for its own sake but for the sake of efficiency and productivity. Discourses of prevention focus on harassment as a workplace issue in part, it seems, because harassment marks the apparent incompatibility of sexual and capitalist pursuits. In the name of progress, harassment must be stamped out because sexuality must be contained.

This is, in effect, the logic of the university's prevention videos. Each of the first two times I taught the oral history and performance course, I made what seemed the perfunctory arrangements for the university's sexual harassment officer to visit. Each time, I was struck by the gap between my own, as yet incipient, understanding of harassment and the official stories represented. Each presentation included a video. The first, presented by the sexual harassment officer, was specifically designed for students. It provided brief scenes for review and discussion: a foreign teaching assistant making sexist comments in class, a sleazy professor pushing a student for a date. The video set a game-like tone for the class. It made the central question definitional—was it or wasn't it harassment?—and encouraged the students to rush to the buzzer with the "right" answer. The room raged with clarity. Confident that they would never be as weak or tremulous as the women on the TV screen, the students issued dire warnings. "If I'd met that guy in a bar, I would have told him 'in your face!' " said one. Others used the language of the policy itself—"unwelcome advances," "hostile environment"—to clobber the foreigner and the lech.

The next semester, a representative from the office of human resources stood in for the sexual harassment officer. He took a kinder and gentler approach. He began by observing a tension between the legal and experiential dimensions of harassment, sympathetically explaining that the process of legal prosecution is so fraught with recrimination and retaliation—or, perhaps more importantly, the fear of retaliation—that it potentially redoubles the harassment itself and keeps reporting low. He expressed the university's consequent commitment to resolving these issues internally and to responding to their attendant trauma on a case-by-case basis. Harassment was, for him, a pervasive but personal problem, requiring a therapeutic response. "Everybody has secrets," he warmly but provocatively explained. He moreover insisted that harassment was color- and gender-blind: He denied racial and gendered determinations in favor of an essentializing perspective that made harassment one more among many regrettable but human experiences.

The video he showed (apparently designed for staff and administrative audiences) similarly tried to avoid politics. Its basic message was sex and work (when sex is apparently what women bring to the workplace) don't mix. Composed of a frame story and a series of exemplary scenes, the film went to great lengths to show that harassment crossed gender, racial, age, and class lines and that it occurred along horizontal as well as vertical power axes—and so made sure that we couldn't locate its damage within any particular power structure. According to the movie, sex rather than power was the primary culprit: Sex was messy, dangerous, and inefficient and should be rousted from the workplace.

The movie began with a smartly dressed white woman explaining the need for harassment awareness to a conference table full of white male "suits." Mirroring the role of the students in the class, they proceeded to discuss scenes in which they see:

1. a lecherous, pock-marked boss practically drool onto his secretary's keyboard as he instructs her to accompany him out of town or else;

2. a totally together personnel officer assure the shaky, mousy secretary that her harassment report will be entirely confidential—but first she has to report the incident to her boss's boss; and

3. a Barbie doll nurse in a starched white uniform respond to a passing doctor's pinch and greeting, "Hey, girls!", with a wagging finger and brusque reprimand: "Don't ever do that again!"

These were grade school skits, exaggerating stereotypes to make a quick and easy point. In the process, however,

1. they portrayed sexual harassment as sexual deviance, committed only by the completely and pathologically perverse, a category of villainy so narrow as to include almost no one (otherwise known as the Orrin Hatch/Clarence Thomas defense);

2. they subtly encouraged viewers to disidentify with the unattractive and overzealous victim, and to avoid reporting for fear of increased risk to their jobs and reputations; and

3. they provided an unrealistic and ultimately undesirable alternative to submission and/or reporting (what is supposed to look like assertiveness in the third scene amounts instead to no more than reverse infantilism: The girl becomes the mother, scolding the bad boy for sexual impropriety; the whore becomes—once again—the Madonna, the paragon of female virtue, the Florence Nightingale of sexual harassment).

These scenes are, of course, punctuated by repeated assurances that as long as all parties behave in a "businesslike" manner, as long as they dress and act "professionally," they will be protected from prosecution under the law—a resolution that obviously serves the interests of the corporate structure but continues to hold women ransom to conventionally masculine standards of professional conduct and conventionally feminine standards of "good" behavior (suggesting the common correlate: If you're a good girl, you won't get raped). In form and content, the videos reiterated the masculinization of desire and narrative de Lauretis laments: They represent sexuality as a feminized obstacle to be overcome by men and women alike.

Toward the end of both class sessions, the students began to challenge the stories they'd heard. They asked: Where was harassment on a broad continuum of gendered behavior? Is it possible or desirable to isolate harassment out of deep cultural patterns of masculine aggression and feminine submission? How do you resolve the competing claims of community and autonomy that gird "professional" life? To what extent is "professionalism" itself a bait for women—requiring women at once to repress their sexualities and to participate in sexual politics? To what extent does the university policy ignore the fact that it is part of the dynamic of harassment to make the harassing behavior seem not entirely "unwelcome"? In the case of the student and the professor, in particular, wasn't it possible that his attentions were flattering enough to confound her sense of appropriateness, to make her want more, to encourage her to feel compensated for the intellectual insecurities that characterize her daily life at the university? Wasn't this unfair not because it was clearly "unwelcome" but because it played on the very extent to which she might find it welcome—the extent to which she might be willing to accept sexual for intellectual power or, more seductive yet, to believe for a moment, in the alienated, Cartesian world of the university, that her body and mind were one, and that attraction to one might be attraction to both? And if so, was she to blame for—must she suffer the consequences of—not immediately and dramatically rebuffing her professor's advances?

In asking these questions, and in their subsequent performance work, the students pressed "official" stories of harassment for the ambivalence and contradictions lying just below their neat and shining surfaces. They challenged the university to speak to a wider range of experience than that encompassed by the videos and to take a more radical stance, to engage an analysis of power that refuses the kind of sentimental, false liberalism that, in the name of "equality," assumes everyone is "equally" oppressed.

They moreover suggested that banning sexuality from the workplace or, in our case, the classroom, would not only be impossible but undesirable. It would repeat the alienation of the life of the body from the life of the mind that already eats away at women students (making them especially vulnerable to harassment) and that maintains the status quo—that is, only when the mind and the body, idea and action, merge in praxis can change occur. To ban sexuality is to throw out the baby with the bathwater; it is to roust power with abuse, to proscribe the possibility of sexual agency with its current constraints. It is to reduce sexuality to having sex (or, in the case of the new codes at the University of Virginia, "amorous relations") and so to delimit and devalue its sphere of influence. In the case of teaching, it is in turn to forsake the powerful resources of play, passion, community, and pleasure in the endeavor to know and to (re)make sexual history.

(UN)BECOMING VOICES

I began this essay with the good news: the possibility of performance to open an alternative discursive space in which the body can read its own pain and so write its own pleasure. I have returned to the bad news: the tendency of prevailing discourses of harassment to recuperate the disciplinary structure of harassment itself by encouraging a juridical or therapeutic response. I'd like to conclude by tracing two emergent themes: the "hug" and the problem of "voice."

Ellen in effect hugged Polly as she massaged her back. Amy hugged her adviser, and I hugged Amy in turn. The class discursively hugged Bill when we offered him the long arms of our sympathy. What was all this hugging about? As I look back, it seems to me—at best—to be about a kind of embarrassed control, control masquerading as openness and support, substituting some kind of equilibrium for what seem the impossible objects of erotic desire—what Peter Gabel (1992) calls desire for "social meaning and connectedness" as well as sexual desire. To greater and lesser degrees, these hugs were empty signs, signs often violently insisting on reference to affection and forgiveness and community and yet, in so doing, mostly signifying lack. They were signs of the very sterility and distance they sought to overcome. They were deceptively kind, stifling opposition and pain under blankets of good intentions. They personalized the political.[20] They individualized pain and circumscribed power—and questions of power—with great shows of sympathy and apology. They thus rehearsed the power of weak or false liberalism generally to violate the very subject/object of its devotion.

To redeem desire, pleasure, agency, and community from the recuperative effects of false liberalism, we must tell our sexual histories. We must remember them in performance. We must bear witness, collectively and individually. As Carole Vance (1984) argues:

Our task is to identify what is pleasurable and under what conditions, and to control experience so that it occurs more frequently. To begin, we need to know our sexual histories, which are surely greater than our own individual experience, surely more diverse than we know, both incredible and instructive. To learn these histories, we must speak about them to each other. . . . Without women's speech, we fall back on texts and myths, prescriptive and overgeneralized. (p. 6)

But before we do so, we must beware of our own capacity for suffocating kindness. In order for story to become the site of the kind of "social meaning and connectedness" both desired and denied beneath all that hugging, we must resist the temptation to "embrace" the past uncritically—to value "voice" for its own sake—in favor of a more rigorous, complex, and reflexive point of view.

Finally, then, the problem of "voice." As I suggested earlier, voice is not something found or realized. It is produced within the immediate context of performative, social relations. It is always already "becoming" as it passes from one context to another. Harassment in many ways trains women's voices to take on a particular timbre—the pitch of penitence, the tone of self-doubt, if not exactly silence. This is the voice that conventionally "becomes" women, the voice that is, by white, middle-class standards, gender appropriate. The performance classroom potentially produces other kinds of voices, including those that are "unbecoming" in the sense of distasteful, transgressive, and irreverent, and those that are "un-becoming" in the sense of unraveling and deconstructing or transforming "backward." I think the massage performance worked on both of these levels. First, it articulated the core dynamics of harassment in and through the body harassment teaches us to keep silent, hidden, withdrawn. It transgressed gender expectations by privileging the body, and it surpassed performance expectations by reiterating what was a largely verbal assault in concrete, immediate, and in some ways repulsively direct terms. Then, it dis-articulated the experience of harassment reported in the interview. It tore it apart. It engaged multiple, alternative voices—the harasser's, the performers', the spectators', an imaginary roommate's or some other woman's—in the re-production of a scene that consequently became infinitely readable, not only open to but demanding diverse interpretations.

Over the three semesters I have taught the Oral History and Performance course, it consistently produced a wide range of voices—some defensive, confessional, contentious, even abusive. But as uncomfortable as this multiplicity often was, it was a welcome alternative to the reductive and regulated positions offered by the videos and harassment itself. In this chapter, as in the course, I have been concerned with representing sexuality in ways that don't further alienate it. As a consequence, I find myself at the intersection of many voices, among them, my own—lyrical, narrative, theoretical, anxious, angry, sardonic, empathic—and Polly's, Amy's, Bill's, bell hooks's, Linda Alcoff's, Carole Vance's. In the performance of this chapter, I am no more a "monolithic being" than was Anita Hill before the Senate Judiciary Committee, despite the committee's attempts to make her serve a single identity.[21]

Among all of the problems Hill presented to the committee, one of the most nagging was that of ethical credibility or "character." The hearings presumed the singularity of moral character. As Orrin Hatch so eloquently put it, for Thomas to have committed the acts of which he was accused he would have had to have been a pervert: It was inconceivable that he could be both good and bad, that the goodness he showed in other places at other times did not imply absolute consistency. Hill, on the other hand, was relentlessly paradoxical. Hard as the senators tried, they couldn't resolve—and dissolve—her into a single myth of femininity. Within the discourses of the hearings, she was simultaneously performed as a spurned lover and a dutiful daughter, a sexual obsessive and a spinster sister, a victim and a bitch, too black and too white, too smart and too dumb. Because the poet-performer of ancient Greece similarly challenged the rationalist idealization of ethos, he was banned from Plato's *Republic*. The poet lied, Plato argued; he portrayed the gods and heroes as authors of evil deeds, capable of shape-shifting and paradox. Republicans, rather, should emulate the true god: They should play one part only, "the manly part," a part cleansed of ambiguity, multiplicity, partiality and feeling—all of which make up the unacceptable "part of a woman" (Plato, 1953, p. 39). Indeed, the "part of a woman" is not a part at all. It is many parts, each fluid and protean. Anita Hill interrupted the judiciary review of Clarence Thomas from the perspective of a woman and a performer who both witnessed and enacted ironic transformations of character. She embodied difference. Whether true in the sense of factually consistent or not, Hill's account challenged the committee to reveal its intolerance for a kind of ethical inconsistency, ambivalence, and contradiction grounded in sexual difference.

To perform the "part of a woman" is thus to resist the "texts and myths, prescriptive and overgeneralized" embedded in idealist models of subjectivity, whether reactionary or liberal. It is to displace masculine narratives in which women appear as the objects of male desire to be "overcome" (tamed and contained) with narratives written by female, desiring subjects, who "overcome" (break out and get past) their containment by multiplicity and performed difference. It is to replenish the eros of social life with the exorbitant possibilities of play. From a performative perspective on narrative and sub-jectivity, the spaces between and within emergent, multiple voices are sites of possibility. Widening or narrowing, cracking and branching out under pressure of a given scene, they evoke the restless instability of any one voice and prom-ise new and more productive ways of talking about and from our respective sexualities, ways that don't repeat the violence already done to them but that enjoy and redeem the plenitude of sexuality itself. It is in the spirit of this promise that I will continue to teach the Oral History and Performance course and to learn from it.

NOTES

I would like to thank Jane Blocker, Judith Farquhar, Jacquelyn Hall, Joy Kasson, Beverly Long, and Carol Mavor for their invaluable help in the preparation of this chapter. I would also like to thank the students in Speech 95/395 (spring 1992), Speech 173 (fall 1992), and History 255/Duke University (spring 1993) for their provocative work and David Shaw for his research assistance. This course was facilitated by a development grant from the Curriculum in Women's Studies, University of North Carolina, Chapel Hill.

1. The course was taught three successive terms in the past two years. In the spring semester of 1992, I team-taught the course with Jacquelyn Hall, director of the South-ern Oral History Program at UNC, as a graduate/undergraduate independent study in history, speech communication, and women's studies. In the fall of 1992, I taught the course as an advanced undergraduate course in the Department of Speech Commu-nication. Jacquelyn and I again team-taught the course as a graduate seminar in the history department at Duke University through the Duke Center for Documentary Studies in the spring of 1993. The first two times the course was taught it focused the students' field and performance projects on sexual harassment in the university com-munity. The third time, sexual harassment was one among several options concerned with sexuality, gender, and power.

2. de Lauretis characterizes the kinds of desire generally expressed in Western narratives as "Oedipal," or the masculine, heroic desire "to denude, to know, to learn the origin and the end," and masochistic, or the "place of a purely *passive* desire" reserved for feminine object- subjects (de Lauretis, 1984, pp. 107, 151). See de Lauretis (1984), esp. pp. 106–107, 155–157, for her development of Claire Johnston's notion of the "working through" of desire, articulated in Johnston's 1974 essay "Women's Cinema as Counter-Cinema" in *Notes on Women's Cinema*, pp. 28, 31.

3. For other approaches to performance as an alternative mode of representing oral history and ethnography, see Conquergood (1991), Turner (1986), and Frisch (1990).

4. Those interested in the general approach, assignments, and readings in the course may obtain a syllabus by submitting a direct request to the author at: Depart-ment of Communication Studies, Bingham CB# 3285, University of North Carolina, Chapel Hill, NC, 27599.

5. Polly Compos, paper for SPCH 395, May 2 1992; quoted with permission. Polly is drawing on Robert Scholes's notion of "textual economy" (1989).

6. See Brecht (1955), esp. scene 4, pp. 65–69.

7. I am, of course, indebted to Helene Cixous (1976) for her mandate to "write the body."

8. Pseudonym; story told with permission.

9. For a complementary perspective, see John Berger's sense of how women assimilate the roles of the "surveyor" and the "surveyed" such that "the surveyor of woman in herself is male: the surveyed female. Thus she turns herself into an object— and most particularly an object of vision: a sight" (1972, p. 47).

10. On spectacles of femininity, see Spitzack (1993) and her primary references, Butler (1990b) and Bartky (1988).

11. I am borrowing the central notion of liminality, explicated in Turner (1969; 1982).

12. See bell hooks's influential essay " 'when i was a young soldier for the revolution': coming to voice," in hooks (1989, pp. 10–18).

13. See "feminist politicization: a comment," in hooks (1989, pp. 110–111).

14. This is the seminal concept in Bakhtin (1981).

15. I am grateful to Marianne Hirsch for encouraging me in this direction.

16. Pseudonym. I understand this to be an account of my own experience and so have not secured Bill's permission to tell it. I did alert the students repeatedly to this writing project and requested their general permission to discuss their work.

17. Pseudonym.

18. Tompkins's essay is a compelling confrontation with lecture-style teaching and the "antipedagogical" bias in higher education, but it is not unproblematic. Of particular concern to me are Tompkins's simplistic and essentialist opposition of emotional empowerment and intellectual disempowerment, and her substitution of an antitheatrical for an antipedagogical bias (implicit in her dismissal of what she calls the "performance model" of teaching in favor of teaching as a "maternal or coaching activity"). See Tompkins, 1990, p. 660.

19. See Stallybrass and White's development of Bakhtin's notion of the "low other" (1986).

20. For critiques of the current tendency to invert the working premise of contemporary feminism—"the personal is the political"—and, in effect, to personalize the political, see Rich, 1986, p. x, and Kaminer, 1992.

21. I should note that this was neither a partisan effort nor one limited to the committee's proceedings. Indeed, the contest over Hill's identity has only intensified in the popular press resulting, on the one hand, in David Brock's spurious and reactionary *The Real Anita Hill: The Untold Story* (New York: Macmillan, 1993) and, on the other hand, in *Ms.* magazine's feminist canonization/commodification of Hill in its subscription offer of video highlights of Hill's testimony during the Thomas hearings.

8

Sexual Harassment as Information Equivocality: Communication and Requisite Variety

Gary L. Kreps

Sexually harassing communication is a ubiquitous feature of modern organizations that seriously degrades the quality of organizational life (Aggarwal, 1987; Fitzgerald et al., 1988; Loy & Stewart, 1984; Popovich, 1988). It causes great pain and suffering to those who are harassed, diminishing their organizational power and position and degrading them as human beings through violation of their personal and professional expectations to be treated fairly and respectfully (Kreps, 1986; Payne, 1993; Quina, 1990). Sexual harassment also seriously constrains the organizing process by breaking down interpersonal trust and cooperation between organizational actors, creating closed and defensive communication climates, and distracting members from the accomplishment of goals (Driscoll, 1981; Kreps, 1990).

Sexual harassment is a product of discursive practices, since it is expressed, reacted to, and sustained communicatively through patterns of interpersonal interaction (Hickson, Grierson, & Linder, 1990). Discursive patterns define sexual harassment by introducing and reinforcing social norms for what is appropriate and acceptable interpersonal interaction (Kreps, 1993b). Dysfunctional discursive practices have fostered the spread of sexual harassment in organizations, leading to the current epidemic of sexual harassment in modern organizational life. Careful examination of the discursive practices that underlie and surround sexual harassment can help increase public understanding and the ability to respond effectively to this troubling phenomenon. This chapter begins such examination by reviewing some of the ways that problematic discursive practices have fostered sexual harassment in organizational life. Weick's (1979) model of organizing and the principle of requisite variety are used as a theoretical foundation for interpreting the influences of communication on sexual harassment and suggesting new discursive strategies for confronting and preventing it in organizational life.

THE DISCURSIVE TRIVIALIZATION OF SEXUAL HARASSMENT

Sexual harassment has flourished because it has not been defined, described, nor perceived as a serious issue by many organizational actors (Collins & Blodgett, 1981; Garcia, Milano, & Quijano, 1989; Kreps, 1993b; Pryor & Day, 1988; Williams & Cyr, 1992; Wood, 1993e). Sexual harassment has been trivialized discursively within organizations by being explained away as a minor social issue. It is discussed and joked about as though acts of sexual harassment were actually misguided expressions of affection, romance, teasing, or playfulness (Booth-Butterfield, 1989; Driscoll, 1981; Kreps, 1993a; Shotland & Craig, 1988; Witteman, 1993). These trivializing messages diminish public concern about and sanctions against sexually harassing behaviors.

Communicatively based cultural ideologies that establish guidelines for "correct" behavior in organizations and society have often served to foster sexual harassment (Kreps, 1993a). For example, those in positions of authority, often operating from a traditional managerial ideology of supervision through control and dehumanization, may believe that harassing behaviors are legitimate supervisory messages. This ideology expects managers to be tough and show workers who's the boss. Harassment is often seen as an inevitable rite of passage that subordinate organization members must bear (Kreps, 1992; Phillips & Jarboe, 1993). It is but a small jump from managerial harassment to sexual harassment, especially when the manager finds his or her (but usually his, since men are much more likely to perpetrate acts of sexual harassment) subordinate to be sexually attractive. The traditional societal ideologies of sex role stereotypes, where men are expected to dominate women, also foster sexual harassment in organizations, since men are more likely than women to hold positions of formal authority, often supervising women, in modern organizations (Payne, 1993; Phillips & Jarboe, 1993).

Those who are sexually harassed are often too ashamed to speak about their plight and may blame themselves (Collins & Blodgett, 1981; Pryor & Day, 1988; Quina, 1990; Williams & Cyr, 1992). The shame of being sexually harassed inadvertently trivializes sexual harassment through silence, by making it invisible. If those who are sexually harassed do not speak of their harassment they become victims. They cannot elicit cooperation from others nor can they receive social support, because others are unaware of their plight. They also shield harassers from public condemnation and punishment, providing the perpetrators with communicative immunity for their acts of abuse.

Due to discursive trivialization, sexual harassment has long been tolerated, swept under the rug, and perpetuated. Harassers have not been seriously admonished and discouraged from engaging in such behaviors. Those who are sexually harassed have been made to feel that they had no legitimate reason nor opportunity for complaint or retribution (Jossem, 1991; Terpstra & Baker, 1988). The organizational trivialization of sexual harassment has legitimized harassment and disenfranchised those who are harassed (Kreps, 1993a).

THE EQUIVOCALITY OF SEXUAL HARASSMENT

Equivocality refers to the relative level of complexity, lack of predictability, and ambiguity one has in responding to a particular event (Kreps, 1990). Highly equivocal phenomena are very complex, unpredictable, and ambiguous. They are most challenging since they are difficult to understand. Weick (1979) refers to the different situations and events that organizational actors encounter as information inputs, emphasizing the importance of information in organizational life. In fact, he posits, based upon sociocultural evolutionary theory and information theory, the primary reason for organizing is to provide individuals with support and feedback in responding to highly equivocal situations. Thus, according to his model, communication plays an important role in social organizing, helping actors cope with the challenges of interpreting and responding to equivocal information situations.

Weick describes organizational environments as information environments. That is, the most salient feature of any organizational environment is the information value of the different situations actors encounter. When organizational actors effectively interpret and respond to the many different information situations they attend to (selected from the enormous population of potential information inputs that are available in organizational life), they are able to make sense of organizational life and direct the accomplishment of individual and collective goals.

Interestingly, equivocality is not merely a characteristic of an event (or information situation), but rather a characteristic of the individual's ability to perceive and respond to the event. That is, a situation is not inherently imbued with a certain level of equivocality. A situation that is of very high equivocality to one person may be quite routine and of low equivocality to another person. It is the ability of the individual to interpret a phenomenon effectively that determines its level of equivocality.

A primary goal in organizational life is to develop the ability (communicative processes) and interpretive resources (organizational intelligence) to enable actors to interpret and respond effectively to a broad range of information situations. Organizational actors, like all human beings, have an insatiable appetite for meaning, for understanding the many different people and events they encounter every day (Kreps, 1990). Some of these events (highly equivocal information inputs) challenge their ability to interpret and respond to unique situations, thus challenging their ability to be in control and make sense of their environments.

Sexual harassment is an organizational event that challenges actors' abilities to interpret, predict, and control organizational life. For many, it is a highly equivocal organizational situation. The equivocality of sexual harassment makes it a major problem in modern organizational life. By examining sexual harassment from a Weickian information equivocality perspective, the discursive practices that are used to interpret and respond to harassment become the primary organizing strategies for handling (information processing) it.

Sexual harassment is a situation that is rife with uncertainty. It is a difficult information situation for organizational actors to understand. Subjects of sexual harassment may have the following unanswered questions: What is happening here? Why is this person acting this way? Is this flirtation? Joking? Intimidation? How can these unwelcome behaviors be stopped? Who, if anyone, should these patterns of sexual harassment be reported to? Bosses? Coworkers? Friends? Family?

Those who are accused of sexual harassment also encounter high levels of uncertainty and shame (Shedletsky, 1993). It is unclear what forms of recourse are available to those who are accused (fairly or unfairly) of sexual harassment. How can those who are accused of sexual harassment prove (without a doubt) that they are innocent? How will such accusations affect their reputations and relationships with other organization members? Accusations of sexual harassment are likely to be very equivocal information situations.

In fact, accusations of sexual harassment can increase the equivocality of organizational life for all members. Supervisors and administrators who are charged with investigating and providing formal responses to charges of harassment have a difficult time deciding what to do. How do they know whether charges are true? They must be very careful to preserve the confidentiality of both the accuser and the accused, who have rights to privacy, yet they must also ask questions and gather information to investigate accusations. Coworkers and subordinates face similar equivocality. How do they know who to believe and support? What kinds of support are most appropriate and effective? There are few easy answers for responding to charges of sexual harassment in modern organizational life.

Sexual harassment is a very complex social phenomenon. It is communicated in many different ways (Hickson, Grierson, & Linder, 1990). It can be subtle or overt. It is expressed verbally and nonverbally. It has many complex, and often negative, influences on organizational life, such as breeding tension and distrust in relationships, degrading climates, and decreasing members' work motivation and job satisfaction (Aggarwal, 1987; Driscoll, 1981; Loy & Stewart, 1984; Popovich, 1988).

Responding to harassment is very unpredictable (Terpstra & Baker, 1988). It is often unclear whether charges of sexual harassment will be treated fairly and confidentially. It is uncertain whether charges will result in retribution, more harassment, poor work evaluations, reduced opportunities for promotion, or loss of employment. When charges of sexual harassment are made, who will be believed, the accuser or the accused? What, if anything, will be done to discourage future harassment? These are very difficult questions to answer in many modern organizational contexts.

SEXUAL HARASSMENT AND THE PRINCIPLE OF REQUISITE VARIETY

The principle of requisite variety suggests that an effective organizational response to an information situation must match its equivocality. In practice this means that simple (low equivocality) situations should be responded to with simple organizational processes, and complex (high equivocality) situations should be responded to with complex processes. When organizations respond to low equivocality situations with complex processes they waste energy and resources, and when they respond to high equivocality situations with simple processes they are unlikely to handle the problem effectively (Kreps, 1990).

In the case of sexual harassment, which is most often a highly equivocal information input in modern organizational life, the principle of requisite variety suggests that the best organizational response is to compose a complex process. Unfortunately, since sexual harassment is trivialized in organizational life, actors often do not recognize the equivocality of such situations, and often respond inappropriately with simple rules. For example, a typical response to an act of sexual harassment is for the subject of harassment, supervisors, and coworkers to ignore the harasser and hope the harassment will stop. This is a rather simplistic, yet understandable, response to an uncomfortable and highly equivocal issue that is not likely to resolve the problem. In fact, ignoring harassment can communicate acquiescence, powerlessness, and vulnerability, encouraging additional acts by making the harasser feel powerful, intimidating, and immune to retribution (Kreps, 1993a).

Simplistic responses to equivocal situations, such as ignoring sexual harassment, violate the principle of requisite variety. Organizations often encourage such violations by failing to provide clear policies and support mechanisms to help those who encounter sexual harassment to respond effectively. Organization members can be empowered to develop situationally sensitive strategies for responding effectively to the equivocality of sexual harassment through institutionalized education programs, social support mechanisms, and organizational policies that demystify sexual harassment and identify clear procedures for handling it (Kreps, 1993a).

EQUIVOCAL INPUTS AND WEICK'S MODEL OF ORGANIZING

Weick's model describes the organizing processes used to respond to equivocal information situations effectively. The model follows the guidelines set in the principle of requisite variety by recommending the use of simple organizational processes (rules) to respond to low equivocality information situations, and the use of complex organizational processes (communication cycles) to respond to high equivocality situations. For example, a response to acts of sexual harassment (high equivocality inputs) that follows Weick's model would be the performance of communication cycles to reduce the equivocality of the information situation. Communication cycles that could be used in this case might include discussing the situation with the perpetrator, coworkers, legal counsel, or supervisors within the organization. Additionally, organizations can provide support mechanisms for members, such as counseling centers, human resource representatives, or ombudspeople, to facilitate the use of communication cycles in response to sexual harassment.

Communication cycles are three-part interlocked sequences of communication, often referred to as double interacts (Kreps, 1980). Each double interact is composed of an act, a response to the act, and an adjustment to the response. For example, a hypothetical communication cycle between a subject of harassment and a lawyer might include an act: the subject asks the lawyer, "What legal recourse do I have?"; a response: the lawyer says, "You can file a grievance with the Equal Employment Opportunity Commission"; and an adjustment: the subject says, "Yes, I would like to file a grievance." While this one communication cycle alone is not likely to resolve all the ambiguities facing the subject of sexual harassment, each cycle (according to Weick's model) should remove some of the equivocality from the information situation and help the individual understand and respond effectively to this instance of sexual harassment. The more equivocal the information situation is, the more cycles are likely to be needed to reduce equivocality to a manageable level (Kreps, 1980).

As a highly equivocal information situation is discussed and examined through cycles of discourse, it becomes less equivocal and more amenable to the selection and use of rules to respond to the problem now and in the future. Not every communication cycle will be equally effective at reducing the equivocality of sexual harassment. In fact, some cycles may be ineffective and may even increase equivocality. Therefore, organization members must be selective in choosing the best communication cycles for reducing equivocality. Selecting the best communication cycles is often accomplished through trial and error, but once effective communication cycles are identified, they can be retained for use as assembly rules for directing future organizational action.

Rules are clear guidelines for guiding organizing actions in interpreting and responding to information situations. In accordance with the principle of requisite variety, a rule can be effectively established and used only when the particular information situation is at a manageable level of equivocality for organizational actors. Thus, communication cycles are performed to reduce highly equivocal situations to a manageable level so effective rules can be developed and employed.

THE ENACTMENT, SELECTION, AND RETENTION
PHASES OF ORGANIZING

Weick's model identifies three interdependent phases of organizing in which rules and communication cycles are used to process information situations: enactment, selection, and retention. In the enactment phase organizational actors use rules and cycles to evaluate the equivocality of information situations, helping them to understand fully the nature of the information input. Communication cycles are performed in this phase to help organizational actors examine, describe, and interpret equivocal situations, and to develop rules for classifying these situations and future situations like them.

The second phase of organizing is selection. In the selection phase situationally specific strategies for responding to specific information situations are constructed and performed. While the information input is processed prior to the selection phase (during the enactment phase to register its level of equivocality and make sense of it), making choices about how to respond effectively to a situation is quite different and more complex than merely interpreting the situation. After engaging in enactment organization members may increase their understanding of the nature of the information situation, but they do not necessarily know what to do about it. If selecting strategies for responding to the situation is highly equivocal, organization members will have to engage in additional communication cycles to reduce equivocality further before selecting appropriate rules for responding to the specific situation. Just as in the enactment phase, communication cycles and rules are used to process information situations during the selection phase of organizing. By engaging in communication cycles during the selection phase organization members are able to process information to develop effective strategies for responding to challenging information situations.

The retention phase is the final, and perhaps most important, phase of Weick's model of organizing. In this phase organization members evaluate enactment and selection processes, identifying rules about how to and how not to respond to similar information situations in the future. There are even assembly rules concerning the selection of communication cycles that are likely to be most helpful in reducing the equivocality of specific situations.

Rules are retained as part of a repertoire within "organizational intelligence." Organizational intelligence gleaned from information-processing activities (communication cycles) are used to guide enactment and selection processes, indelibly connecting the three phases of organizing (enactment, selection, and retention). For example, if similar information situations have been effectively handled in the past and preserved within organizational intelligence, there is no need for organization members to "reinvent the wheel" and process the inputs all over again. On the other hand, if situations have not been handled satisfactorily in the past organizational actors will have to engage in communication cycles to develop new rules for responding to these situations effectively. Old and ineffective strategies for responding to sexual harassment, such as ignoring or sweeping these situations under the rug, should be changed through the performance of new communication cycles. New rules are added to organizational intelligence to guide future actions.

In effective organizations, rules from past experiences are used to enlighten enactment and selection of new messages. Even if new messages are significantly different from past messages, organizational intelligence can be used to compare and contrast these new inputs with ones already processed, identifying how they are similar or different. Such information can help guide present interpretation and action. Information stored in the retention phase is used to guide current enactment and selection processes, and current enactment and selection processes provide relevant information to the retention phase for expanding organizational intelligence.

APPLICATION OF WEICK'S MODEL OF ORGANIZING TO RESPONDING TO SEXUAL HARASSMENT

Sexual harassment has become a serious and ubiquitous problem in modern organizational life, largely because organizational responses have all too often violated the principle of requisite variety. Due to discursive trivialization, the equivocality of sexual harassment has been routinely underestimated. Many instances go unreported due to shame and fear of retribution, making harassment invisible and harassers invulnerable. Inappropriate rules have been used to interpret and respond to acts of sexual harassment, exacerbating the problem.

Application of Weick's model of organizing in interpreting and responding to sexual harassment can help organizational actors cope with the equivocality of this epidemic and promote the development and preservation of situationally based intelligence for combatting sexual harassment. According to the principle of requisite variety, the high equivocality of sexual harassment in modern organizational life demands an equally complex communicative response. Weick's model of organizing suggests the performance of communication cycles to help organization members better understand this phenomenon and develop specific strategies for effectively responding to sexual harassment.

Communication cycles for enactment of sexual harassment can take many forms. For example, educational programs (such as seminars and workshops during orientation and training sessions) can be conducted to help organizational actors recognize the seriousness and complexity of sexual harassment (see Berryman-Fink, 1993; Galvin, 1993). Similarly, organizational media (such as pamphlets, handbooks, audiotapes, videotapes, and interactive computer programs) can be designed to help promote greater understanding of the issues surrounding sexual harassment. These educational and media programs can discourage discursive trivialization by clearly and persuasively describing the individual and organizational detriments of sexual harassment.

Communication cycles can be used to facilitate selection of strategies for responding effectively to sexual harassment. For example, opportunities to interact formally or informally in support groups with others who have been sexually harassed can help those who are targets of sexual harassment use communication cycles to work through the equivocality of coming to grips with being harassed and help them develop effective strategies for responding to such harassment (Kreps, 1992). Similarly, counselors and ombudspeople can be made available in organizations to help both subjects and perpetrators of sexual harassment work through their confusion and concerns, as well as help them identify strategies for interacting more effectively and satisfyingly in the future (Howard, 1991; Kreps, 1992).

Communication cycles can also be used to develop a repertoire of organizational rules for responding to and discouraging acts of sexual harassment. Instances of sexual harassment should not be swept under the rug; they should be confronted swiftly, forcefully, and vocally. Organizational leaders should make it clear, through public and private communications, that they will not stand for sexually harassing behaviors in their organizations. Perpetrators of sexual harassment should be dealt with severely (within the boundaries of organizational and societal laws) and publicly to let all organization members know that sexual harassment is a problem that is taken very seriously (Kreps, 1993a). Furthermore, formalization and institutionalization of organizational programs concerning sexual harassment (such as relevant educational and media programs, support groups, counselors, ombudspeople, and policies) can help preserve organizational intelligence for handling future acts. Information about these programs and policies should be actively disseminated both formally and informally to make organizational intelligence for confronting sexual harassment available to all organizational actors. However, it should be noted that educational programs, organizational media, support groups, and other communication can effectively combat sexual harassment only to the extent that they reduce equivocality, help actors identify effective response strategies, and preserve these strategies as organizational intelligence.

It is also important to note that intelligence is not necessarily transferable from one organization to another. Rules that work well for one organization may or may not work equally well in others. In fact, every organizational event has to be evaluated as a unique situation, and each organization should develop its own situationally sensitive rules for responding to equivocal situations. This means that there is not a perfect set of universal rules for responding to all instances of sexual harassment in all organizations. Each situation will be somewhat different and will demand unique response strategies. Effective responses to sexual harassment must be developed situationally in each organization.

At the end of the first edition of Weick's book *The Social Psychology of*

Organizing (1989), he tentatively suggests five general implications for organizational practice that can be profitably applied to coping with sexual harassment in organizational life.

1. "Don't panic in the face of disorder" (p. 106). Sexual harassment causes disorder for many organizational actors because it is often highly equivocal. To respond to this disorder actors should follow the principle of requisite variety by engaging in an equally complex set of interlocked communication cycles to demystify sexual harassment and create specific situationally responsive strategies for responding to it.

2. "You never do one thing all at once" (p. 106). Sexual harassment is a complex organizational phenomenon which will not be eradicated overnight. The more equivocal a problem is, the more communication cycles may be needed to help organization members cope with it. By developing a wide range of creative communication cycles (educational and media programs, counseling, social support mechanisms, discussion groups, legal counsel), actors begin the process of responding to and eliminating sexual harassment in organizational life.

3. "Chaotic action is preferable to orderly inaction" (p. 107). The most damaging response to sexual harassment is discursive trivialization and avoidance. Equivocal problems like sexual harassment become even more equivocal if they are not addressed directly. The best response to the equivocality of sexual harassment is communication, even if such communication is uncomfortable or strained. By engaging in communication cycles organizational actors learn how to respond to and solve the specific difficult situations (such as sexual harassment) they encounter.

4. "The most important decisions are often the least apparent" (p. 107). The process of demystifying equivocal organizational situations is often haphazard. It is only after different communication cycles are performed that we find out which are most effective. Active communicative experiences, rather than a priori strategies, provide organizational actors with the creative information they need to reduce the equivocality of challenging social situations, such as understanding and responding to sexual harassment.

5. "You should coordinate processes rather than groups" (p. 107). Actors should not be constrained by organizational structures in responding to sexual harassment. New and creative sources for communication cycles must be identified to reduce equivocality and direct organizational action. The emphasis of organizing is on process rather than structure. To respond effectively to sexual harassment organizational actors need to share relevant information, seek social support, and coordinate efforts in developing new rules and increasing organizational intelligence.

CONCLUSION

Sexual harassment is a serious and all too common problem that significantly degrades the quality of modern organizational life. This chapter has described sexual harassment as a highly equivocal information situation that is often underestimated and trivialized. Organizational actors' failure to recognize fully the complexity and serious implications of sexual harassment leads to their selection of overly simplistic and ineffective responses, violating the principle of requisite variety and exacerbating the problem. Weick's model of organizing is described as a theoretical model for guiding the development of effective situationally appropriate discursive strategies for: (1) accurately registering and reducing the equivocality of interpreting acts of sexual harassment (enactment); (2) developing strategies for effectively responding to instances of sexual harassment (selection); and (3) compiling and preserving organizational intelligence to guide the implementation of rules for interpreting, responding to, and preventing sexual harassment in the future (retention).

The use of discursive practices, such as communication cycles, can diminish and eventually prevent sexual harassment in organizational life by reducing its equivocality and establishing situational rules for handling it. By developing well-stocked repertoires of communication rules about sexual harassment, stored in organizational intelligence, the equivocality of sexual harassment can be reduced. Clear, situationally appropriate rules, well established through past experiences, for interpreting, responding to, and preventing sexual harassment can be made available to all organization members. If actors experience high equivocality when encountering acts of sexual harassment, they can use communication to reduce this equivocality and develop creative and situationally appropriate strategies for responding. If such communication cycles are enacted, sexual harassment will be out of the closet; it will be openly talked about, it will become less equivocal, and organization members will eventually come to realize the inappropriateness and inadvisability of it.

NOTE

My thanks to Julia Wood and Shereen Bingham for their helpful comments and suggestions on an earlier version of this chapter.

9

Secrets of the Corporation: A Model of Ideological Positioning of Sexual Harassment Victims

Dana M. Kaland and Patricia Geist

It is clear that sexually inappropriate conduct is rampant in organizations. What is not clearly understood, however, is why legal and organizational efforts to eliminate harassment and to provide assistance to victims have done little to reduce the frequency of cases or experiences with it. Seventy-five percent of the membership companies of the American Management Association have organizational policies discouraging sexual harassment (Lee, 1992). In addition, in 1986 the Supreme Court ruled that sexual harassment is an illegal form of sex discrimination prohibited by Title VII of the Civil Rights Act, and holds employers liable for sexual harassment in the workplace (Krohne, 1991; Lee, 1992; Webb, 1992). Given these sanctions, one might expect that the victims would pursue formal recourse when dealing with harassers; however, that is not the most common response to the phenomenon (Collins & Blodgett, 1981; Krohne, 1991).

Although research has found that victims typically respond to sexual harassment by avoiding the harasser rather than registering a formal report, women respond in a variety of ways. In *Sexual Harassment: Women Speak Out*, the editors comment on the hundreds of written narratives they received which describe very diverse responses to incidents of sexual harassment:

[W]omen write not only of their experiences but also of how they responded to them. Some went into extreme depression or experienced physical symptoms; some fought back; some denied the harassment was happening, wanting to believe it was unintentional or something they themselves had provoked. Some found humorous ways and creative ways of dealing with the harasser. (Sumrall & Taylor, 1992, p. vii)

However, we really do not understand *why* different women respond differently. If institutions are to be given the grave and challenging responsibility of eliminating sexual harassment from the workplace, then it is important to understand the thinking process, the choices, and the responses of the victims. Ultimately, victims and their responses to the experience of sexual harassment are the key to understanding how organizations can best assist and empower individuals faced with it.

This chapter explores victims' responses to sexual harassment and shows a link between their perceptions and empowerment in an organization's culture. These perceptions are important in explaining why victims exercise such a wide variety of choices, even when they are faced with the same type of harassment experience. Using a case study approach our objective is to examine how discourse contests and reconstructs understandings of sexual harassment in one organization, which we call Mastermark. The interviews at Mastermark produced rich and varied narratives of participants' views of the organization, power structures, and the way they would, and in some cases did, handle incidents of sexual harassment.

WOMEN'S RESPONSES TO SEXUAL HARASSMENT

Research studies are conclusive in suggesting that the most often used strategy for dealing with sexual harassment is to avoid the perpetrator and hope the behavior stops (Gruber, 1989; Lee, 1992; Milwid, 1990; Sandroff, 1992). Passive approaches such as avoiding or ignoring the harassment are often used when the offender is the supervisor of the victim, but they are also utilized when the victim perceives that, upon confrontation, the perpetrator will be unlikely to view the situation as she did or will trivialize the allegations (Terpstra & Baker, 1986a). Avoidance may also result from a concern for maintaining a positive or manageable working relationship with the boss and coworkers, and adds to the complexities of utilizing individual strategies (Bingham, 1991). Some argue that individual tactics such as assertively expressing discomfort or disinterest to the harasser may be effective, but Bingham and Burleson (1989) found that women were not optimistic that communicative responses would succeed in stopping harassment behavior, avoiding retaliation, or minimizing relational damage. In many cases the victim will quit her job rather than confront the harasser or seek assistance in the organization (Coles, 1986).

The inability to define the phenomenon of sexual harassment effectively and consistently is pivotal to understanding why it continues to be a part of organizational life. Though the term "sexual harassment" was created in the late seventies (Farley, 1978), legal and organizational definitions have been refined and revised numerous times over the last decade. Mongeau and Blalock (1992) suggested that most definitions are too narrow and offer a useful definition: "any number of behaviors or interactions which are sexual in nature and/or are perceived as offensive. These behaviors can vary from those being explicitly sexual to those with implicit sexual reference" (p. 4). This definition is particularly effective for defining and studying sexual harassment because it allows for a broad range of behaviors and is not dependent on relationship or status dimensions or the presence of explicit sanctions or rewards.

Many experts assert that sexual harassment is a manifestation of the division of power in organizations and between the sexes (Booth-Butterfield, 1987; Collins & Blodgett, 1981; Farley, 1978; Gutek & Morasch, 1982; Milwid, 1990). Though power is often equated with positional authority in organizations, it may also stem from control of resources, associations with opinion leaders, and personal qualities (Bingham & Scherer, 1993). These types of power are not formally acknowledged by the organization but are still perceived by organizational members. The notion that sexual harassment is an abuse of power is supported by research which revealed that victims are often the "powerless" in the organization (Gutek, 1985).

As one would expect, supervisor communication that is sexual in nature is more threatening than collegial and creates a dilemma for the victim (Booth-Butterfield, 1987). Over two-thirds of the complaints filed by women in the 1989 *Working Woman* survey were made against a supervisor or senior manager (Sandroff, 1992). It is argued that without the presence of a power division, harassment is simply ignored or inadequately dealt with by the victim (Rowe, 1981). Milwid (1990) interviewed over twenty-five women about their experiences in organizations and found that many women could cite experiences of harassment with coworkers at similar levels in the organization, and that many of these situations were bothersome. However, it was those situations of sexual harassment by a superior or significant power holder that caused the greatest degrees of anxiety and frustration. Moreover, Bingham and Scherer (1993) found that as the formal authority of the harasser relative to the victim increased (less, equal, more), victims reported less satisfaction with the way the sexual harassment situation was resolved.

In light of varied definitions of sexual harassment, the dynamics of power, and the dilemmas in reporting incidents, it is not surprising that victims do not frequently step forward to make formal allegations or seek organizational assistance with the problem. The subtleties of sexual communication and the evolution of legal and organizational definitions of harassment are significant contributing factors to the pervasiveness of sexual harassment in organizations and to the hesitance of women to register formal complaints. Nevertheless, not all women try to avoid or ignore sexual harassment; different women respond differently. The perceptions of sexual harassment held by victims may influence the responses they utilize to diffuse incidents of it. These perceptions can be said to represent an ideological positioning of the victim.

IDEOLOGICAL POSITIONING

Ideology refers to the meanings people formulate and use to understand an organization, how it works, their place in it, and what is expected (Geist

& Hardesty, 1990; 1992; Hall, 1985). Discourse produces, reproduces, and/or contests ideologies which, in turn, sustain power structures of privilege and oppression in organizations (see chapters 1 and 4). Ideological positioning occurs as individuals communicate their perceptions of an organization's culture, and their discourse reveals the ways that culture defines, clarifies, or constrains the position they can take on an issue (Geist & Hardesty, 1990). Therefore, ideological positioning in response to the issue of sexual harassment emerges from experiences with the dominant culture's handling of sexual harassment in the organization, from perceptions of the severity of the harassment experience, and from perceptions of the range of response strategies available to victims. Variation in ideological positioning reveals that victims' perceptions of the strategy they selected or would select in diffusing sexual harassment experiences are based on their views of power structures in the organization. It can be argued that ideological positioning can be used by victims, perpetrators, and the organization to rationalize and explain the choices made by individuals in response to sexual harassment.

Through a naturalistic case study we found that women's ways of thinking about and dealing with sexual harassment are not all alike. Interpretation of narratives gathered through interviews provides evidence of different ideological positioning. The following discussion outlines the methods used for this naturalistic study of sexual harassment.

CASE STUDY

The organization selected for this study, Mastermark, is a division of a major international corporation in a high-tech industry. The division in which the case study was conducted employs approximately seven-hundred people ranging from highly educated designers and technologists to assemblers on the manufacturing floor. A sample of thirty employees, sixteen men and fourteen women, was randomly selected from all levels of the organization. Included in the sample were employees from the lower secretarial ranks all the way up to top management, in order to uncover a broad range of organizational perspectives. Participants were informed by internal electronic mail that they were encouraged but not mandated to participate.

Face-to-face interviews, ranging in length from fifteen to fifty minutes, were conducted in a conference room of the organization. The first part of the interview was designed to determine the interviewees' basic definition of what constitutes sexual harassment, information about their personal experience with or observation of the phenomenon within Mastermark, their degree of awareness as to the official channels to pursue if sexual harassment were being experienced in the organization, and the perceived barriers to using those channels. The second half of the interview was designed to understand the range of possible responses that a victim may have to hypothetical cases of harassment. The following three scenarios were created to fit the legal definition of sexual harassment and ranged in severity from a hostile work environment situation in which the victim was uncomfortable with comments being made by a coworker, to a quid pro quo incident of harassment perpetrated by a supervisor on a subordinate.

Scenario A

A male employee frequently compliments his coworker on her attire and physique. The man makes comments in front of others such as, "You ought to wear short skirts like that more often, you have great legs." Often in meetings the male employee announces to his coworker to "sit closer" because he "likes the view." These comments appear to other coworkers to make the female employee uncomfortable and to embarrass her, and on two occasions she was overheard asking him not to make such personal comments.

Scenario B

A male supervisor discusses with a female subordinate in detail his sexual fantasies and activities. These discussions take place in private meetings with her in his office. He describes his sexual exploits and interests and frequently jokes with her that she would "never be the same after being with him." He often invites her for drinks after work and on two occasions arrived unannounced at her home after hours.

Scenario C

On a business trip, a male supervisor subtly suggests to his female subordinate that if she will "join him in his hotel room during the trip," a very visible and important project may be assigned to her in the near future. This supervisor continues throughout the trip to suggest that a "close" relationship with him could benefit her greatly in her career goals with the company.

Women were asked to put themselves in the place of the victim and describe how they would handle the situation, and men were asked to describe how they thought a man committing such acts might protect himself from an embarrassing or damaging complaint.

All interviews were taped and transcribed verbatim. Upon completion of the interviews, open coding of transcribed interviews and field notes was conducted to discover categories of ideological positioning (Strauss & Corbin, 1990). Ideological positioning of victims was derived by the researchers through an analysis of responses to the actual situations employees had encountered at Mastermark or to the hypothetical scenarios they were asked to discuss. Most of the narratives analyzed were extracted from interviews with female employees. Interviews with male employees provide support or clarification of a given ideological position and are presented in the results to illuminate the model.

A TYPOLOGY OF VICTIM RESPONSES

Segments of interviews that provided narratives of employees' responses to sexual harassment revealed two dimensions. The first dimension, severity, included phrases and statements in which participants' responses ranged from a low degree of concern to a high degree of concern about the seriousness of the incident. In the second dimension, power, participants' statements indicated a range from "empowered" to "powerless" responses to incidents of sexual harassment. The two dimensions of severity and power, as described in the next sections, intersect to form four ideological positionings.

Severity

Just as the experience of sexual harassment is defined differently by different people, severity of sexual harassment can be determined only by the victim. In describing their own experiences of harassment, the employees at Mastermark revealed implicitly and explicitly what they perceived to be the severity of the incident. Though they were not asked to rate the severity of the incident, the degree of severity was identified in their narratives by assessing their language and emotional reaction to the experience.

Three types of severity were described in the interviews. High severity incidents were those actual or hypothetical situations which were specifically directed at the victim and were blatant or even physical. These extreme cases were intentional and overt behaviors which created anxiety, fear, or hostility. In a description by a victim of a coworker's inappropriate and offensive sexual behavior, she nervously explained: "I work with this guy who used to always come up behind me when I was leaning over [the assembly table] and reach around my waist and put his body up against mine and say things I didn't want to hear. It was really scary. He heard about this [the interview] and knew I was going to be interviewed and asked me if I was going to tell you his name today." The same woman described an occasion in which her supervisor found her kneeling on the floor to fix something and commented to his fellow supervisor that she could "service him while she was down there." Both these examples are blatant and personal and were perceived by the victim as extreme and highly disturbing.

Moderate severity instances were described as situations in which the harassing behavior was directed at the victim but was subtler and left open for interpretation. These cases seem to be perceived as less severe in part because the victims had the option of interpreting the sexual harassment in a variety of ways and of even minimizing it in their own minds. A woman described the experience of a coworker which occurred on a regular basis. "A friend of mine is pretty frustrated with a situation she's in. There's this guy, a coworker in her group, and whenever he gets the opportunity to be alone with her in her cubicle he 'comes on' to her. She doesn't like him and she really has no interest in him and she is uncomfortable around him." This illustrates an incident of moderate severity because the victim was specifically targeted by the harasser and she expressed discomfort.

Harassment considered of low severity included behaviors that were sexual in nature but not blatant and not directed specifically at a particular person. This type of low-severity harassment may include joking or comments of a sexual nature or even what is considered sexism in the workplace. A male manager identified a situation in which he perceived harassment had taken place but wasn't sure:

We were sitting around in a formal meeting with a mix of men and women and we were just laughing and joking about nothing in particular before the meeting got started—we joked about something and everybody laughed and laughed—I mean it was really funny—we couldn't leave it alone—it was really funny. I don't remember what it was now, but I realized that one of the ladies was really uncomfortable and I thought we might have overstepped it a bit on that one.

In this incident a hostile work environment may have been created for the woman, but it was not directed at her specifically and it was not blatant or intentionally wielded.

The severity of any sexual harassment situation will undoubtedly influence the communicative choices made by the victim. Literature on individual strategies for dealing with harassers often advocates direct and assertive approaches to diffuse the problem. Strategies that advocate taking "the bull by the horns" assume that most victims perceive that confrontation will resolve the problem. However, the results of this investigation reveal that in part the perception of power or powerlessness influences the determination of responses victims of sexual harassment deem appropriate, and assertiveness is not always considered viable or productive. The following discussion delineates the dimensions of empowerment and powerlessness identified in the narratives.

Power

There are diverse decisions and choices an individual can make in response to sexual harassment. Inherent in the strategies indicated by participants to both the three hypothetical cases and their actual experiences are elements of personal and organizational power. Personal power is exhibited through confident and aggressive strategies and language, and usually evolves to reporting the harassment to the organization. The category of empowerment also included responses that communicated a confidence in the organization, either through a utilization of the system or an overt expression that the problem would be handled effectively by the company. Whether that empowerment is based on self-confidence, perceived organizational support, or both, the response is created in light of the victim's power, not the harasser's.

Responding to Scenario C, a participant describes how she would respond to her manager: "I would just say shove it! If that's what you'd use to promote your career then you'd do it anyway and if it's not what you do to promote your career then nothing is worth that kind of compromise. I would let him know that if this affected my career in any way I would elevate this to management." The victim demonstrates a sense of power that discounts or minimizes the positional power or authority of the harasser.

One interviewee describes a sense of power and control in the face of her supervisor (Scenario B): "In the very first instance (when the manager began to discuss sex) I would say that I don't care to hear about this and walk out of his office. I would go to his manager and report the incident." The act of marching out of her manager's office during a meeting and reporting inappropriate behavior takes the focus off the positional power of the manager and places it on the victim.

In contrast to empowerment, powerlessness is exhibited as a distrust of the organization or a sense of fear about the consequences of pursuing a formal complaint. Powerlessness is found in the perception that the victims have little influence over the dilemma they are facing and frequently involves an unconscious decision to accept the responsibility for handling it, live with the harassment, or leave the situation.

Though it could be argued that the choice to leave the department or organization in order to get away from harassment is an assertion of influence in the situation, it places the burden of managing the harassment on the individual and little or none on the harasser or the organization. This represents powerlessness on the part of the victim because she is not utilizing the system established to empower her to protect her job and her rights. Empowerment, in contrast, is exhibited through a joint process of individual strategies and an activation of the system.

Ideological Positioning of Victims

The ideological positioning of victims offers a set of responses and rationales for the strategies chosen by victims in sexual harassment situations. The model of ideological positioning demonstrates how victims determine what is an appropriate strategy for addressing sexual harassment in a given culture or context and contributes to a greater understanding of the phenomenon of harassment. Four types of ideological positioning are identified in the narratives: the Peacemaker, the Hostage, the Rebel, and the Activist.

The Peacemaker. Many of the women at Mastermark expressed that frequent but mild cases of sexual harassment and sexism are a part of everyday life which must be tolerated in order to get along in the workplace. Numerous respondents identified scenarios in which they were mildly concerned about the harassing behaviors and where their response was a reflection of power-lessness. Powerlessness can be seen when the solution is one in which the victim does not disclose the problem to anyone for the purpose of seeking help or terminating it. Though the peacemaker may discuss the problem with female coworkers to find out if others are also being harassed or to vent her feelings, her goal is not to pursue formal assistance but to avoid "making a big deal out of it": "I wouldn't take it to personnel [in reference to Scenario A]. It doesn't seem like it's worth making a big deal of it. I'd start avoiding him without making a big to-do about it."

A peacemaker weighs the lack of severity of the behavior and perceives the outcome of reporting the problem as a greater problem:

I don't think I would go to personnel [in response to comments about attire and appearance]. I wouldn't do anything except repeat my request [to stop making comments]. It's not blatant enough. If I want to make an issue of it, it will reflect more negatively on me than on the man. I'm not going to tell my manager—I'm the only woman in the group—I have to be careful of what I make an issue out of. I might go to my manager if she were a woman.

The goal of the Peacemaker is to take the path of least resistance. In recognition that the situation is not severe, and it may be trivialized by the organization, even if the victim is uncomfortable with the situation, she chooses to say nothing. The Peacemaker makes a conscious or unconscious decision to live with a certain amount of inappropriate conduct and to interpret it as harmless.

The Peacemaker frequently articulates a degree of personal responsibility for resolving the problem herself or in some cases even provoking it. A young woman explained how a big deal was made out of a leather skirt she wore to work to the extent that employees in another building were teasing her about it over a week later:

I have learned—like one day I was going out on a Friday and I didn't want to drag clothes with me, so I wore a leather skirt to work. It was just above the knee, very modest, not tight. It just happened to be leather. I wore a shirt up to here [pointing to the neck] and sleeves down to here [pointing to the wrists], you know, pumps, but still what I thought was professional. Of course, Fridays here are casual day. I heard about that leather skirt for a week! So the leather skirt doesn't come to work anymore! You know, that is all I have learned, the ways I deal with it [sexually related comments], if it causes a problem, you don't wear it, you don't do it, you don't say it!

Changing attire was a common response Peacemakers offered which implicitly suggested that responsibility for harassment falls, in part, on the victim.

The Peacemaker attempts to rationalize harassing behaviors and take part of the responsibility for the harassment. In certain cases the victim may allow the element of guilt to cause her to develop a concern for the possible consequences to the perpetrator, which again restrains her from reporting the incident. She might think, "I wouldn't want him to lose his job. I mean, I'm single, maybe I've been too friendly or something—and because I'm single he thinks it's okay to do it [make sexual innuendos]."

Another theme that can be found in the Peacemaker ideology is an explanation of harasser behavior that implies that it is unintentional or innocent. The Peacemaker would like to believe that the harasser is unaware that his behavior is offensive or inappropriate. Essentially, the perpetrator is frequently characterized by the Peacemaker as someone who doesn't really know what he is doing and in essence should not be held responsible.

Being a Peacemaker is about adapting and living with what is mildly offensive behavior at work—behavior that may not be viewed as offensive or may even go unnoticed outside the professional context. The Peacemaker desires a positive working relationship with others and assesses that if the harassing behavior is not overwhelming, disturbing, or affecting job performance, it is better left alone. When the intensity or severity of harassment increases, the decision to remain silent is more painful and significant. In moderate or extreme harassment, a victim who chooses to endure the situation for fear of retaliation, inaction by the organization, or alienation by peers exhibits a sense of powerlessness and becomes trapped in an impossible dilemma.

The Hostage. Some victims who perceive they are experiencing a moderate or extreme case of sexual harassment—that is, one that is blatant and targeted at them directly—decide upon a strategy that will alleviate the situation without aggravating the harasser. These victims choose to remain silent in hopes of handling it themselves or simply out of fear that doing something about it will be worse than living with it.

I would apply for a job transfer, and try to get out of the situation rather than challenge it [in reference to Scenario B—explicit sexual discussions and unannounced visits at the victim's home]. I don't like conflict, and I will usually appease the situation. If you report it what would you gain? Now he's angry and still making sexual comments—it's not going to make the situation any better. I suppose you could report it for the sake of other women, you know, to help society, but I'm not going to do that.

The Hostage will remain in a difficult situation, or seek alternative positions or organizations, before externalizing her problem to the institution. In cases in which the Hostage chooses to transfer or seek a new employer, though she does not remain a Hostage once the move is complete, the ideological positioning of the Hostage places the burden of resolution on the victim. The hostage may repeat her request to the harasser to terminate the behavior or tell close friends, coworkers, or family to gain their support but not necessarily their intervention: "I can't imagine being in this situation [in reference to scenario B], my husband would call this guy! I guess I would have to transfer. I'm not going to change his behavior—filing a complaint won't help. I'd have to get away from him." Though the decision to transfer or leave the organization is not taken lightly, the ideological positioning of the hostage focuses in part on fears of not being believed by others or of being viewed as a troublemaker if she makes a report.

A primary reason victims may remain in oppressive situations is that they are not sure management or coworkers will believe their story if they come forward. In describing reasons why a victim might not come forward a female manager explained, "We've all followed the Tyson case and the Kennedy case and all the cases on the news and I mean if you can't win a rape case in some cases, something like sexual harassment is probably the hardest to substantiate and deal with so I think it's just basically the belief that it won't be effective [reporting it] for whatever reason, that they [victims] can't win."

The Hostage faces the fear that because she will not be believed, she may jeopardize her own standing in the organization. One male interviewee described what he believed to be the barriers to reporting an incident of sexual harassment:

Sexual harassment is pretty hard to prove and I would think a lot of people elect to ignore it. People who are making comments are pretty professional—they know how to cover it up. Let me put it this way, I've never seen a new college grad making sexual or inappropriate comments. If you try to take a senior manager to personnel you may have a problem. Most of the direct labor force is so immediately replaceable, I think they [a victim] might fear for their job.

In describing the avenues available for reporting harassment, one woman postulated that you must try to complain to the person and maybe, depending on your manager, you could go to him or her. "Then you just shut up and live with it or you quit. I've survived here a long time because I haven't made waves. I'd rather look for another job than deal with trying to report a problem."

The Peacemaker and the Hostage determine that the institution's system for handling sexual harassment is either unnecessary or ineffective. In contrast, the Rebel and the Activist position themselves ideologically to trust the system to a certain degree or to determine what action must be taken to address the problem, even if the outcome is unclear.

The Rebel. In contrast to the fundamental tenets of tolerance and endurance of the Peacemaker and the Hostage, the ideological positioning or tenet of the Rebel is one of intolerance. The Rebel is poised for any battle deemed worthy of pursuit. In other words, confrontation and utilization of organizational means are the weapons for the protection of the rights of the victim. The Rebel perceives a sense of power that any situation of harassment is unacceptable, and she is empowered by the organization to act. The Rebel's was the least reported strategy at Mastermark, with only six responses identified in the category.

In response to the male coworker making comments about appearance and attire, which in most scenarios was identified by Mastermark employees as a low-severity incident, the Rebel utilizes the formal system to seek intervention:

First I would go to my manager and explain that it made me uncomfortable, and if I wasn't satisfied with the results of that, then I would go to human resources and report him. If he didn't want to transfer, then I would push pretty hard to have something done about him. . . . I hope that it would jeopardize his career and that they [human resources] would tell him that.

The Rebel's language is often unequivocal and definitive, and responses are offered quickly. Most often the Rebel does not begin with a report to the institution, but if confronting the harasser does not produce the desired result, then the Rebel's immediate reaction is to go to management and human resources and to "expect" something to be done about it.

Though the Rebel was the least frequently cited ideological positioning at Mastermark, fear of the Rebel surfaced repeatedly, particularly from men. The Rebel ideology is often communicated visibly and assertively, even in violation of cultural norms and expectations. The Rebel may be viewed as someone who is unaware of the political margins of the organization and who lacks judgment. She is frequently perceived by her male counterparts as the cause of an oversensitivity to relationships between men and women.

This stuff [sexual harassment] is way overblown. We've gotten into an area of social contact between the genders. You can't even be loose and talk to somebody anymore, that's where it's gotten really harmful. A female gets into a male environment and she reacts—"I'm gonna get harassed!" To have to be intimidated to talk to your fellow coworkers—we've missed the point of working with genders.

Frequently, the Rebel starts out as a Peacemaker and, if a single attempt to deal with the perpetrator fails, the Rebel may take a bold overt strategy: "I would talk to all other females in the group [in reference to Scenario A]. I would go to his manager if I found out it was something other women were dealing with. Then I would address it [his comments] in a meeting in front of others [so he would be embarrassed]."

The ideological position of the Rebel may contribute to fears in the organization that every slip of the tongue or backward glance will trigger a sexual harassment investigation. In contrast, the Activist seeks organizational assistance only when a situation is severe, and thus may be perceived as more politically astute or sensitive.

The Activist. Victims who face extremely severe experiences with harassers and who seek individual and organizational solutions demonstrate an Activist ideology. By far the most frequently identified ideology, the Activist understands that living with abusive or disturbing conduct is not acceptable. The Activist expresses a belief in the system and in herself and is not willing to tolerate or flee from an unbearable situation: "My very first reaction [referencing Scenario B] would be to say, 'I don't care to hear about this,' and get up and walk out of the room. I would go to his manager and report his behavior and insist on a transfer—one of us has to go!"

Another woman reacted to the same scenario, and although she articulated her fears on taking a stand, she was certain that she would: "I would be scared! But I would tell him he'd have to stop and then I'd go straight to human resources and to his boss. I guess I might be fired—he might try and turn it around."

An Activist, holding to an ideology that reflects a belief that no job is worth the sacrifice of putting up with immoral behavior, is motivated to activate the system designed to protect the rights of employees. In essence, by feeling empowered to act, the Activist empowers the organization to create a culture that strongly discourages harassment. The Activist ideology is sometimes fueled by a sense that the organization will respond appropriately and sensitively to allegations and also by an individual confidence in one's own ability to deal with a sticky situation.

Unlike the Hostage, who frequently expressed fear of being disbelieved in Scenario C, the Activist does not seem to concern herself with what the reactions of others will be or what consequences may surface after reporting the experience. In fact, the Activist has a difficult time understanding or relating to the behavior of the Hostage.

Though the response of the Activist is much the same as that of the Rebel, it is likely that the Activist will be perceived more positively in the organization because her response is more fitting with the offense. Activists do not place their focus on doubts that they will be believed, but on a clear sense that wrongdoing has occurred and it must be dealt with. One of the male participants expressed beliefs that may contribute to the confidence level of the Activist at Mastermark. This was his response to the question, "Can you describe for me any incidence of sexual harassment that you have experienced, observed, or heard about at Mastermark?"

I'm not sure I can. I'm sure they're going on. If I knew any I would certainly do something about it. As far as devastating someone's career or morale—something that makes you uncomfortable at work everyday, it shouldn't be tolerated. I guess I am unobservant—no, I'm just very businesslike—only discussing the task at hand, not participating in a lot of joking around. I may miss this stuff because I am not in situations where it is facilitated.

This male participant articulates a high degree of concern about acts of sexual harassment and reinforces the ideological positioning of the Activist by recommending that action be taken.

An Activist is instrumental in alleviating the problem of sexual harassment in organizations by exposing it and empowering the institution to deal with the perpetrator. Activists do not always accept organizational solutions if they deem insufficient measures have been taken, and they may seek external help, such as from the EEOC, an attorney, or both.

The ideological positioning of victims provides decision rules and frames the thinking of sexual harassment victims. Ideological positioning is embedded in the context in which harassment occurs and is helpful in understanding the reasons victims deem certain options more appropriate than others. In the following section the implications of the model of ideological positioning are outlined, and movement between ideological positions is explicated. In addition, organizational and theoretical implications and recommendations for future research are described.

THE DYNAMICS OF IDEOLOGICAL POSITIONING

Many scholars have sought to uncover the complexities of sexual harassment in organizations and to identify effective and ineffective strategies for dealing with harassers at work (Bingham & Burleson, 1989; Clair & McGoun, 1991; Maypole, 1986). The typology of responses to sexual harassment identified in this research may provide a greater understanding of how variances in handling harassing situations is dependent on victims' assessment of the severity of their experience and assessments of their power within the organization. The ideological positioning of victims (see Figure 1) reveals the discursive practices that legitimate or challenge an organization's dominant ideology concerning sexual harassment.

As the model suggests, movement in ideological positioning represents a change in discursive practice motivated by a perceived change in the victim's assessment of her degree of empowerment or the severity of the harassment. Through discourse victims "test" a situation, respond, and then retest with a new response, reconstructing their own or others' understanding of incidences of sexual harassment. Unsuccessful attempts to address situations individually may lead victims to engage in practices that perpetuate the sexual harassment rather than challenge it, or such attempts may prompt victims to reconstruct understandings of sexual harassment in ways that discourage harassment, thus empowering victims.

The discursive practices of the Peacemaker and the Hostage reveal their efforts to take the path of least resistance. Peace and tolerance are central to their ideological positioning as evidenced in discourse that references not wanting to "make a big deal" out of the harassment, or in stating that seeking intervention is not "worth the trouble it might cause." The discourse of the Peacemaker and the Hostage exhibits complacency, fear, self-protection, and an ideology of institutional inadequacy. The ideological positioning of the Peacemaker infers that institutional intervention would be both ineffective and

Figure 1
Ideological Positioning of Sexual Harassment Victims

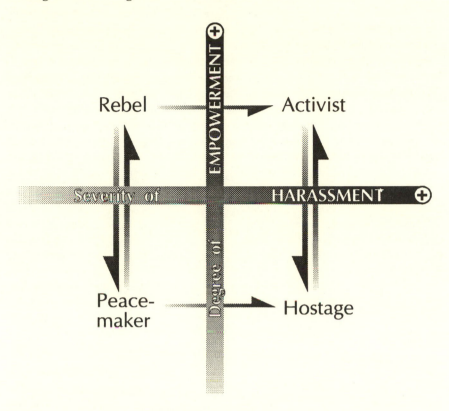

unnecessary, while the Hostage constructs a position whereby the system is powerless in effectively addressing the harassment. The discourse of the Peacemaker and the Hostage does not contest the sexual harassment. In order to reduce the degree of disruption in their lives they legitimate tolerance of others' offensive behavior and thus domination of them as victims in the working environment.

The discursive practices of the Rebel and the Activist place a higher priority on the need to terminate the harassment than on the consequences of the act of seeking intervention. The Rebel and the Activist communicate attitudes of self-confidence and self-respect that often are fueled by an indignation or anger at the situation or the perpetrator. In expressing that the behavior of the harasser is just "not right," or that the victim "should not have to put up with this stuff," the Rebel and the Activist reconstruct understandings of sexual harassment, empowering victims to engage in practices to discourage harassment. Rebels and Activists envision a social order in which individuals and/

or institutions are capable of contesting ideologies in ways that eliminate harassing behavior.

The model of ideological positioning of sexual harassment victims contributes to theory about how victims' discursive practices represent an ideology of the way sexual harassment is viewed in one organization's culture (see Figure 1). The continua identified in this study, severity of harassment and power, are revealed in the model to demonstrate the dynamic nature of ideological positioning. Though a minority of participants' ideological positioning could be found to be consistent regardless of the scenario or incident being discussed, more often the ideological positioning of the respondent was fluid.

The implications of ideological positioning as dynamic and fluid are significant. In January 1991 the Ninth Circuit Court ruled that a hostile work environment must be judged from the perspective of the victim (Sumrall & Taylor, 1992). As Julia Wood explains in chapter 1, this ruling, most commonly referred to as the "reasonable woman standard," suggests that cases of sexual harassment must be carefully weighed to understand fully the perception of the alleged victim, and that a hostile work environment case can be established by alleging conduct that a reasonable woman would perceive as sufficiently severe or threatening.

A change in ideological positioning represents in part a reconstruction of what is considered reasonable or acceptable in an organization. However, the model also illuminates that a "reasonable woman" standard is determined through an assessment of power relationships in an organization and the seriousness of the offense, which may change during the experience. A victim may change her willingness to tolerate certain behaviors from a harasser after attempting to address the problem through one ideological position, and at that point, she may reconstruct her definition of what a "reasonable woman" should be expected to endure.

Many authors have argued that the power of the harasser is central to the issue of sexual harassment and the manner in which victims respond to it. The ideological positioning of victims suggests, however, that while the victim assesses the power of the harasser, she may be more acutely aware of *her* relative power or powerlessness within the workplace. The focus seems to be not on the power of the perpetrator but on the degree of power or powerlessness the victim perceives she possesses. The ideological positioning of the Hostage and the Peacemaker articulates that the power of the harasser is not as influential as the victim's own powerlessness. Articulating powerlessness is common for Peacemakers and particularly Hostages, and it illuminates the power focus being placed on the victim more so than on the perpetrator. In contrast, the Rebel and the Activist tend to discount the power of the harasser and embrace their own power or the organizational resources they need to eliminate the problem. Understanding the central role of power in sexual harassment is commonly held, but it is equally important to gain further insight into victims' understandings of and access to power in the organization and to discover whose interests are served by particular ideological positions.

Future research on sexual harassment should test the model in other types of organizations and across industries to develop an understanding of the nuances of ideological positioning of victims. Future studies need to address the frequency of each ideological position in certain types of cultures. For example, in organizations where there are very few reports of sexual harassment, it would be useful to discover what types of ideological positionings are most frequently identified, and what discursive practices reveal about the dominant ideology concerning sexual harassment. Organizations that have explicit guidelines, frequent training, and that handle grievances quickly and with sensitivity may over time see relatively few complaints as harassment is reduced. However, organizations like Mastermark, which believe they don't have a problem with sexual harassment, may need to examine the discursive practices that perpetuate oppressive ideologies, discouraging ideological positioning that empowers victims.

The issue of sexual harassment is one of great importance, and future research focusing on an understanding of its causes and of strategies for reducing its occurrence in the workplace is needed (Alberts, 1992; Taylor & Conrad, 1992). It is unlikely that sexually implicit communication will be eliminated from organizations as long as men and women work together, but it is important to understand the causes and seek solutions to the damaging, costly, and painful effects of sexual harassment.

Part IV

Critical Reflections

10

Particularities and Possibilities: Reconceptualizing Knowledge and Power in Sexual Harassment Research

Karen A. Foss and Richard A. Rogers

As we talked through our reactions to the chapters in this volume, we came to realize—in the dual sense of becoming aware and making real—that a discursive approach opens up the project of researching sexual harassment in a multiplicity of ways. These chapters address this multiplicity substantively by dealing with a range of issues—definition, organizational structure, gender-socialization experiences, oral history and performance, and more. Despite wide variations in subject matter as well as theoretical framework and style, these chapters are, however, relatively homogeneous in terms of two closely related issues: what is to count as "knowledge" in an academic context and what is to count as "power" in a social context. We feel the discursive approach is an ideal framework for examining the importance of these points of convergence and making evident the strengths and limitations of various approaches to sexual harassment.

Discursive approaches, as Julia Wood explains in her chapter, highlight the processes by which social structures and experiences are constituted. Any discourse, then, is necessarily constraining and enabling, constituting some objects, ideas, and relationships while excluding others. This implication applies, in our view, both to the patriarchal discourses that enable and legitimize sexual harassment and to the feminist, legal, political, and organizational discourses that name sexual harassment for what it is. Thus, the discursive approach enables individual women to alter their awareness and evaluation of their experiences and makes possible the implementation of various educational, legal, and political programs to address sexual harassment.

A second implication of the discursive approach is that these chapters, as discourses, do not simply reflect and discover some preexisting set of objects and experiences (discourse, sexual harassment, women's experiences, gender socialization, organizational climate, and so on). Instead, this book is a part of the discourse on sexual harassment, and as such, is equally constitutive of its objects. Texts, as discourses, are facts of power. Texts are of and in the world. They are positioned and interested. They displace. They direct our attention in some directions and not others. They enable some thoughts, utterances, and nondiscursive actions and not others.

The constitutive nature of all discourse—including academic texts like this one, produced by and/or for oppressed or marginalized groups—demands that we attend to the possibilities and consequences of our discourses. We believe that, as academics and feminists, we ought to be consistently self-reflexive and self-critical, recognizing the powers as well as the limits of the particular approach in which we are framing an issue such as sexual harassment. Thus, we want to call attention to the investments, the affiliations, and the identities we enact and perform under the banner of "research."

To this end, we want to extend the implications of a discursive approach in a different direction than that implicit in these chapters—in a tactical, pragmatic direction rather than a theoretical one. In sketching some alternative research directions, we do not intend to construct these chapters as unproductive or inferior in any way. As hopefully will become clear, we believe the approaches embodied in these chapters are absolutely necessary for a comprehensive understanding and examination of the practice called sexual harassment. Our purpose is to suggest another conceptual framework implicit in a discursive perspective that addresses a different set of necessities—and thus may inspire important research directions that are not yet central to the research conducted about sexual harassment.

ACADEMIC DISCOURSE AND POWER

In general, two characteristics of the chapters in this volume stood out for us. First, they are primarily theory-driven, in the sense that the authors sought to uncover the enabling structures of sexual harassment from top-down, macro-level perspectives—legal, definitional, sociological, and organizational. The desire for an overall explanation of sexual harassment seemed to take precedence over affective reactions, the articulation of specific experiences, and responses based on the contingencies of context and relationship. This is not to say that particularities are entirely absent from this volume. For example, Muir and Mangus's starting point is women sharing their personal experiences with sexual harassment; Kaland and Geist collect individual stories about harassment in an organization; Hale, Cooks, and DeWine demonstrate how Anita Hill's experiences as an African-American woman could not be understood within the framework of fairness under which the Senate hearings operated; and Pollock uses her own experiences in a performance course to grapple with the nature of and possible responses to sexual harassment. Furthermore, we recognize that definition is an important step in the discursive approach: Unless something is named and its boundaries delineated, it is not available for examination.

Second, in offering possible remedies to the problem of sexual harassment, the authors focus on the implementation of policy, the pursuit of legal avenues of redress once policies are in place, the need for ongoing education, and the facilitation of fundamental social change. While seemingly quite variable, these solutions have one trait in common: They are located at the structural level, working to eliminate specific instances of sexual harassment from the top down. That these solutions are generic and rather abstract is not surprising, given the highly generalized approach to knowledge from which they are derived.

Despite the recognition of the inadequacy of covering laws and theories to explain human behavior (Wood, 1992), the impulse toward broad generalizations and explanations continues to dictate, as a residual yet hegemonic force, what counts as "theory." The requirements of generalizability demand that research move beyond specificity and contingency to a broad explanation of the phenomena under investigation. We see in these chapters, then, efforts to identify broad discursive structures—whether those that function within organizations, contribute to gender socialization, inform hegemonic processes, or construct narratives and frameworks of believability.

While the linguistic turn has undermined notions of objectivity, it, too, remains influential in knowledge production. Researchers continue to be expected to construct and maintain a distanced relationship with the object of study. Objectivity is retained in that the distinction between subject and object, knower and known, is maintained in the form and style of academic writing. The result is the neglect, if not absence, of the researcher's interests, passions, and experiences. While the discourse produced within the parameters of objectivity would indicate otherwise, these authors *are* participants in the very discourses they are attempting to explain theoretically.

The form of discourse being used and the type of knowledge it produces are important because discourse and knowledge are linked to power: Any form of knowledge enables certain structures of power; any structure of power enables certain forms of knowledge. Knowledge, as much as the discourses that produce it, is a thing of this world (Foucault, 1980). While the knowledge produced by macro-level social theory is assumed to be accessible to everyone, not everyone has the power or capability to act on the basis of that knowledge.

The authors of the essays in this book make the point that women and other disempowered groups are sexually harassed precisely because of their relatively powerless positions. Yet the proposed solutions—which follow from a particular form of knowledge—more often than not assume agents who have access to certain resources and have been granted certain levels of authority. Thus, many of the solutions offered are generated from the standpoint of the institutional structures and not from the standpoint of those who are "pow-erless." The Muir and Mangus chapter on women's stories about sexual ha-rassment constitutes one exception; they discuss how the act of telling about harassment is itself a first step toward women collectively generating their own solutions. Kaland and Geist, in exploring responses to real and hypo-thetical cases of sexual harassment in an organization, also do not assume access to authority and resources. The typology they generate, however, seems imposed on the stories from above, and we wonder whether the women them-selves would be comfortable with the ideological labels—Peacemaker, Hos-tage, Rebel, and Activist—chosen to characterize their responses.

A central implication of a discursive approach is that those "things" we so often take for granted as "real" are constituted by human discursive activity. For example, Foucault (1977) argues that power is not possessed but is prac-ticed. In other words, it is not a "real" thing but is constituted through certain formations of discourse and knowledge. If we assume there is one type of power—such as that implied by macro-level, top-down social theory—it be-comes reified. When one form of power is successfully reified (universalized, essentialized) a dichotomy is created whereby some have it and others do not. From the standpoint of a commitment to producing social change, this may not be particularly productive.

In order to escape the dichotomy of "powerful" versus "powerless" and to generate solutions that also address the condition from those in the "power-less" position, we first need to recognize the efficacy of alternative forms of power practiced by the "powerless" (De Certeau, 1984). The form of power typically associated with those in positions of institutional authority can be characterized by its reliance on the establishment and control of space. The act of distinguishing between spaces—spaces from which to act and spaces over which to exert control—presumes access to and management of re-sources, bodies, and authoritative discourses. This kind of power is also visually oriented: It relies heavily on surveillance and often depends on the visible manifestations of its authority. The spatial/visual configuration made possible by access to institutional resources characterizes this form of power as stra-tegic. Military institutions typify this form of power as they rely on the cate-gorization, occupation, and colonization of space.

In contrast to strategic power, the form of power exercised by subordinated groups is tactical. Given that these groups do not have the resources necessary to occupy and control space, this form of power relies on time. As with guer-rilla warfare, tactical power is based on well-timed interventions and tempo-rary incursions into the spaces established by the powerful. It relies on secrecy, underground networks, and forms of communication not recognized or valued by those with strategic power (Scott, 1990). A sensitivity to the contingencies and possibilities of the local is opposed to the homogenizing and globalizing of strategic power.

The focus on structure and definition that pervades the chapters in this volume positions them as part of institutional, strategic knowledge. Definitions establish boundaries; in legal and political terms, they establish a place from which to act by allowing for the representation, and hence the universalization and legitimation, of experience. Discourses such as this book tend to constitute sexual harassment as a singular object, an environment, a space distinct from "policymaker" and/or "researcher." These agents of strategic power and knowledge can then engage in the examination (dare we say surveillance?) of this space. These examinations can lead to the development of policies or solutions which, in turn, establish additional structures that function to channel the energies of the bodies over which they preside in certain directions rather than others. While research at the institutional level is a necessary part of understanding how sexual harassment is constituted and how it functions, it is not nor should it be the only direction for research.

In order to propose solutions that take into account local conditions and social positions of individual experiences with sexual harassment, we feel a need to shift to a tactical conception of power. Since forms of knowledge are connected to forms of power, this move requires a reconceptualization of what counts as knowledge. Tactical power necessitates sensitivity to the particularities of context; the accompanying form of knowledge would value the local, the specific, and the contingent rather than the universal, the abstract, and the constant. This is not to deny the existence of institutional structures and power relations or the value of studying the discourse constituted at that level. On the contrary, successful use of tactical power relies on a knowledge of the nature and relevance of those structures—and the chapters in this volume provide an excellent summary of this knowledge as it currently is constructed in terms of sexual harassment. At the same time, a tactical knowledge of these structures is necessarily positioned differently than that of the strategic knowledge of policymakers and enforcers.

In addition to sensitivity to context, tactical knowledge also highlights personal experience. It erases the stable and impermeable barriers between the knower and the known, makes evident the necessary interdependence of entities, and produces knowledge that is radically contingent. Tactical knowledge, therefore, departs from strategic knowledge in at least three ways. First, it calls for a focus on the particularity of individual experiences, narratives, and interactions more than on the articulation of general patterns. Narratives, for instance, are not treated as means to demonstrate theoretical constructs but as moments from which to investigate and understand the meanings and interpretations of the women themselves.

Second, in tactical knowledge the demise of the subject/object distinction recasts the relationship between knower and known as horizontal instead of vertical: Both parties interact as participants in a dialogue in which both are open to influence and change. When the participants recognize their interdependence, neither becomes objectified nor instrumental and both are vulnerable to and accountable for their roles in the research process (which is not to argue that the relationship magically transcends the problems of representation and power). Julie Brown (1993) argues that the distancing between knower and known in scholarly discourse is not merely in service of a certain system of power/knowledge, but is motivated by fear—a fear of vulnerability:

The remarkably uniform way in which we structure "scholarly" writing . . . protects by isolating. It does so by interposing itself between writers and their material such that the particular qualities of the material at hand have little power to set the terms in which the material is discussed. . . . I suspect that the resistance to major variations in form—and to taking our own forms seriously as themselves political practices—is so endemic, so ubiquitous, and so well hidden that it seems insurmountable. So on we go protecting ourselves and others from fully contacting our subject matter. In so doing, we ward off the fear of contacting ideas that may jumble, sully, or in some way open us up to them. (p. 5)

The third implication follows closely from the second—the positions and interests of the researcher need to be acknowledged and addressed. All of the authors in this anthology are participants in at least one institution—the university—in which sexual harassment is a daily and ongoing occurrence. But because they have stayed, for the most part, within the conventions of strategic knowledge (and thus have the opportunity to exercise strategic power), we know little about their personal investments in, experiences with, or positions with regard to sexual harassment.

Given this perspective, we should not pretend to ignore our own relationships—to our subject matter, to this text, and to one another—that enter into the discourse on sexual harassment. A conversation we had while writing this chapter illustrates the process and importance of making explicit the positions from which we write. We began by sharing our general responses to the chapters and discovered that what was most powerful for both of us were the narratives that served as data in some of the studies. Our respective positions were made evident through our different responses. Karen reacted emotionally, recalling similar situations and the feelings of shame and guilt associated with them. While Rich has recognized that sexual harassment regularly occurs, reading the narratives gave him a glimpse into a lived, emotional experience that he usually does not have to think about or face and thus raised fundamentally different feelings of shame and guilt. Both of us experienced a sense of powerlessness in regard to sexual harassment, although these feelings originated from very different vantage points.

Generalizing about either of our relationships to sexual harassment as a personal experience or a topic for study is problematized because of the specificity and multiplicity of our positions. Institutionally, as a graduate student, Rich is in a more vulnerable position. However, being male not only reduces the likelihood of his being a target of sexual harassment, it makes it less likely that he will perceive how others treat him through that lens. His role as a teacher, on the other hand, places him in a position perceived as filled with potential for harassment. His feminist commitments and explicit discussions of gender issues in the classroom both heighten his awareness and foster the dangerous illusion that he is conscious enough of his actions to avoid behaving in ways that could legitimately be interpreted as harassment.

Karen's institutional position also places her in a position of authority, creating the power differential so central to sexual harassment. She is also a woman in a society still saturated with patriarchy. Sexual harassment can become, for example, a means for male students and colleagues to reduce the felt tension of having a woman in a position of authority. Her feminist agenda in both the classroom and in her research only increases the possibilities for antagonism from males unable or unwilling to accept her presence in the academy. These tensions led in part to our ambivalence about strategic proposals: The specificity and multiplicity of any individual's social positions complicate the application of generalizations about sexual harassment.

As academics, too, we acknowledge that we are comparatively privileged in terms of access to the resources of strategic power. We are both ensconced in academic institutions and accept that we exercise strategic power ourselves by virtue of our positions in the academy. Indeed, the act of writing this chapter can be seen as a means of furthering and guaranteeing our privileged positions; neither of us is planning on leaving the citation for this work off our résumés despite our recognition of the limitations of academic knowledge production.

Just as we need to be aware of and take into account the particular experiences and positions we bring to this chapter, so, too, does research need to address the particularities as well as the theoretical aspects of sexual harassment so as not to gloss over crucial differences in the lives of women: class, region, ethnicity, race, religion, sexuality, and many other factors (the chapters by Hale and her colleagues and Muir and Mangus provide examples of how these lived differences can be taken into account). Generally speaking, however, the discourse on sexual harassment functions to constitute a single, unitary object called "woman"—an abstraction made possible only by ignoring the multiplicity of position and experience (James, 1992). Statements are made about what "women have been taught" concerning their value and role, about the consequences for "men who force sexual attention on uninterested women," about how "women and men experience sexuality and power in different ways," about "women's stories."

Little attention is paid to how the sex roles taught to African-American women, Asian-American women, Native American women, and Hispanic women are different from those taught to Euro–American women, or how working-class women are given different conceptions of their bodies and sexuality than upper-middle-class women. Many of the explanations for sexual harassment rely on culturally specific factors without recognizing that specificity. For example, the public praise of men for forcing sexual attention on women is often cited as a discursive condition enabling sexual harassment. In these discussions, rarely is it mentioned that African-American men historically have been lynched for public displays of their sexuality. In fact, the history of lynching and other racial violence motivated by discursive constructions of blacks as sexually different led many African-Americans to fear public discussions of the sexual relations between black women and men (Chrisman & Allen, 1992; Morrison, 1992).

As another example, the status of African-Americans as a subordinated group within society places black women in a bind between an allegiance to their race and sex—two intimately fused aspects of their identity which legal and political discourses artificially separate and, in the Hill-Thomas hearings, set in opposition (Crenshaw, 1992). Black women's experiences of sexual harassment are not necessarily separable from their racial status: Interracial sexual relations, the use of stereotypes about black women's sexuality, and the combination of racist and sexist slurs are but a few of the factors potentially involved. This intersection would exist for other racial and ethnic groups, including Euro-American women; the danger is in generalizing on the basis of one group's experience (Butler, 1990a).

We recognize that in attempting to address the problem of sexual harassment from the particularities rather than the abstractions of experience, we ourselves are continuing to operate at the level of "theory" and that generalizations are virtually unavoidable. That we posit new reifications in our attempt to denaturalize old ones is also undeniable. Strategic and tactical power are as much discursive constructions as sexual harassment. In establishing "strategic" and "tactical" as endpoints of a continuum, we risk reifying some of the same dualisms that pervade conventional approaches to communication and society: individual/social, micro/macro, concrete/abstract, experience/theory, top/bottom. At the very least, we would want to argue that strategic-tactical is a continuum and is only one of many by which academic discourses could be classified. Research that addresses every aspect of the continuum from every conceptual position is necessary to understand the complex set of practices that constitute sexual harassment.

ALTERNATIVE DIRECTIONS FOR RESEARCH

Given our interest in elaborating the tactical implications of discursive practices, what suggestions can we offer that address sexual harassment from the tactical side—the side of those who experience it and do not necessarily have access to the resources and knowledge available to those who control institutional structures? In the hopes of stimulating research from this perspective, we will offer suggestions in three areas: definitions of sexual harassment, the handling of personal narratives, and tactical possibilities for those experiencing sexual harassment.

First, we suggest that the definition of sexual harassment—and the need to define it with such singularity—be subjected to ongoing examination. We acknowledge that a monolithic definition of sexual harassment needs to exist for legal purposes and that the creation of such a definition proves empowering to many women who would not have previously defined certain behaviors as harassing. But from the standpoint of tactical knowledge and power, such a definition is not always necessary or appropriate. If we are to take seriously the notion that sexual harassment is constituted discursively and that such discourses vary across the social formation, we need to take into account all of the reactions and definitions women have about sexual harassment. Often these individual views are invalidated in the quest for agreement about the legal definition.

For instance, rather than listening to the woman who says she did not consider a particular behavior to be harassment, even though it might be considered so legally, a frequent reaction is to attempt to get her to redefine it as harassment. This action in effect disempowers her by invalidating her perceptions, meanings, and feelings. We need to spend more time with the narratives of women to hear what comprises their socially positioned definitions of sexual harassment, how these behaviors mesh with how they frame their lives, and the actions they have in their repertoires for handling such incidents. A fixed definition of sexual harassment is not that important from a tactical perspective, and indeed, such a definition may be counterproductive to the women such definitions are allegedly put in place to help (Butler, 1990a; Crenshaw, 1992).

One site for examining these definitional issues is women's narratives. Narratives of sexual harassment can be reread to understand the local conditions and perceptions involved in a particular case and to see what tactics women utilize to address their conditions. From this perspective, we must also be sensitive to how they choose to address their conditions: If we impose the standards of certain political programs (i.e., various versions of academic feminism) we may be likely to interpret their choices as too accommodating. Instead, in engaging in a dialogue with these narratives, we can open ourselves to a wide range of tactics from passive acceptance to coping to active intervention. In any particular narrative, we will likely see the operation of both strategic and tactical power—the active, ongoing, fluid push and pull of different discourses, interests, and power relations.

The narratives in the chapters by Conrad and Taylor, Muir and Mangus, and Clair, for instance, are read to demonstrate, respectively, the institutionally powerless position of victims of sexual harassment and the processes by which they give their consent to oppressive structures. In rereading these narratives, we are not claiming these authors' readings to be wrong, but partial (as is ours) and positioned in terms of strategic assumptions about power. What we are attempting to do here is not to provide *the* interpretation of these narratives—such a task would be presumptuous—but to demonstrate the different kinds of readings highlighted by the approach developed here.

Many of the narratives presented by Conrad and Taylor include strong emotional reactions as well as revealing recognition of lack of power within an organizational hierarchy. One woman recalls the response of a colleague who opposed a policy on gender-neutral language in department discourse:

He called me into his office to show me a pair of foam breasts that he had put on his phone as a shoulder rest. He didn't say anything, but the message was clear. I left his office without saying a word, seething but realizing that there was little I could do to stop his sexism until such time as I got tenure.

A strategic approach, in focusing on institutional structures and definitions, would tend not to be as concerned with the significance of her feelings as a tactical approach would be. In addition, a tactical approach would be interested in further investigating the specifics of such reactions: how they serve these women as sources of energy, how they are affirmed by and passed on to other women, how they help address specific instances of harassment.

Many of the narratives refer to a learning process. How is learning defined and valued by these women? How is it made relevant and put to practical use? In this narrative from Conrad and Taylor, notice how the woman has constructed her own agency: "While I remained silent . . . I learned not to feel inferior and to name the thing for what it was—a political act of intimidation, an attempt to keep me in my place." What processes are involved in her learning, in her taking charge of the situation? In addition, notice her focus on specific behaviors and goals: "Now that I have graduated, I no longer remain silent in the face of offensive remarks. I wish every speech department in the country had a feminist scholar who could empower female graduate students to name the oppression they undoubtedly also experience and to fight back." Her emphasis is not so much on structures and power relations—although those are necessarily there—but on the particularities of her condition and on ways to deal with it. Finally, she demonstrates an understanding of the strategic system of power: "a political act . . . an attempt to keep me in my place." These factors, characteristic of a tactical orientation, are what she indicates as important for her empowerment.

Similarly, one of the narratives presented by Muir and Mangus includes the statement that "males obviously have low self-esteem." What conditions and relationships enable this belief? How is the statement itself used in discussions about sexual harassment or as a well-timed intervention in response to particular cases of harassment? To whom is it performed and under what conditions?

These narratives can also be read for the kind of verbal interventions available to strategically powerless groups. Clair, for example, presents this narrative from a nurse who was pregnant at the time of the encounter: "He came up to me a couple of days ago and said he gets turned on by pregnant women. I told him I felt sorry for him . . . it was really an injustice to his wife." While Clair reads this as an example of how privatizing harassment enables its continuation, the reported response strikes us as an attempt to reframe the event in a way that belittles the harasser, thereby potentially avoiding negative feelings of blame and guilt on the part of the woman. It can be read, therefore, as a creative use of existing discursive structures. Such appropriations of the materials provided by those in power are a central part of tactical resistance.

Similarly, Clair presents several narratives she reads as trivializing the harassment by calling it a joke. While a less active form of resistance, joking can be seen as a coping mechanism: If the woman is relatively powerless to change the structures that enable harassment, attempts to cope with its existence should not be belittled. Turning the harassment into a joke may not only let the harasser off the hook, but the woman as well. People reliant on tactical power must choose their confrontations carefully based on the energy and resources available, the particular conditions and relationships in play, and the like. In this frame, the following narrative can be read not only as perpetuating the conditions of harassment but as a case of practical decision making:

Well, if it's subtle and it's jokingly, and it's not hurting me or my position, I'm okay with it, because it's not harming me. And it's nothing really direct. But then it annoys you and you want to do something about it. You almost want to dish it back really bad.

To be fair to Clair, she does acknowledge that victims who do not internalize the cultural ideology that supports harassment may in fact use the same strategies as those who do, but she continues to focus on how these tactics perpetuate the oppression of women. We want to raise other possibilities for interpretation: Perhaps the most subversive forms of resistance are the use of expected responses against the status quo—but in ways that empower the victim without the establishment realizing it. We are reminded of the women in Suzette Haden Elgin's futuristic novel *Native Tongue* (1984), in which the women hide their creation of a women's language in their recipe files and under the needlework in their laps. The woman who knows exactly what she is doing when she makes a joke about harassment likewise may be highly empowered because she recognizes that even the most innocuous and seemingly submissive strategy can contain the seeds of subversion and resistance.

While we empathize with desires to change structures so that women do not have to learn to cope, do not have to make choices for more "passive" forms of resistance to "get by," the conditions in which women live seem to require that we pay attention to how the existence of these structures, discourses, and behaviors are dealt with on a daily basis. What conditions led this woman to decide the harassment is not really harming her, that she shouldn't act even if she wants to? How does she use that pent-up annoyance? When does she decide to act and in what ways?

From a tactical perspective, the development and dissemination of responses and interventions, such as those suggested by these narratives, is given priority over "knowledge" in the traditional sense. We are interested in empowering women who face sexual harassment regardless of their familiarity with legal definitions or with the existence of policies established at their place of employment. We want to be able to offer suggestions to women who are unable even to ask the "right" questions to "proper" authorities about harassment—because of lack of time, "limited" (from a strategic standpoint) verbal skills, or unfamiliarity with how middle-class bureaucracies function. We propose, then, an investigation into various acts of resistance that take advantage of the resources of the supposedly powerless.

A variety of solutions make use of female networks that are often in place—even if they are used only infrequently and quite casually. Graffiti in women's toilet stalls is one example of such a network: In some communities, women have "published" the names of known sexual harassers as well as rapists on bathroom walls. As another example, women new to an organization are often warned by other women to "watch out for" someone's roving hands, or "never let the boss close the door when you're alone with him in the office." While these networks by themselves do not prevent the harassment, they function to let women know they are not alone in dealing with the problem and often offer forewarning and support to the women in a particular environment so they can avoid situations in which harassment is likely to occur.

We also recommend research on the verbal tactics that women can use effectively to step out of the response mode in a harassing situation—because often any kind of reaction that responds in some way to the harassment is precisely what the harasser wants. The suggestions that follow work to allow women to "step aside" and out of the one-on-one system that the harasser hopes to establish. Suzette Haden Elgin (1992), for instance, suggests that when confronted with a harassing comment, one response is for the woman simply to "get boring." If the harasser says, "Why won't you go out with me," the woman does not try to respond rationally with answers such as "I'm married," "I'm not interested," or "I don't date people I work with." Rather, she simply launches into a long and boring response such as "Well, the reason I won't go out with you probably has something to do with what happened in my childhood. I grew up on a farm in North Dakota, and I loved to sit on my swing set in the summer and watch the sun set over the wheat fields. I lived on that farm until I was ten . . ." The woman continues for as long as she perceives necessary or until her storytelling skills are taxed to the maximum. This response works because the woman isn't challenging the harasser; she has simply gone elsewhere with her talk. The harasser typically becomes bored himself by this lengthy narrative, and the tension just wears itself out without a loss of face on either side.

Another tactic that also moves the focus away from an emphasis on the sexually harassing behavior per se is a form of neutral affirmation of part of the harasser's statement. If the harasser says, "If you really cared about the morale of this organization, you'd at least go out with me," the woman can respond in very general terms to the content of the "really" proposition and not the harassing phrase itself. She might say, "You know, organizational morale is an interesting thing . . ." She avoids using "I" or "you," so she has not bought into the personal intent of the interaction; she has shown no emotion beyond a kind of neutral interest, and she has not blamed the harasser in any way (Elgin, 1980). A response like this has the advantage of surprise—a discourse on organizational morale is not what he was expecting—and she will have moved the conversation to another level and probably put an end to the harassing episode.

Such techniques are especially effective if, using the informal network, women in an organization decide to employ the same tactic consistently whenever one of them is harassed. The boss who routinely harasses his female employees and is suddenly greeted with boring stories from all of them about growing up may find it no longer beneficial—in terms of his desired payoff or the waste of time—to listen. We believe women are tactically resourceful in managing sexual harassment; as researchers, we simply need to listen to and read their narratives from their position in society in order to grasp the whole range of tactics that are part of the subterranean approach to resistance.

PARTING COMMENTS

Given the position and assumptions of the tactical knowledge we have outlined here, these responses and interventions cannot be offered as "solutions"—that is, as universally relevant or effective. Tactical knowledge is offered as contingent; this strategic weakness is its tactical strength. We are suggesting that, as researchers, we need to look at how knowledge is constructed at every level of society.

Different social positions provide widely divergent constraints and opportunities. Any one form of knowledge is likely to enable some socially situated actors more than others. A plurality of perspectives does more than affirm abstractions such as "diversity" and "academic freedom"; it offers academics the opportunity to address a variety of social conditions for a variety of social actors.

A potential concern is that this approach seems to accept the game as rigged, that the task of macro-level change has proved too daunting, that we are settling for "making do." This is not our sense of our motives. Top- down, structurally driven research has a vital role to play in addressing sexual harassment. However, given the very real constraints—the inadequacy of legal and organizational mechanisms for many women's circumstances, the (at best) incremental process of changing socialization and education processes, the tenacity of patriarchal discourses and practices—researchers also need to study those approaches that address the conditions of everyday life. Much feminist work has been driven by a focus on the personal and a recognition of its political character. We need not only to move the personal into the political (i.e., sexual harassment into legal and policy realms), but the political (power, intervention, resistance) into the personal.

Epilogue: Research on Sexual Harassment—Continuing the Conversation

Shereen G. Bingham

An underlying premise of this book is that new ideas emerge out of contesting voices. While the preceding chapters explore conceptions of sexual harassment as discursive practice, oppositions and inconsistencies arise within and between the chapters, and these have potential to provoke novel thinking. This volume reminds us that meanings of concepts such as sexual harassment, discourse, power, and ideology are diverse and contested rather than monolithic and stable. The authors do not attempt to resolve incongruities, nor will I try to provide resolution here. Instead, I want to discuss briefly two of the many unsettled issues that emerge from this collection as challenges for sexual harassment researchers. Readers are encouraged to contemplate these and other ideas-in-tension for insights they may inspire.

First, discursive understandings of sexual harassment challenge researchers to locate intersections between theoretical understanding and lived experience. Although it might be easier to view theory and individual experience as mutually exclusive and antithetical, conceptualizing sexual harassment as discursive activity seems to demand that we envision both of these as simultaneously authentic and interactive. The chapters in this volume are examples of the kind of self-conscious work that is needed in our struggle to meet this challenge.

At the crux of this first challenge is the concept of individual subjectivity. Discursive perspectives view direct experience as the basis of a person's knowledge, but one's subjective reality is seen as crafted by material conditions and discursive practices. Thus, what sexual harassment means to someone who experiences it is understood to be shaped by material conditions and the dis-

courses available for interpreting and talking about the world. As Foss and
Rogers suggest in chapter 10, a potential danger of discursive conceptions is
that they may imply distrust of individuals' accounts of their own experiences.
A researcher might interpret victims' sexual harassment narratives as inaccu-
rate or impoverished and might impose alternative explanations that would
not ring true for the victims.[1] For example, if a person claims that a harassing
incident was not serious or provides excuses for the harasser, researchers and
activists may view the person's narrative as naive and might impose their own
"superior" interpretations onto the experiences.

The risks of imposing an outsider's perspective on individual experiences
are not limited to the study of sexual harassment. Houston (1992) points out,
for example, that white feminists have tended to distort the experiences of
minority women rather than to allow those women's perspectives to guide
interpretations of their own behavior. If researchers and activists fail to listen
to victims' experiences in their own terms, we may inadvertently foist on them
disempowering interpretations of their behavior or advise idealistic solutions
that have no pragmatic value. Worse, we may position ourselves as powerful
and knowing experts prepared to save the ignorant and helpless.

Although interpretations imposed without respect for lived experiences potentially yield research and advice that are useless and even harmful, embracing the other extreme by renouncing theory can be equally dangerous. As
Wood and Cox (1993, p. 281) contend, "We can listen and observe carefully
to grasp the intrinsic integrity of what and whom we study. If that is the extent
of our work, however, we add nothing beyond what a perceptive actor can
make of her or his own experience." If researchers fail to understand the ways
individual accounts of sexual harassment are shaped and influenced by dominant discourses and material conditions, they limit their work to clarifying
sexual harassment from the point of view of victims, harassers, and other
participants. Lannamann (1991) suggests that when researchers study subjective experience without addressing ideological issues, "the field risks generating findings that reify existing cultural practices and legitimize current social
orders" (p. 179). Similarly, a study of sexual harassment experiences that is
detached from larger understandings of cultural patterns and structures potentially reifies oppressive practices and structures that legitimate and normalize sexual harassment.

The challenge for researchers, as demonstrated in this volume, is to devise
theoretical orientations and methods of study that respect the integrity of
individual experiences while also recognizing the influence of discursive practices and material life on individual subjectivity (see Wood & Cox, 1993).
Sexual harassment narratives can be understood as "true but partial accounts
of sexual harassment" (Brodkey & Fine, 1991, p. 112). This means that researchers understand narratives as valid accounts of experience, and read them
with awareness that they are shaped by social and organizational structures
and practices. Without this layering of knowledge we fail to offer any illumi-

nation, much less critique, of prevailing social structures and practices that have legitimized sexual harassment and other forms of oppression.

A second and related challenge for researchers working from discursive understandings of sexual harassment is to bridge the apparent rift between individual tactics for surviving sexual harassment within the current system and strategies that contribute to changing the system itself. Although these two forms of resistance may be viewed as polar opposites, the most effective methods for combatting sexual harassment may emerge as researchers and activists find ways in which these forms interact and merge. The chapters in this volume demonstrate the efforts of authors engaged in the struggle to find solutions to sexual harassment that incorporate multiple viewpoints and approaches.

Central to this second challenge is the way discursive conceptions of sexual harassment envision victims' responses. A discursive perspective recognizes that victims' responses to sexual harassment and the choices that seem possible for responding occur within systems, situations, and relationships that are themselves discursively constituted and constrained. There is a potential danger that this perspective will lead a researcher to view individuals as inept or weak if their responses do not contest sexual harassment in the manner a researcher or activist would recommend. Only strategies that overtly oppose the status quo might be valued, and victims who do not speak up more forcefully might be blamed or belittled because they are allowing themselves to be oppressed. In contrast, Foss and Rogers argue that the tactics women use to cope with sexual harassment in daily life should be valued as strong and skillful means for survival, especially in the absence of social and organizational support. An individual's power and ability to cope with oppressive conditions and practices should not be discounted, and an individual's feelings of empowerment that may arise through successful coping in these contexts should not be underestimated.

However, the chapters in this book suggest that it ought to be possible to acknowledge that victims' responses to sexual harassment occur within contexts that are both materially and discursively constructed, without belittling the tactics that individuals use to cope with and survive sexual harassment in daily life. Tactics for deflecting sexual harassment do little or nothing to disrupt the social and organizational practices and structures that have been exposed repeatedly throughout this volume as forces that legitimate sexual harassment. If researchers do not move beyond respecting coping tactics and those who use them skillfully in constrained situations, we are in danger of reifying and perpetuating the status quo.[2] Thus, the study of survival tactics is an important but not sufficient research focus if we hope to understand, resist, and undermine the practices sustaining sexual harassment. Figuring out how discursive practices operate actually is a way—one of perhaps many—to generate strategies of resistance as well as discover ways the prevailing practices, and, thus, their consequences, can be undermined.

The challenges of integrating theory with lived experience and of bridging
survival tactics with oppositional discourses inspire a range of specific ideas
for future research. As we continue to struggle with these challenges, our
research may provide a basis for developing activist strategies that both empower individual actors and contest the discursive practices and material conditions sustaining sexual harassment. I want to suggest just two of many
possible ideas for future research with implicit implications for activist efforts.

First, researchers might explore educational strategies that may help individuals gain access to discourses that oppose sexual harassment. Della Pollock's chapter hints at precisely what I am suggesting here, and in so doing,
reveals the rich complexity of this line of inquiry. Although victims of sexual
harassment may become empowered through education, the chapters in this
volume, and Pollock's in particular, suggest that not just any kind of education
will do. Knowledge can invite people to move out of self-perceptions as victims, which are perceptions of passivity and helplessness. However, "personal
knowledge does not necessarily become grounds for political action" (Brodkey
& Fine, 1991, p. 112). For example, if women realize they are being treated
unfairly but cannot envision ways to change the conditions and practices that
normalize and sustain sexual harassment, they may become "transfixed rather
than transformed by their knowledge of oppression" (Brodkey & Fine, 1991,
p. 112).

Brodkey and Fine (1991) demonstrate how research on sexual harassment
as discursive practice can inform educational strategies when they present a
feminist pedagogy that arises from their reading of the narratives of female
graduate students. The narratives revealed that the students could not envision
the kind of institutional change that would enable them to report sexual harassment. The authors describe an educational project designed "as a first step
toward interrupting the illusion that institutional authority is literally anony-
mous" (p. 115). According to them, "[t]his is the illusion feminists must first
seek to dispel if we hope to enable young women and men to see oppression
as mutable through critical and collective reflection and action" (p. 113). The
project begins with students imagining how various university representatives
might respond to different versions of a particular sexual harassment narrative
and then interviewing the representatives. Students redefine institutional authority by "revealing heterogeneity within what only appears to be a single
voice to outsiders" (p. 114).

Second, researchers might study how individuals who already have access
to discourses of resistance talk about and respond to sexual harassment. When
people gain access to oppositional discourses, they are not suddenly released
from ideological frames that sustain sexual harassment. Instead, individuals
may develop what Spender (1985) describes as a "double view of the world"
(p. 309). The ability to move from one ideological frame to another helps one
question the "truth" of all perspectives and to understand that all frames of
reference are partial.

Vision through opposing ideological frames can also be stressful, however, and the ways in which individuals work out the tension between competing discourses warrants attention by researchers. Huspek (1993) argues that some individuals have access to "dueling structures of meaning" and rival or competing ideologies. These speakers may be under pressure to both express and disguise resistance to dominant structures in their ways of speaking. Although Huspek focuses on linguistic structures and dialects, victims of sexual harassment who have access to opposing discourses may also be understood as dealing with simultaneous pressure to express and cloak resistance in their speech. For example, a woman who knows her employer or professor is sexually harassing her and treating her unfairly may feel pressure to challenge the harassment while also to mask her resistance. According to Huspek (p. 18), "[t]his appearance/nonappearance of resistance is accomplished by means of ambiguity, veiled sarcasm, irony, humor, and other artful techniques." As Huspek suggests, it would be fruitful for researchers to "[analyze] discursive productions . . . in terms of the degree to which resistance in discourse extricates itself from domination, and how it is constrained in its efforts to do so" (p. 21). For example, communication strategies for responding to sexual harassment might be analyzed in terms of the extent to which they both resist and are constrained by dominant discourses. Envisioning responses to sexual harassment as a speaker's effort to negotiate dueling structures of meaning suggests a theoretical perspective for research that values tactics of resistance while also viewing them as constrained by oppressive discursive practices and structures.

Conceptualizing sexual harassment as discursive activity means calling attention to how discursive practices and the cultural and personal phenomena implicated in them constitute, sustain, legitimize, and sometimes resist sexual harassment. A primary value of this book is that it problematizes taken-for-granted meanings and encourages open dialogue among contesting voices. Any informed understanding of discursive activity must take into account the ambiguities in symbolic behavior and must deliberately problematize processes such as interpretation and response. To do otherwise is to misrepresent the tensions that inhere in discursive practice by focusing on one set of impulses and meanings and falsely implying, whether implicitly or explicitly, that no other impulse and meanings complicate this interpretation. Although questioning our understandings of sexual harassment and discursivity is unsettling and a difficult process, it is precisely this kind of reflection that is instrumental to envisioning and instigating change, both in ourselves as social actors and in our work as researchers who study social practice.

NOTES

1. I use the term "victim" here and elsewhere because I find that those on whom sexual harassment is imposed are being harmed. I fully recognize, however, that there are good arguments for using alternative terms such as "survivor" or "target."

2. Brodkey and Fine (1991) make this point when they argue that the strategies women students devise to deflect individual incidents of sexual harassment "neither interrupt nor disrupt the material and ideological gender asymmetries organizing the academy," and thus the strategies do nothing to change the "pervasive, routinized, and institutionalized sexual intimidation" that women speak of in their narratives (p. 109).

References

Abbey, A. (1982). Sex differences in attributions for friendly behavior: Do males mis-perceive females' friendliness? *Journal of Personality and Social Psychology* 42: 830–838.

Adams, K., & Ware, N.C. (1989). Sexism and the English language: The linguistic implications of being a woman. In J. Freeman (ed.), *Women: A feminist perspective*. Mountain View, CA: Mayfield, 470–484.

Aggarwal, A. P. (1987). *Sexual harassment in the workplace*. Toronto: Butterworth.

Alberts, J. K. (1992). Teasing and sexual harassment: Double-bind communication in the workplace. In L.A.M. Perry, L. H. Turner, & H. M. Sterk (eds.), *Constructing and reconstructing gender: The links among communication, language, and gender*. Albany: State University of New York Press, 185–208.

Alcoff, L. (1990). Feminist politics and Foucault: The limits to a collaboration. In A. Dallery & C. Scott (eds.), *Crises in continental philosophy*. Albany: State University of New York Press, 69–86.

Alcoff, L., & Gray, L. (1993). Survivor discourse: Transgression or recuperation? *Signs* 18: 260–290.

Allen, D., & Okawa, B. (1987). A counseling center looks at sexual harassment. *Initiatives. Journal of the National Association for Women Deans, Administrators, and Counselors* 51: 9–16.

Allen, K. R., & Baber, K. M. (1992). Ethical and epistemological tensions in applying a postmodern perspective to feminist research. *Psychology of Women Quarterly* 18: 1–15.

Althusser, L. (1977). *For Marx*. (Trans. B. Brewster). London: NLB.

Ardener, S. (ed.), (1975). *Perceiving women*. London: Malaby.

Arliss, L. P. (1991). *Gender communication*. Englewood Cliffs, NJ: Prentice-Hall.

Bakhtin, M. (1981). Discourse in the novel. In M. Holquist (ed.), C. Emerson and M. Holquist (trans.), *The dialogic imagination*. Austin: University of Texas Press, 259–422.

Baldridge, J. V. (1978). *Policy-making and effective leadership*. San Francisco: Jossey-Bass.

Baldridge, K., & McLean, G. (1980). Sexual harassment: How much of a problem is it . . . really? *Journal of Business Education* 55: 294–297.

Balsamo, A. (1985, September). Beyond female as variable. Paper prepared for the Critical Perspectives in Organizational Analysis Conference, Boston.

Bartky, S. (1988). Foucault, femininity, and the modernization of patriarchal power. In I. Diamond and L. Quinby (eds.), *Feminism and Foucault: Reflections on resistance*. Boston: Northeastern University Press, 61–86.

Beneke, T. (1982). *Men on rape: What they have to say about sexual violence*. New York: St. Martin's Press.

Benson, D., & Thompson, G. (1982). Sexual harassment on a university campus. *Social Problems* 29: 236–251.

Berger, J. (1972). *Ways of seeing*. London: British Broadcasting Corporation and Penguin Books.

Bernard, J. (1981). *The female world*. New York: The Free Press.

Berryman-Fink, C. (1993). Preventing sexual harassment through male-female communication training. In G. L. Kreps (ed.), *Sexual harassment: Communication implications*. Cresskill, NJ: Hampton Press, 267–280.

Bingham, S. (1991). Communication strategies for managing sexual harassment in organizations: Understanding message options and their effects. *Journal of Applied Communication Research* 19: 88–115.

——— (1993, March 10). Personal communication.

Bingham, S. G., & Burleson, B. R. (1989). Multiple effects of messages with multiple goals: Some perceived outcomes of responses to sexual harassment. *Human Communication Research*, 16: 184–216.

Bingham, S. G., & Scherer, L. L. (1993). Factors associated with responses to sexual harassment and satisfaction with outcome. *Sex Roles*, 29: 239–269.

Blumenfeld, L. (1992, October 13). One year, after Hill: Women and sexual harassment in America. *Washington Post*, E5.

Booth-Butterfield, M. (1987, May). Assessing personal boundaries: Organizational application of harassment guidelines. Paper presented at the International Communication Association Convention, Montreal.

——— (1989). Perceptions of harassing communication as a function of locus of control, work force participation, and gender. *Communication Quarterly* 37: 262–275.

Box, S. (1983). *Power, crime, and mystification*. London: Tavistock.

Bravo, E., and Cassedy, E. (1992, July). Is it sexual harassment? *Redbook*, 53–54, 56.

Brecht, B. (1955). *Mother Courage*. (Trans. E. Bentley.) New York: Grove Press.

Brennan, J. B. (1989, Summer). Words with Walker. *San Francisco Review of Books*, 13.

Brodkey, L., & Fine, M. (1991). Presence of mind in the absence of body. In Henry A. Giroux (ed.), *Postmodernism, feminism, and cultural politics*. Albany: State University of New York Press, 100–118.

Brooks, L., & Perot, A. (1991). Reporting sexual harassment: Exploring a predictive model. *Psychology of Women Quarterly* 15: 31–47.

Brown, J. (1993, February). The habits of fear/the habits of love: Self, criticism, and community. Paper presented at the Western States Communication Association convention, Albuquerque.

Brownmiller, S. (1993, January 4). Making female bodies the battlefield. *Newsweek*, 37.

Bunch, C. (1986). Making common cause: Diversity and coalition. *Ikon* 7: 49–56.

Burk, T. L., Nickless, J. L., and Sutherland, C. L. (1991). Family stories. In K. A. Foss & S. K. Foss (eds.), *Women speak: The eloquence of women's lives*. Prospect Heights, IL: Waveland.

Burke, K. (1968). *Counter-statement*. Berkeley: University of California Press.

Burrell, G., & Hearn, J. (1989). The sexuality of organization. In J. Hearn, D. L. Sheppard, P. Tancred-Sherrif, & G. Burrell (eds.), *The sexuality of organization*. Newbury Park, CA: Sage, 1–28.

Buss, D. M. (1981). Sex differences in the evaluation and performance of dominant acts. *Journal of Personality and Social Psychology* 54: 616–628.

Butler, J. (1990a). *Gender trouble: feminism and the subversion of identity*. New York: Routledge.

———— (1990b). Performative acts and gender constitution: An essay in phenomenology and feminist theory. In S. E. Case (ed.), *Performing feminisms: Feminist critical theory and theatre*. Baltimore: Johns Hopkins University Press, 270–282.

Camitta, M. (1990). Gender and method in folklore fieldwork. *Southern Folklore* 47: 21–32.

Caraway, N. (1991). *Segregated sisterhood: Racism and politics of American feminism*. Knoxville: University of Tennessee Press.

Carothers, S. C., & Crull, P. (1984) Contrasting sexual harassment in female and male dominated occupations. In K. Broadkin-Sacha and D. Remy (eds.), *My troubles are going to have trouble with me*. New Brunswick, NJ: Rutgers University Press, 219–228.

Castaneda, C. J. (1992, August 3). Tailhook investigation 'no help.' Women go public, may file suit. *USA Today*, 3A.

Charles, N., & Kerr, M. (1987). Just the way it is: Gender and age differences in family food consumption. In J. Brannen & G. Wilson (eds.), *Give and take in families: Studies in resource distribution*. London: Unwin Hyman, 155–174.

Chatman, S. (1978). *Story and discourse: Narrative structure in fiction and film*. Ithaca, NY: Cornell University Press.

Chrisman, R., & Allen, R. L. (eds.) (1992). *Court of appeal: The black community speaks out on the racial and sexual politics of Clarence Thomas vs. Anita Hill*. New York: Ballantine.

Cixous, H. (1976). The laugh of the Medusa. *Signs* 1: 875–893.

Clair, R. P. (1993a, May). The bureaucratization, commodification, and privatization of sexual harassment through institutional discourse: A study of the "Big Ten" universities. Paper presented at the annual meeting of the International Communication Association, Washington D.C.

———— (1993b, November). Four facets of hegemony with implications for sexual harassment. Paper presented at the annual meeting of the Speech Communication Association, Miami.

———— (1993c). The use of framing devices to sequester organizational narratives: Hegemony and harassment. *Communication Monographs* 60: 1–24.

Clair, R. P., & McGoun, M. (1991, November). A study of strategic responses to sexual harassment: An analysis of women's narratives. Paper presented at the Speech Communication Association convention, Atlanta.

Clair, R. P., McGoun, M. J., & Spirek, M. M. (1993). Sexual harassment responses of working women: An assessment of current communication-oriented typologies and perceived effectiveness of the response. In G. L. Kreps (ed.), *Communication and sexual harassment in the workplace.* Cresskill, NJ: Hampton Press, 200–224.

Clarke, E. (1980). Stopping sexual harassment. Detroit: Labor Education and Research Project.

Clegg, S. R., & Dunkerley, D. (1980). *Organization, class and control.* London: Routledge & Kegan Paul.

Coles, F. S. (1986). Forced to quit: Sexual harassment complaints and agency response. *Sex Roles* 14: 81–95.

Collins, E.G.C., & Blodgett, T. B. (1981). Sexual harassment: Some see it . . . some won't. *Harvard Business Review* 59: 76–95.

Collins, P. H. (1990). *Black feminist thought.* New York: Routledge.

Conquergood, D. (1991). Rethinking ethnography: Towards a critical cultural politics. *Communication Monographs* 58: 179–194.

Cordes, H. (1993, January/February). The blue balls bluff. *Utne Reader,* 62–63.

Cowan, G., & Hoffman, C. D. (1986). Gender stereotyping in young children: Evidence to support a concept-learning approach. *Sex Roles* 14: 211–224.

Crenshaw, K. (1992). Whose story is it, anyway? Feminist and antiracist appropriations of Anita Hill. In T. Morrison (ed.), *Race-ing justice, en-gendering power: Essays on Anita Hill, Clarence Thomas, and the construction of social reality.* New York: Pantheon, 402–440.

Crull, P. (1979). The impact of sexual harassment on the job. Working Women's Institute Research Series Report no. 3.

———— The impact of sexual harassment on the job: A profile of the experiences of 92 women. In D. A. Neugarten & J. M. Shafritz (eds.), *Sexuality in organizations: Romantic and coercive behaviors at work.* Oak Park, IL: Moore Publishing, 67–71.

———— (1982). Stress effects of sexual harassment on the job: Implications for counseling. *American Journal of Orthopsychiatry,* 52, 539–544.

Daly, M. (1973). *Beyond God the Father: Toward a philosophy of women's liberation.* Boston: Beacon Press.

———— (1975). The qualitative leap beyond patriarchal religion. *Quest* 1: 20–40.

———— (1983). *Gyn/ecology: The metaethics of radical feminism.* Boston: Beacon Press.

Davis, H. V. (1992). The high-tech lynching and the high-tech overseer: Thoughts from the Anita Hill/Clarence Thomas affair. In R. Chrisman & R. L. Allen (eds.), *Court of appeal.* New York: Ballantine Books, 59–62.

De Certeau, M. (1984). *The practice of everyday life.* (Trans. S. Rendall.) Berkeley: University of California Press.

de Lauretis, T. (1984). Desire in Narrative. *Alice doesn't.* Bloomington: Indiana University Press, 103–157.

DiTamaso, N. (1989). Sexuality in the workplace. In J. Hearn et al. (eds.), *The sexuality of organization.* Newbury Park, CA: Sage, 71–90.

Dowd, M. (1991, October 8). The Senate and sexism. *New York Times,* A1, A22.

Driscoll, J. B. (1981). Sexual attraction and harassment: Management's new problems. *Personnel Journal* 60: 33–36, 56.

Duke, L. (1992, October 16). Hill says racial perceptions undercut her credibility. *Washington Post*, A10.

Dworkin, A. (1987). *Intercourse*. New York: Macmillan.

Dziech, B. W., & Weiner, L. (1990). *The lecherous professor*. 2d ed. Urbana: University of Illinois Press.

Edwards, L. (1992, March). Gag rule: How the Republicans and one weak-kneed Democrat—Joe Biden—suppressed the truth about Clarence Thomas and saved his nomination. *Spy*, 40–50.

Ehrenreich, N. (1990). Pluralist myths and powerless men: The ideology of reasonableness in sexual harassment law. *Yale Law Journal* 99: 1177–1234.

Elgin, S. H. (1980). *The gentle art of verbal self-defense*. New York: Dorset Press.

———— (1992, March). Washing utopian dishes, sweeping utopian floors. Keynote address presented at the Conference on Gender and Communication Research, Roanoke, VA.

Epstein, C. F. (1988). *Deceptive distinctions: Sex, gender and the social order*. New Haven: Yale University Press.

Evans, L. J. (1978). Sexual harassment: Women's hidden occupational hazard. In J. R. Chapman & M. Gates (eds.), *The victimization of women*. Beverly Hills, CA: Sage, 203–223.

Fain, T. C., & Anderton, D. L. (1987). Sexual harassment: Organizational context and diffuse status. *Sex Roles* 5–6: 291–311.

Falbo, T., & Peplau, L. A. (1980). Power strategies in intimate relationships. *Journal of Personality and Social Psychology* 38: 618–628.

Farley, L. (1978). *Sexual shakedown: The sexual harassment of women on the job*. New York: McGraw-Hill.

Fechner, H. B. (1990). Toward an expanded conception of law reform: Sexual harassment law and the reconstruction of facts. *Journal of Law Reform* 23: 475–505.

Fisher, B. A. (1978). *Perspectives on human communication*. New York: Macmillan.

Fisher, W. R. (1985). The narrative paradigm: An elaboration. *Communication Monographs* 52: 347–367.

———— (1987). *Human communication narration: Toward a philosophy of reason, value, and action*. Columbia: University of South Carolina Press.

Fishman, P. M. (1978). Interaction: The work women do. *Social Problems* 25: 397–406.

Fitzgerald, L. F., et al. (1988). The incidence and dimensions of sexual harassment in academia and the workplace. *Journal of Vocational Behavior* 32: 152–175.

Forell, C. (1993, March). Sexual and racial harassment: Whose perspective should control? *Trial*, 70–76.

Foss, K. A., & Foss, S. K. (1989). Incorporating the feminist perspective in communication scholarship: A research commentary. In K. Carter & C. Spitzack (eds.), *Doing research on women's communication: Perspectives on theory and method*. Norwood, NJ: Ablex, 65–91.

———— (1991) *Women speak: The eloquence of women's lives*. Prospect Heights, IL: Waveland.

Foss, S. K. (1989). *Rhetorical criticism: Exploration and practice*. Prospect Heights, IL: Waveland.

Foucault, M. (1973). *The order of things: An archeology of the human sciences.* New York: Random House.
———— *Discipline and punish: The birth of the prison.* New York: Random House.
———— Politics and the study of discourse. *Ideology and Consciousness* 3: 7–26.
———— (1980a). *The history of sexuality.* Vol. 1. (Trans. R. Hurley.) New York: Vintage.
———— (1980b). *Power/knowledge: Selected interviews and other writings 1972–1977.* (Ed. C. Gordon.) New York: Pantheon.
———— (1982). The subject and power. *Critical Inquiry* 8: 777–789.
Fraser, N. (1990). The uses and abuses of French discourse theories for feminist politics. *Boundary 2,* 17: 82–101.
Freedman, E. B. (1992, January 8). The manipulation of history at the Clarence Thomas hearings. *Chronicle of Higher Education* 38: B2–B3.
French, M. (1992). *The war against women.* New York: Summit.
Frisch, M. (ed.). (1990). Oral history performance. *Oral History Review* 18.
Gabel, P. (1992, January–February). Roundtable: Sexuality after Thomas/Hill. *Tikkun* 7: n.p.
Galvin, K. M. (1993). Preventing the problem: Preparing faculty for the issue of sexual harassment. In G. L. Kreps (ed.), *Sexual harassment: Communication implications.* Cresskill, NJ: Hampton Press, 257–266.
Garcia, L., Milano, L., & Quijano, A. (1989). Perceptions of coercive sexual behavior by males and females. *Sex Roles* 21: 569–577.
Gaylin, W. (1992). *The male ego.* New York: Viking.
Geertz, C. (1973). *The interpretation of cultures.* New York: Basic.
Geist, P., & Hardesty, M. (1990). Ideological positioning in professionals' narratives of quality medical care. *Studies in Symbolic Interaction* 11: 257–284.
———— (1992). *Negotiating the crisis: DRGs and the transformation of hospitals.* Hillsdale, NJ: Erlbaum.
Geras, N. (1987). Post-Marxism? *New Left Review* 163: 40–82.
Giddens, A. (1979). *Central problems in social theory.* Berkeley: University of California Press.
Gillespie, M. A. (1992, January–February). We speak in tongues. 41–43.
Gilligan, C., Lyons, N. P., & Hanmer, T. J. (eds.). (1990). *Making connections: The relational worlds of adolescent girls at Emma Willard School.* Cambridge: Harvard University Press.
Gitlin, T. (1980). *The whole world is watching: Mass media in the making and unmaking of the new left.* Berkeley: University of California Press.
Goffman, E. (1977). The arrangements between the sexes. *Theory and Society* 4: 301–331.
Gordon, L. (1991). On difference. *Genders* 10: 91–111.
Gramsci, A. (1971). *Selections from the prison notebooks.* (Trans. Q. Hoare and G. N. Smith). Newark: International.
Grauerholz, E. (1985). Power and intimacy: Power relations between men and women. Ph.D. dissertation, Indiana University.
Grauerholz, E., & Serpe, R. (1985). Initiation and response: The dynamics of sexual interaction. *Sex Roles* 12: 1041–1059.
Greif, E. B. (1979, March). *Sex differences in parent-child conversations: Who interrupts whom.* Paper presented at the meetings of the Society for Research on Child Development, San Francisco.

Grieco, A. (1987). Scope and nature of sexual harassment in nursing. *Journal of Sex Research* 23: 261–266.

Gronbeck, B. E. (1983). Narrative, enactment, and television programming. *Southern Speech Communication Journal* 48: 229–243.

Grossberg, L. (1979). Marxist dialectics and rhetorical criticism. *Quarterly Journal of Speech* 65: 235–249.

Gruber, J. E. (1989). How women handle sexual harassment: A literature review. *Sociology and Social Research* 74: 307.

———— (1992). A typology of personal and environmental sexual harassment: Research and policy implications for the 1990s. *Sex Roles* 26: 447–464.

Gutek, B. (1981, August). Experiences of sexual harassment: Results from a representative sample. Paper presented at the annual APA convention, Los Angeles.

———— (1985). *Sex and the workplace: The impact of sexual behavior and harassment on women, men and organizations.* San Francisco: Jossey-Bass.

———— (1989). Sexuality in the workplace. In J. Hearn et al. (eds.), *The sexuality of organization.* Newbury Park, CA: Sage, 56–70.

———— (1993). Responses to sexual harassment. In S. Oskamp & M. Costanzo (eds.), *Gender issues in social psychology.* Newbury Park, CA: Sage, 197–216.

Gutek, B., & Cohen, A. (1987). Sex ratios, sex role spillover, and sex at work: A comparison of men's and women's experiences. *Human Relations* 40: 97–115.

Gutek, B., & Koss, M. (1993). Changed women and changed organizations: Consequences of and coping with sexual harassment. *Journal of Vocational Behavior* 42: 28–48.

Gutek, B., & Morasch, B. (1982). Sex-ratios, sex-role spillover, and sexual harassment of women at work. *Journal of Social Issues* 38: 55–74.

Gutek, B., Morasch, B., & Cohen, G. (1983). Interpreting social-sexual behavior in a work setting. *Journal of Vocational Behavior* 22: 30–48.

Habermas, J. (1984). *The theory of communicative action.* Vol. 1: *Reason and the rationalization of society.* (Trans. T. McCarthy.) Boston: Beacon.

Hall, S. (1985). Signification, representation, ideology: Althusser and the poststructuralist debate. *Critical Studies in Mass Communication* 2: 91–114.

Hanley, J. M. (1979). *Sexual harassment in the federal government.* Hearings before the Subcommittee on Investigations of the Committee on Post Office and Civil Service, U.S. House of Representatives, Ninety-sixth Congress, First session, October 23, 1979, serial no. 96–57. Washington, D.C.: U.S. Government Printing Office.

Haraway, D. (1988). Situated knowledges: The science question in feminism and the privilege of partial perspective. *Signs* 14: 575–599.

Harding, S. (1991). *Whose science? Whose knowledge? Thinking from women's lives.* Ithaca, NY: Cornell University Press.

Hart, R. (1991). *Modern rhetorical criticism.* Glenview, IL: Scott Foresman.

Hartley, R. (1959). Sex-role pressures and the socialization of the male child. *Psychological Reports* 5: 457–468.

Hartsock, N.C.M. (1983). The feminist standpoint: Developing the ground for a specifically feminist historical materialism. In S. Harding & M. B. Hintikka (eds.), *Discovering reality.* Boston: Reidel, 283–310.

———— (1990). Foucault on power: A theory for women? In J. Nicholson (ed.), *Feminism/postmodernism.* New York: Routledge, 157–175.

Hemming, H. (1985). Women in a man's world: Sexual harassment. *Human Relations* 38: 67–79.

Henley, N. M. (1977). *Body politics: Power, sex, and nonverbal communication*. Englewood Cliffs, NJ: Prentice-Hall.

Hennessy, R. (1993). *Materialist feminism and the politics of discourse*. New York: Routledge.

Hickson, M., III, Grierson, R. D., & Linder, B. C. (1990, October). A communication model of sexual harassment. *Association for Communication Administration Bulletin* 74: 22–33.

——— (1991). A communication perspective on sexual harassment: Affiliative nonverbal behaviors in asynchronous relationships. *Communication Quarterly*, 39, 111–118.

Hill, A. (1992, October 16). Conference on Race, Gender and Power in America. Washington, D.C.: Georgetown University Law School.

Hoffman, C. D., et al. (1984). A comparison of adult males' and females' interactions with girls and boys. *Sex Roles* 11: 799–811.

hooks, b. (1989). *Talking back: thinking feminist, thinking black*. Boston: South End Press.

——— (1990). *Yearning: Race, gender and cultural politics*. Boston: South End Press.

Houston, M. (1992). The politics of difference: Race, class, and women's communication. In L. F. Rakow (ed.), *Women making meaning*. New York: Routledge, 45–59.

Howard, E., Stuart, C., and Crisp, W. (1992, December). Sexual harassment continues to haunt the halls of Congress: What do men think? Press release, National Association for Female Executives, 1–9.

Howard, S. (1991). Organizational resources for addressing sexual harassment. *Journal of Counseling and Development* 69: 507–511.

Huspek, M. (1993). Dueling structures: The theory of resistance in discourse. *Communication Theory* 3: 1–25.

Israeli, D. N. (1983). Sex effects or structural effects? An empirical test of Kanter's theory of proportions. *Social Forces* 62: 153–165.

James, J. (1992). Anita Hill: Martyr heroism and gender abstractions. In R. Chrisman and R. L. Allen (eds.), *Court of appeal: The black community speaks out on the racial and sexual politics of Thomas vs. Hill*. New York: Ballantine, 110–115.

Johnson, S. (1986). Telling the truth. *Trivia: A Journal of Ideas* 9: 9–33.

Johnston, C. (ed.). (1974). *Notes on women's cinema*. London: SEFT.

Jordan, M., and Buckley, S. (1991, October 20). In the workplace, closing mouths and opening minds. *Washington Post*, A1, A23.

Jossem, J. H. (1991). Investigating sexual harassment complaints. *Personnel Journal* 68: 9–10.

Kaminer, W. (1992). *I'm dysfunctional, you're dysfunctional: The recovery movement and other self-help fashions*. Reading, MA: Addison-Wesley.

Kanter, R. (1977). *Men and women of the corporation*. New York: Basic Books.

Kelly, L. (1988). *Surviving sexual violence*. Minneapolis: University of Minnesota Press.

Kenig, S., & Ryan, J. (1986). Sex differences in levels of tolerance and attribution of blame for sexual harassment on a university campus. *Sex Roles* 15: 535–549.

Kersten, A. (1986). A critical-interpretive approach to the study of organizational communication: Bringing communication back into the field. In L. Thayer (ed.),

Organization—Communication: Emerging perspectives I. Norwood, NJ: Ablex, 133–150.

King, V. (1992). *Manhandled black females.* Nashville, TN: Winston-Derek Publishers.

Kollock, P., Blumstein, P., & Schwartz, P. (1985). Sex and power in interaction: Conversational privileges and duties. *American Sociological Review* 50: 34–36.

Kramarae, C. (1992). Harassment and everyday life. In L. F. Rakow (ed.), *Women making meaning. New feminist directions in communication.* New York: Routledge, 100–120.

Krauss, C. (1991, October 11). Biden, women's rights advocate, finds his sensitivity questioned. *New York Times,* A18.

Kreps, G. L. (1980). A field experimental test and reevaluation of Weick's model of organizing. In D. Nimmo (ed.), *Communication yearbook 4.* New Brunswick, NJ: Transaction Press, 389–398.

——— (1986). Ethical dimensions of organizational communication. In W. Hamel (ed.), *Human resources management and organizational behavior proceedings: 1986 national conference.* Virginia Beach, VA: Maximilian Press, 1: 285–289.

——— (1990). *Organizational communication: Theory and practice.* 2d ed. White Plains, NY: Longman.

——— (1992). The value of therapeutic communication in organizational life. *Journal of Communication Therapy* 5: 154–173.

——— (1993a). Promoting a sociocultural evolutionary approach to preventing sexual harassment: Metacommunication and cultural adaptation. In G. L. Kreps (ed.), *Sexual harassment: Communication implications.* Cresskill, NJ: Hampton Press, 310–318.

——— (1993b). Sexual harassment and communication. In G. L. Kreps (ed.), *Sexual harassment: Communication implications.* Cresskill, NJ: Hampton Press, 1–5.

Kristeva, J. (1982). Women's time. (Trans. A. Jardim & H. Blake.) In N. Keohane, M. Rosaldo, & B. Gelpi (eds.), *Feminist theory: A critique of ideology.* Chicago: University of Chicago Press, 31–53.

Krohne, D. (1991). The effect of sexual harassment on female naval officers: A phenomenological study. Ph.D. dissertation, University of San Diego.

Laclau, E., & Mouffe, C. (1985). *Hegemony and socialist strategy: Towards a radical democratic politics.* London: Verso.

LaFontaine, E., & Tredeau, L. (1986). The frequency, sources, and correlates of sexual harassment among women in traditional male occupations. *Sex Roles* 15: 433–442.

Lannamann, J. W. (1991). Interpersonal communication as ideological practice. *Communication Theory* 1: 179–203.

Lee, C. (1992). Sexual harassment: After the headlines. *Training* 29: 3, 23–31.

Lever, J. (1978). Sex differences in the complexity of children's play and games. *American Sociological Review* 43: 471–483.

Lewis, M., & Simon, R. I. (1986). As discourse not intended for her: Learning and teaching within patriarchy. *Harvard Educational Review* 56: 457–472.

Lewis, W. F. (1987, August). Telling America's story. *Quarterly Journal of Speech* 73: 280–302.

Lips, H. M. (1981). *Women, men and the psychology of power.* Englewood Cliffs, NJ: Prentice-Hall.

Littler-Bishop, S., Seidler-Feller, D., & Opaluch, R. E. (1982). Sexual harassment in the workplace as a function of initiator's status: The case of airline personnel. *Journal of Social Issues* 38: 137–148.

Livingston, J. A. (1982). Responses to sexual harassment on the job: Legal, organizational, and individual actions. *Journal of Social Issues* 38: 5–22.

Loy, P. W., & Stewart, L. P. (1984). The extent and effects of sexual harassment of working women. *Sociological Focus* 17: 31–43.

Maccoby, E. E., & Jacklin, C. N. (1974). *The psychology of sex differences*. Stanford, CA: Stanford University Press.

MacCorquodale, P. (1989). Gender and sexual behavior. In K. McKinney & S. Sprecher (eds.), *Human sexuality: The societal and interpersonal context*. Norwood, NJ: Ablex, 91–112.

Machlowitz, D. S., & Machlowitz, M. M. (1987). Preventing sexual harassment. *ABA Journal* 73, pt. 2: 78–80.

MacKinnon, C. (1979). *Sexual harassment of working women*. New Haven: Yale University Press.

———— (1987). *Feminism unmodified: Discourses on life and law*. Cambridge: Harvard University Press.

Maihoff, N., & Forrest, L. (1983). Sexual harassment in higher education: An assessment study. *Initiatives. Journal of the National Association for Women Deans, Administrators, and Counselors* 46: 3–8.

Malovich, N. J., & Stake, J. E. (1990). Sexual harassment on campus: Individual differences in attitudes and beliefs. *Psychology of Women Quarterly* 14: 63–81.

Maltz, D. N., & Borker, R. A. (1983). A cultural approach to male-female miscommunication. In J. A. Gumperz (ed.), *Language and social identity*. New York: Cambridge University Press, 195–216.

Mantilla, K. (1992, Spring). Hill-Thomas II: Minoritizing and universalizing. *Matrix* 1: 1, 6.

Marche, T. A., & Peterson, C. (1993). The development and sex-related use of interruption behavior. *Human Communication Research* 19: 388–408.

Martin, J. (1990). Deconstructing organizational taboos: The suppression of gender conflict in organizations. *Organizational Science* 1: 339–359.

Maypole, D. (1986). Sexual harassment of workers at work: Injustice within? *Social Work* 31: 1, 29–34.

Mazer, D. B., & Percival, E. F. (1989). Students' experiences of sexual harassment at a small university. *Sex Roles* 20: 1–22.

McCaghy, M. D. (1985). *Sexual harassment. A guide to resources*. Boston: G. K. Hall.

McKinney, K. (1993, March 28). Personal communication.

McKinney, K., & Maroules, N. (1991). Sexual harassment. In E. Grauerholz & M. Koralewski (eds.), *Sexual coercion: A sourcebook on its nature, causes and prevention*. Lexington, MA: Lexington Books, 29–44.

McNamee, S. (1989). Challenging the patriarchal vision of social science: Lessons from a family therapy model. In K. Carter & C. Spitzack (eds.), *Doing research on women's communication: Perspectives on theory and method*. Norwood, NJ: Ablex, 95–117.

Mead, G. H. (1934). *Mind, self, and society*. Chicago: University of Chicago Press.

Metts, S., & Cupach, W. R. (1989). The role of communication in human sexuality. In K. McKinney & S. Sprecher (eds.), *Human sexuality: The societal and interpersonal context*. Norwood, NJ: Ablex, 139–161.

Milwid, B. (1990). *Working with men: Professional women talk about power, sexuality, and ethics*. Hillsboro, OR: Beyond Words Publishing.

Moi, T. (1985). *Sexual/textual politics: Feminist literary theory*. London: Methuen.

Money, J., & Earhardt, A. (1972). Man and woman, boy and girl. Baltimore: Johns Hopkins University Press.

Mongeau, P. A., & Blalock, J. (1992, February). Differentiating sexual harassment from immediacy attempts: A replication and extension. Paper presented at the Western States Communication Association convention, Boise, ID.

Morgan, R. (1992, January–February). Bearing witness. *Ms.*, 1.

Morin, R. (1992, December 18). Harassment consensus grows: Poll finds greater awareness of misconduct. *Washington Post*, A1, A22.

Morrill, C. (1992). The private ordering of professional relationships. In D. M. Kolb and J. M. Bartunek (eds.), *Hidden conflict in organizations*. Newbury Park, CA: Sage, 92–115.

Morrison, T. (1987). *Beloved*. New York: Knopf.

———— (1989, May 22). The pain of being black. *Time*, 120.

———— (ed.). (1992). *Race-ing justice, en-gendering power: Essays on Anita Hill, Clarence Thomas, and the construction of social reality*. New York: Pantheon.

Muir, J. K. (1992). Discovering C-SPAN. *C-SPAN in the communication classroom: Theory and applications*. Annandale, VA: Speech Communication Association.

———— (1993). C-SPAN's coverage of the gulf war: Television as town square. In R. J. Denton, Jr. (ed.), *Media coverage of the Persian Gulf*. New York: Praeger.

Nielsen, J. M. (ed.). (1990). *Feminist research methods. Exemplary readings in the social sciences*. Boulder, CO: Westview Press.

Norment, L. (1992, January). Black men, black women and sexual harassment. *Ebony*, 119–122.

O'Farrell, B., & Harlan, S. L. (1982). Craftworkers and clerks. *Social Problems* 29: 252–264.

Orton, J. D., & Weick, K. (1990). Loosely-coupled systems. *Academy of Management Review* 15: 208–223.

"Our stories": Communication professionals' narratives of sexual harassment. (1992). *Journal of Applied Communication Research* 20: 363–391.

Paludi, M. A., & Barickman, R. B. (1991). *Academic and workplace sexual harassment. A resource manual*. Albany: New York Press.

Paetzold, R., & O'Leary-Kelly, A. (1993). The legal context of sexual harassment. In G. L. Kreps (ed.), *Communicative perspectives on sexual harassment*. Cresskill, NJ: Hampton Press, 63–77.

Payne, K. (1993). The power game: Sexual harassment on the college campus. In G. L. Kreps (ed.), *Sexual harassment: Communication implications*. Cresskill, NJ: Hampton Press, 133–148.

Phillips, G. M., & Jarboe, S. (1993). Sycophancy and servitude: Harassment and rebellion. In G. L. Kreps (ed.), *Sexual harassment: Communication implications*. Cresskill, NJ: Hampton Press, 281–309. (Trans. B. Jowett.)

Plato. (1953). *Republic*. In H. Adams (ed.), (1971), *Critical theory since Plato*. New York: Harcourt Brace, 19–41.

Pleck, J. (1980). *The American man*. Englewood Cliffs, NJ: Prentice-Hall.

Polanyi, L. (1985). *Telling the American story: A structural and cultural analysis of conversational storytelling*. Norwood, NJ: Ablex.

Pollack, W. (1990). Sexual harassment: Women's experience vs. legal definitions. *Harvard Women's Law Review* 13: 35–85.

Poole, M. S., & Van de Van, A. H. (1989). Using paradox to build management and organization theories. *Academy of Management Review* 14: 562–578.

Popovich, P. M. (1988). Sexual harassment in organizations. *Employee Responsibilities and Rights Journal* 1: 273–322.

Powell, G. N. (1986). Effects of sex role identity and sex on definitions of sexual harassment. *Sex Roles* 14: 9–19.

Pryor, J. B. (1987). Sexual harassment proclivities in men. *Sex Roles* 17: 269–290.

Pryor, J. B., & Day, J. D. (1988). Interpretations of sexual harassment: An attributional analysis. *Sex Roles* 18: 405–417.

Putnam, L. (1983a). Preface. In L. Putnam & M. E. Pacanowsky (eds.), *Communication and organizations: An interpretive approach*. Newbury Park, CA: Sage, 7–11.

———— (1983b). The interpretive perspective. An alternative to functionalism. In L. Putnam & M. E. Pacanowsky (eds.), *Communication and organizations: An interpretive approach*. Newbury Park, CA: Sage, 31–54.

Quina, K. (1990). The victimization of women. In M. A. Paludi (ed.), *Ivory power: Sexual harassment on campus*. Albany: State University of New York Press, 93–102.

Rabidue v. Osceola Refining Company. (1986). 805 F.2d 611, 626 Cir (6th Cir).

Ramazanoglu, C. (1987). Sex and violence in academic life, or you can keep a good woman down. In J. Hanmer & M. Maynard (eds.), *Women, violence and social control*. Atlantic Highlands, NJ: Humanities Press International, 61–74.

Randall, M. (1992). Doublespeak and doublehear, Anita Hill in our lives. In A. C. Sumrall & D. Taylor (eds.), *Sexual harassment: Women speak out*. Freedom, CA: Crossing Press, 18–22.

Range, P. R. (1992, July 18). C-SPAN: The little network that could. *TV Guide*, 12–15.

Reilly, T., Carpenter, S., Dull, V., & Bartlett, K. (1982). The factorial survey, An approach to defining sexual harassment on campus. *Journal of Social Issues* 38: 99–119.

Rich, A. (1986). Ten years later: A new introduction. *Of woman born*, 10th anniversary ed. New York: W. W. Norton.

Ricoeur, P. (1980). Narrative time. In W.J.T. Mitchell (ed.), *On narrative*. Chicago: University of Chicago Press, 165–186.

Rizzo, A.-M., & Brosnan, D. (1990). Critical theory and communication dysfunction. *Administration and Society* 22: 66–85.

Roberts, H. (ed.). (1981). *Doing feminist research*. London: Routledge & Kegan Paul.

Roscoe, B., Goodwin, M. P., Repp, S. E., & Rose, M. (1987). Sexual harassment of university students and student-employees: Findings and implications. *College Student Journal* 21: 254–273.

Rowe, M. (1981). Dealing with sexual harassment. *Harvard Business Review* 59: 3, 42–44.

Rowe, M. (1985, May 10). Dealing with harassment concerns. Paper delivered at Yale University, New Haven.

Rowland, R. C. (1987). Narrative: Mode of discourse or paradigm? *Communication Monographs* 54: 264–275.

Rubin, J. Z., Provenzano, F. J., & Luria, Z. (1974). The eye of the beholder: Parents' views on sex of newborns. *American Journal of Orthopsychiatry* 44: 512–519.

Russell, D.E.H. (1982). *Rape in marriage*. New York: Collier.

Rybacki, K., and Rybacki, D. (1991). *Communication criticism: Approaches and genres*. Belmont, CA: Wadsworth.

Salisbury, J., Ginorio, A. B., Remick, H., & Stringer, D. M. (1986). Counseling victims of sexual harassment. *Psychotherapy* 23: 316–324.

Sanders, J. S., & Robinson, W. L. (1979). Talking and not talking about sex: Male and female vocabularies. *Journal of Communication* 29: 22–30.

Sandroff, R. (1992, June). Sexual harassment: The inside story. *Working Woman*, 47–52, 78.

Schiappa, E. (1991). Defining reality: The politics of meaning. Unpublished manuscript, Purdue University.

——— (in press). Arguing about definitions. *Argumentation* 6.

Schneider, B. (1982). Consciousness about sexual harassment among heterosexual and lesbian women workers. *Journal of Social Issues* 38: 75–97.

Scholes, R. (1989). *Protocols of reading*. New Haven: Yale University Press.

Scott, J. C. (1990). *Domination and the arts of resistance: Hidden transcripts*. New Haven: Yale University Press.

Sennett, R. (1977). *The fall of public man*. New York: Knopf.

Shedletsky, L. J. (1993). Accused of sexual harassment. In G. L. Kreps (ed.), *Sexual harassment: Communication implications*. Cresskill, NJ: Hampton Press, 81–89.

Shotland, R. L., & Craig, J. M. (1988). Can men and women differentiate between friendly and sexually interested behavior? *Social Psychology Quarterly* 51: 66–73.

Shott, S. (1979). Emotions and social life: A symbolic interactionist analysis. *American Journal of Sociology* 84: 1317–1334.

Siegel, D. L. (1992). *Sexual harassment: Research and resources*, 2d. ed. (Ed. S. A. Hallgarth & M.E.S. Capek.) New York: National Council for Research on Women.

Smith, D. (1987). *The everyday world as problematic: A feminist sociology*. Boston: Northeastern University Press.

Smith, J. H., and Morris, H. (eds.). (1992). *Telling facts: History and narration in psychoanalysis*. Baltimore: Johns Hopkins University Press.

Somers, A. (1982). Sexual harassment in academe. *Journal of Social Issues* 38: 23–32.

Spender, D. (1984). Defining reality: A powerful tool. In C. Kramarae, M. Schultz, & W. O'Barr (eds.), *Language and power*. Beverly Hills, CA: Sage, 9–22.

——— (1985). On feminism and propaganda. In P. A. Treichler, C. Kramarae, & B. Stafford (eds.), *For alma mater: Theory and practice in feminist scholarship*. Urbana: University of Illinois Press, 307–315.

Spitzack, C. (1993). The spectacle of anorexia nervosa. *Text and Performance Quarterly* 13: 1–20.

Spitzack, K., & Carter, K. (1989). Research on women's communication: The politics of theory and method. In K. Carter & C. Spitzack (eds.), *Doing research on women's communication: Perspectives on theory and method*. Norwood, NJ: Ablex, 11–39.

Spivak, G. (1987). *In other worlds: Essays in cultural politics*. New York: Methuen.

——— (1988). Can the subaltern speak? In C. Nelson & I. Grossberg (eds.), *Marxism and the interpretation of culture.* Chicago and Urbana: University of Illinois Press, 271–316.

Stallybrass, P., & White, A. (1986). *The politics and poetics of transgression.* Ithaca, NY: Cornell University Press.

Steinbacher, R., & Holmes, H. B. (1987). Sex choice: Survival and sisterhood. In G. Corea et al. (eds.), *Man-made women: How new reproductive technologies affect women.* Bloomington: Indiana University Press, 52–63.

Stern, M., & Karraker, K. H. (1989). Sex stereotyping of infants: A review of gender labeling studies. *Sex Roles* 20: 501–522.

Stockard, J., & Johnson, M. M. (1992). *Sex and gender in society.* Englewood Cliffs, NJ: Prentice-Hall.

Strauss, A., & Corbin, J. (1990). *Basics of qualitative research: Grounded theory procedures and techniques.* Newbury Park, CA: Sage.

Strine, M. S. (1992). Understanding "how things work": Sexual harassment and academic culture. *Journal of Applied Communication Research* 20: 391–400.

Stryker, S. (1964). The interactional situational approaches. In H. Christensen (ed.), *Handbook of marriage and the family.* Chicago: Rand-McNally, 124–170.

———— (1980). *Symbolic interactionism: A social structural version.* Menlo Park, CA: Benjamin/Cummings.

Suleiman, S. (1990). *Subversive intent: Gender, politics, and the avant-garde.* Cambridge: Harvard University Press.

Sumrall, A. C., and Taylor, D. (eds.). 1992. *Sexual harassment: Women speak out.* Freedom, CA: Crossing Press.

Survey (1992, February). *Working Woman,* 14–16.

Survey: More young viewers are tuning in C-SPAN (1991, March 3). *C-SPAN Update* 9: 1–3.

Tangri, S. S., Burt, M. R., & Johnson, L. B. (1982). Sexual harassment at work: Three explanatory models. *Journal of Social Issues* 38: 33–54.

Tannen, D. (1990). *You just don't understand: Women and men in conversation.* New York: William Morrow.

Taylor, B., & Conrad, C. (1992). Narratives of sexual harassment: Organizational dimensions. *Journal of Applied Communication Research* 20: 401–418.

Terpstra, D. E. (1986). Organizational costs of sexual harassment. *Journal of Employment Counseling* 23: 112–119.

Terpstra, D. E., & Baker, D. D. (1986a). A framework for the study of sexual harassment. *Basic and Applied Social Psychology* 7: 1, 17–34.

———— (1986b). Psychological and demographic correlates of perception of sexual harassment. *Genetic, Social, and General Psychology Monographs* 112: 459–478.

———— (1988). Outcomes of sexual harassment charges. *Academy of Management Journal* 31: 185–194.

Thomann, D. A., & Wiener, R. L. (1987). Physical and psychological causality as determinants of culpability in sexual harassment cases. *Sex Roles* 17: 573–591.

Thompson, J. B. (1984). *Studies in the theory of ideology.* London: Polity.

Thorne, B., & Henley, N. (eds.). (1975). *Language and sex: Difference and dominance.* Rowley, MA: Newbury House.

Thorne, B., & Luria, Z. (1986). Sexuality and gender in children's daily worlds. *Social Problems* 33: 176–190.

Tiffs, S., & VanOsdol, P. (1991, February 4). A setback for pinups at work. *Time,* p. 61.

Tompkins, J. (1990). Pedagogy of the distressed. *College English* 58: 653–660.

Tuana, N. (1985). Sexual harassment in academe. Issues of power and coercion. *College Teaching* 33: 53–64.

Turner, V. (1969). *The ritual process: Structure and anti-structure.* Ithaca, NY: Cornell University Press.

——— (1982). Liminal to liminoid, in play, flow, ritual. In *From ritual to theatre: The human seriousness of play.* New York: PAJ Publications, 20–60.

——— (1986). Performing ethnography. In *The anthropology of performance.* New York: PAJ Publications, 139–155.

Tyler, S. (1987). Postmodern ethnography. In *The unspeakable: Discourse, dialogue, and rhetoric in the postmodern world.* Madison: University of Wisconsin Press, 199–216.

U.S. Merit Systems Protection Board (1981). *Sexual harassment in the federal workplace: Is it a problem?* Washington, D.C.: U.S. Government Printing Office.

Valentine-French, S., & Radtke, L. (1989). Attributions of responsibility for an incident of sexual harassment in a university setting. *Sex Roles* 21: 545–555.

Van Dijk, T. A. (1993). Principles of critical discourse analysis. *Discourse and Society* 4: 249–283.

Vance, C. S. (1984). Pleasure and danger: Towards a politics of sexuality. In C. S. Vance (ed.), *Pleasure and danger: Exploring female sexuality.* Boston: Routledge and Kegan Paul, 1–27.

Wagner, E. J. (1992). *Sexual harassment in the workplace. How to prevent, investigate, and resolve problems in your organization.* New York: AMACOM.

Walker, A. (1989). *The temple of my familiar.* San Diego, CA: Harcourt Brace Jovanovich.

Warnick, B. (1987). The narrative paradigm: Another story. *Quarterly Journal of Speech* 73: 172–182.

Webb, S. (1992). *Step forward, sexual harassment in the workplace: What you need to know!* New York: MasterMedia Limited.

Weedon, C. (1987). *Feminist practice and poststructuralist theory.* London: Basil Blackwell.

Weick, K. (1979). *The social psychology of organizing.* 2d. ed. Reading, MA: Addison-Wesley.

Weinraub, M., et al. (1984). The development of sex role standards in the third year: Relationship to gender labeling, gender identity, sex-typed toy preferences, and family characteristics. *Child Development* 55: 1493–1503.

Weitzman, L. (1979). *Sex role socialization.* Palo Alto, CA: Mayfield.

Westkott, M. (1983). Women's studies as a strategy for change: Between criticism and vision. In G. Boweles and R. D. Klein (eds.), *Theories of women's studies.* London: Routledge and Kegan Paul, 210–218.

Whiting, B., & Edwards, C. P. (1973). A cross-cultural analysis of sex differences in the behavior of children aged three to eleven. *Journal of Social Psychology* 91: 171–188.

Williams, K. B., & Cyr, R. R. (1992). Escalating commitment to a relationship: The sexual harassment trap. *Sex Roles* 27: 47–72.

Wilson, K. R., & Kraus, L. A. (1983). Sexual harassment in the university. *Journal of College Student Personnel* 24: 219–224.

Wise, S., & Stanley, L. (1987). *Georgie Porgie. Sexual harassment in everyday life.* New York: Pandora.

Witteman, H. (1993). The interface between sexual harassment and organizational romance. In G. L. Kreps (ed.), *Sexual harassment: Communication implications.* Cresskill, NJ: Hampton Press, 27–62.

Wood, J. T. (1992). Telling our stories: Narratives as a basis for theorizing sexual harassment. *Journal of Applied Communication Research* 20: 349–362.

———— (1993a). Engendered relationships. In S. Duck (ed.), *Understanding relationship processes.* Beverly Hills: Sage, 4: 26–54.

———— (1993b). Gender and moral voice: From woman's nature to standpoint theory. *Women's Studies in Communication* 15: 1–24.

———— (1993c). *Gendered lives: Gender, culture and communication.* Belmont, CA: Wadsworth.

———— (1993d). Naming and interpreting sexual harassment: A conceptual framework for scholarship. In G. L. Kreps (ed.), *Sexual harassment: Communication implications.* Cresskill, NJ: Hampton Press, 9–26.

———— (1994). Engendered identities: Shaping voice and mind through gender. In D. Vocate (ed.), *Intrapersonal communication: Different voices, different minds.* Hillsdale, NJ: Erlbaum, 145–167.

Wood, J. T., & Cox, J. R. (1993). Rethinking critical voice: Materiality and situated knowledges. *Western Journal of Communication* 57: 278–287.

York, K. M. (1989). Defining sexual harassment in workplaces: A policy-capturing approach. *Academy of Management Journal* 32: 830–850.

Young, M., and Muir, J. K. (1992, April). Perspective, evidence, and credibility: The case of Anita Hill. Paper presented at the annual meeting of the Eastern Communication Association, Portland, ME.

Zalk, S. R. (1990). Men in the academy: A psychological profile of harassment. In M. A. Paludi (ed.), *Ivory power: Sexual harassment on campus.* Albany: State University of New York Press, 141–175.

Zimmerman, D., & West, C. (1975). Sex roles, interruptions and silences in conversations. In B. Thorne & N. Henley (eds.), *Language and sex: Difference and dominance.* Rowley, MA: Newbury House, 105–129.

Index

About the Editor and Contributors

SHEREEN G. BINGHAM (Ph.D., Purdue University) is an Assistant Professor of Communication at the University of Nebraska at Omaha, where she teaches in the areas of gender, interpersonal, and organizational communication. Her research focuses on sexual harassment and communication, primarily on individual and institutional responses to the former. Her publications have appeared in *Human Communication Research*, *Journal of Applied Communication Research*, *Sex Roles*, and *Case Studies in Organizational Communication*, edited by Beverly Davenport Sypher.

ROBIN P. CLAIR (Ph.D., Kent State University) is an Assistant Professor of Communication at Purdue University. Her work focuses on sexual harassment, and recent publications appeared in *Communication Monographs* and *Management Communication Quarterly*.

CHARLES CONRAD (Ph.D., Kansas University) is an Associate Professor of Speech Communication at Texas A&M University. His primary research interests involve social and organizational power relationships and the ways in which communicative processes influence power asymmetries. He is the author of *Strategic Organizational Communication*, editor of *The Ethical Nexus*, and has published articles in a number of journals.

LEDA M. COOKS (Ph.D., Ohio University) is an Assistant Professor of Communication at the University of Massachusetts. Her research interests include critical pedagogy, media/film criticism, feminist theory, empowerment, and interpretive approaches to interpersonal communication. She has presented numerous convention and conference papers as well as having published in *Discourse & Society, Western Journal of Communication*, and *Howard Journal of Communication*.

SUE DeWINE (Ph.D., Indiana University) is a Professor and Director of the School of Interpersonal Communication at Ohio University and operates her own consulting firm for private industry, government, and educational institutions. Her research interests include gender differences in organizational communication, memorable messages for women, consulting practices, communication networks in organizations, and requests for support. Her latest book is *The Consultant's Craft: Coping with Communication Failures in Organizations*.

KAREN A. FOSS (Ph.D., University of Iowa) and RICHARD A. ROGERS (M.S., University of Utah) have been working together in the areas of feminism and the analysis of discourse since 1987. Early in their relationship, Karen introduced Rich to feminist thought and pushed the boundaries of his understanding of rhetorical theory. More recently, Karen has been exploring alternative frameworks for understanding women's communication, while Rich's interests have turned toward post-structuralist theories of discourse and the intersections between race and gender. These and other commonalities and differences in theoretical orientations, subjects of study, political commitments, and social positions have given rise to a variety of dialogues concerning sexual harassment and academic discourse. Karen is an Associate Professor of Communication and Journalism at the University of New Mexico; Rich is finishing his Ph.D. in Communication at the University of Utah.

PATRICIA GEIST (Ph.D., Purdue University) is an Associate Professor of Communication at San Diego State University. Her research interests in the area of organizational and health communication focus on the study of power, control, gender, and negotiated order. She has published work in journals such as *Communication Monographs, Western Communication Journal, Health Communication Journal*, and *Management Communication Journal*. Her book *Negotiating the Crisis: DRGs and the Transformation of Hospitals* (1992) centers on communicating and negotiating order in the hospital under a controversial Medicare policy.

ELIZABETH GRAUERHOLZ (Ph.D., Indiana University) is an Associate Professor of Sociology at Purdue University. Her primary area of interest is violence against women, especially sexual harassment and rape. She is the editor of *Sexual Coercion: A Sourcebook on Its Nature, Causes, and Prevention*.

CLAUDIA L. HALE (Ph.D., University of Illinois), is an Associate Professor of Interpersonal Communication at Ohio University. Her research interests focus on the relationship between social cognition and communication competence, particularly in situations involving interpersonal conflict. Her articles have appeared in *Communication Monographs*, *International Journal of Conflict Management*, *Journal of Language and Social Psychology*, and *Discourse and Society*.

DANA M. KALAND (M.A., San Diego State University) is a Senior Partner in Partners in Change Consulting, where she provides organizational development services to public and private organizations throughout the country. She offers leadership development training, managerial assessment programs, sexual harassment workshops, as well as other forms of consultation.

GARY L. KREPS (Ph.D., University of Southern California) is a Professor of Communication Studies and a member of the Gerontology Faculty (Social Science Research Institute) at Northern Illinois University. He has published fifteen books and more than one hundred articles and chapters examining the role of communication in organizational life, health promotion, and education. Some of his most recent books include *Sexual Harassment: Communication Implications* (1993), *Qualitative Research: Applications in Organizational Communication* (1993, with Sandra L. Herndon), and *Perspectives on Health Communication* (1993, with Barbara C. Thornton).

KATHRYN MANGUS (M.A., George Mason University) is an Adjunct Instructor in the Department of Communication at George Mason University, where she teaches small group and interpersonal communication and works with the internship program. She is also employed as a consultant and trainer, teaching a variety of courses in communication for organizations such as the USDA and the Commonwealth of Virginia. She has done public relations writing for the *Washington Post* and has assisted in the construction of instructors' manuals for basic communication courses.

JANETTE KENNER MUIR (Ph.D., University of Massachusetts) is an Assistant Professor and the Basic Course Director in the Department of Communication at George Mason University. One of her primary research interests is concerned with how citizens participate in the political process. She has published book chapters on citizen talk about the Persian Gulf War, C-SPAN's coverage of the 1992 presidential campaign, and is currently working on President Clinton's use of town hall meetings. Muir was also the editor of *C-SPAN in the Communication Classroom: Theories and Applications*, a volume co-produced by C-SPAN and the Speech Communication Association.

DELLA POLLOCK (Ph.D., Northwestern University) is an Associate Professor of Speech Communication at the University of North Carolina at Chapel Hill. She teaches in the area of performance studies and concentrates her research on the politics of performance. She has published in such journals as *Text and Performance Quarterly, Communication Monographs, The Oral History Review*, and *Journal of Dramatic Theory and Criticism*.

BRYAN TAYLOR (Ph.D., University of Utah) is an Assistant Professor of Speech Communication at Texas A&M University. His research involves the use of critical theory and interpretive methods to study relations among discourse, knowledge, power, and consciousness. His research has appeared in the *Quarterly Journal of Speech, Journal of Applied Communication Research*, and *Western Journal of Speech Communication*.

JULIA T. WOOD (Ph.D., Pennsylvania State University) is a Professor of Communication at the University of North Carolina at Chapel Hill, where she teaches and conducts research on feminist theory, gender and communication, and personal relationships. Her scholarship on sexual harassment appears in a number of journals and edited books. She has also organized and participated in activist efforts on college campuses to reduce the incidence of sexual harassment, enhance victims' awareness of their rights, and restructure institutional policies and practices.

ISBN 0-275-94593-6

HARDCOVER BAR CODE